PATERNOSTER THEOLOGICAL MONOGRAPHS

Is World View Neutral Education Possible and Desirable?

A Christian Response to Liberal Arguments

Series Preface

In the West the churches may be declining, but theology—serious, academic (mostly doctoral level) and mainstream orthodox in evaluative commitment—shows no sign of withering on the vine. This series of *Paternoster Theological Monographs* extends the expertise of the Press especially to first-time authors whose work stands broadly within the parameters created by fidelity to Scripture and has satisfied the critical scrutiny of respected assessors in the academy. Such theology may come in several distinct intellectual disciplines—historical, dogmatic, pastoral, apologetic, missional, aesthetic and no doubt others also. The series will be particularly hospitable to promising constructive theology within an evangelical frame, for it is of this that the church's need seems to be greatest. Quality writing will be published across the confessions—Anabaptist, Episcopalian, Reformed, Arminian and Orthodox—across the ages—patristic, medieval, reformation, modern and counter-modern—and across the continents. The aim of the series is theology written in the twofold conviction that the church needs theology and theology needs the church—which in reality means theology done for the glory of God.

Series Editors

David F. Wright, Emeritus Professor of Patristic and Reformed Christianity, University of Edinburgh, Scotland, UK

Trevor A. Hart, Head of School and Principal of St Mary's College School of Divinity, University of St Andrews, Scotland, UK

Anthony N.S. Lane, Professor of Historical Theology and Director of Research, London School of Theology, UK

Anthony C. Thiselton, Emeritus Professor of Christian Theology, University of Nottingham, Research Professor in Christian Theology, University College Chester, and Canon Theologian of Leicester Cathedral and Southwell Minster, UK

Kevin J. Vanhoozer, Research Professor of Systematic Theology, Trinity Evangelical Divinity School, Deerfield, Illinois, USA

Is World View Neutral Education Possible and Desirable?

A Christian Response to Liberal Arguments

Signe Sandsmark

Foreword by John Shortt

MILTON KEYNES · COLORADO SPRINGS · HYDERABAD

THE
STAPLEFORD
CENTRE

Copyright © Signe Sandsmark 2000

First published 2000 by Paternoster and The Stapleford Centre

Paternoster is an imprint of Authentic Media
9 Holdom Avenue, Bletchley, Milton Keynes, Bucks, MK1 1QR
1820 Jet Stream Drive, Colorado Springs, CO 80921, USA
OM Authentic Media, Medchal Road, Jeedimetla Village,
Secunderabad 500 055, A.P., India
www.authenticmedia.co.uk
Authentic Media is a division of IBS-STL UK, a company limited by guarantee
(registered charity no. 270162)

03 02 01 00   7 6 5 4 3 2 1

British Library Cataloguing in Publication Data
A catalogue record for this book is available from the British Library

ISBN 978-0-85364-973-1

Typeset by Norsk Lærerakademi
and printed and bound in Great Britain
for Paternoster and The Stapleford Centre by
Nottingham AlphaGraphics

To Aksel

Contents

FOREWORD

Having had the pleasure of getting to know Signe Sandsmark through the
years of gestation of her doctoral thesis, it has been a delight to see it come
forth in this finished form. It is with quite unreserved enthusiasm that I
commend it to all those who wish to engage in serious reflection on the
relationship between Christian faith and education.

Signe Sandsmark brings a distinctive evangelical Lutheran perspective to
bear on issues such as worldview perspectives, neutrality, pluralism, liberal
education, common schooling, personal autonomy and many more in an
account which is not only wide-ranging but also thorough-going and sensitive. She moves to and fro easily and sure-footedly between her own Norwegian context, in which state education is avowedly Christian, and other
cultural contexts with differing relationships between state education and
Christian faith.

The pages of this book echo throughout with the themes of God-centred
education, service, Christian freedom, truth and love. Signe Sandsmark
develops a vision and task for Christian education which both warms the
heart and stretches the mind. She engages clearly with the issues without
over-simplifying them. She goes to the heart of the supposedly world view
neutral positions she criticises with both precision and humility; their presuppositions are identified clearly and their arguments are responded to
fairly, often with simple demonstration of counter-examples.

All in all, this is an original work of Christian scholarship which both deserves and will repay careful study. In my view, it contributes significantly
to the cause of Christian reflection on education and I warmly commend it
to the reader.

John Shortt
Head of Research & Development
The Stapleford Centre

PREFACE

This book is a somewhat revised version of my PhD thesis, submitted at the Institute of Education University of London in 1998. When I started this work some years ago, the aim was to find out what Norwegian teachers were thinking about the state school's Christian basis. What could it mean that the common school should give 'a Christian and moral upbringing' and that it was based on 'Christian and humanistic values'? The plan was to interview some teachers about these central, political statements: what they mean, what they should mean in a more or less secular and pluralistic society, how the teachers themselves put them into practice, and what problems they saw.

After four test interviews I gave up. I found out that the teachers did not have a very refined language for talking about these things. After a while I also realized that I myself did not know enough to give any fruitful input. The interviews led nowhere. It was necessary to turn to more theory.

As I worked to find out the differences between Christian education and secular education, the focus changed, as this work will show. However, the last chapter is about the possibility of having Christian education in state schools and the problems this might cause, particularly for non-Christian teachers. And one day, only weeks before the completion, I found myself asking a teacher for an interview about the Christian basis for the state school: what it means, what it should mean, how he himself and his colleagues put it into practice, and what problems he saw.

It was satisfying to realize that these years of reading and thinking made a difference to the interview. I was able to dig deeper, to see the crucial points, to give some fruitful input. The next step may be to follow up with more interviews, to get some empirical knowledge about how teachers think in this area, including reflections about world view neutrality.

Many colleagues and friends have given help and encouragement during the process. First of all, my PhD supervisor Graham Haydon deserves thanks for discussions and advice, both on the overall argument and on details, including gentle warnings when needed. Others have read and commented on parts of drafts at different stages. I am grateful to Arve Brunvoll, Trevor Cooling, Terence H. McLaughlin, Shirley Pendlebury,

Svein Rise, Jorun Sandsmark, John Shortt, Paul Standish, and John White. I have also gained much from discussions of papers that in some form are included in this work, and I am thankful to the participants at seminars at the then Department (now School) of Education University of Cambridge, Institute of Education University of London, branch meetings of the Philosophy of Education Society of Great Britain in Cambridge, Birmingham and Gregynog, and at the 1996 conference about church schools in Durham. Finally, my two examiners, Richard Pring and Andrew Wright, gave comments that have been useful in the revision.

My college in Norway, Norsk Lærerakademi (Norwegian Teacher Academy), has given me research leave twice, and in the same periods I was a Visiting Scholar at the Department of Education University of Cambridge. I am grateful to both these institutions. Library staff both places have been of great help.

The interviewees should be mentioned as well, their main merit being to show me a better way: Roger H. Boon, Marguerite Roberts, Hildegunn Sandven, Tor Olav Sønnervik, Bjarne Aakre. Ingeborg Breivik, Arvan Pritchard, and Jeremy Mudditt have helped in more technical ways. Last, but not least, I want to thank colleagues, family and friends in Norway, England and elsewhere for their prayers and their marvellous support.

Bergen, July 1999
Signe Sandsmark

CHAPTER 1

Introduction

1.1 Background for choice of topic

1.1.1 Puzzlement over assumptions that education can be neutral between world views

It is commonplace that upbringing and education cannot be neutral. Lately it is also often emphasized that value neutrality is not even desirable, and society tries to find values we can all agree on which can be the basis for upbringing and education in schools. But when it comes to religions, or world views in general, the picture is different. Both in Norway and England there are many voices claiming that schools ought not to influence children towards a particular religion, faith, or world view, but to give them knowledge about different views and encourage them to make their own choice. In discussions about the role of Christianity - or religion in general - in education, something like the following is often heard: 'We shouldn't tell them that one religion is better than others, they have to choose for themselves.'

The underlying assumption often seems to be that if we tell children that one particular religion is true, they cannot make their own choice. I am puzzled by this implicitly assumed link. Does saying that something is true, when we have no scientific proof, necessarily intrude on children's autonomy?

The 'quotation' above is certainly a popular and not very sophisticated version, but thoughts along the same lines can easily be found in writers advocating liberal education. The rational, autonomous choice is the ideal. As long as children do not choose something that hinders other people's choice, educators have no right to direct their choice. Common values are to be transmitted, but apart from this, liberal educators do not even want to direct children, what they make of life is their own choice. In the Norwegian discussion, the emphasis is not always on choice, it is often on strengthening each child's identity.[1]

What puzzles me even more than this link between neutrality and truth is that so many people, teachers and philosophers of education included, still believe that such neutrality is possible. They believe that school can avoid taking a stand between religions, or between world views in general. And even when they doubt the possibility of such neutrality, they keep arguing for a liberal education that is as neutral as possible.

My own view is that world view neutrality is impossible and not even desirable. In all upbringing and education something more than the explicitly taught content will be conveyed. It may be called ethos, hidden curriculum, or a perspective on life. It will always include religious or non-religious world view presuppositions. God's existence will be assumed or not assumed, a certain view of human nature will come across, beliefs about the meaning of life will be implicitly conveyed, etc. Aims for education are often expressed in terms of helping children to become persons, or helping them to understand and live in this world, and for such purposes educators need to know what it is to be a person and what this world is like, which to a large degree depend on beliefs and faith.

Sometimes it seems that even if, in theory, people know that we all have our own prejudices and that no presentation of knowledge or reality is neutral, they still implicitly assume that education can avoid promoting a specific view of life. In some cases it is acknowledged that education cannot be neutral between world views, or at least between religions, but still there seems to be this presupposition that a secular education is more neutral, more desirable, and better for autonomy, than a religiously based education.

1.1.2 The situation in Norway

I come to this topic from two different perspectives, a Norwegian and an English. This is not just accidental - being a Norwegian who happens to study in England, it is also an interesting combination. The two countries belong to the same culture and there has been a lot of contact over the centuries, but they are still quite different in many respects related to this discussion - politically, educationally, philosophically and theologically. I believe that my Norwegian and Lutheran perspective can give a different and useful contribution to the ongoing discussion about common education in England and elsewhere.

In Norway, we still have a Christian basis for the state school, the law saying that the school should help parents to give a Christian upbringing. Religious Education (RE) has until recently been mainly the teaching of Christianity, based on an evangelical Lutheran understanding. In 1997 this was changed. The content is now both Christianity and other religions and world views, but it is very unclear what the basis for the education is. Some documents try to present the subject as being as neutral as possible, others emphasize our Christian culture and heritage, and there is still the law's requirement of Christian upbringing in the school in general.

In the discussion about the subject, individuals and groups have been arguing for getting rid of the Christian basis for the school, saying that it should not favour one view before others. They seem to think that removing this clause from the law will solve the problem of the school having a particular influence, then it could be based on common values and we would all be happy.

There is a strong tradition in Norway for emphasizing the parents' rights and responsibilities in upbringing and education. The focus is then the parents as opposed to the state, not to the children. Recognizing the parents' rights and responsibilities does not mean that they can do what they want. But somebody has to make decisions on behalf of the children, somebody will inevitably influence very heavily what they will think about themselves and the world. If the state is to decide what the good life is for everybody, there is a danger of uniformity.

1.1.3 The situation in England

In England, the situation is different in many respects. Christianity seems to be less prevalent in society, and although RE is taught and the law requires an act of collective worship, the common school seems to be more secular than in Norway. When the basis for education in the common school is discussed, the focus is on values, not on world view.[2] It seems more or less taken for granted that the common school in a pluralistic society must be secular, and there seems to be an underlying presumption that secular schools are more acceptable for believers of different religions than religious schools could be for various groups of secular people.

Another side to my background is coming to England and trying to understand what 'liberal education' is, with its many uses. There is no equivalent concept in Norway. There is a concept for liberal (allmenn) used as the opposite of vocational education, but not for the frequent, more recent use as in 'liberal education in a pluralist society', where the emphasis is on helping pupils to make rational autonomous choices among all the options pluralism provides. In this context I find the same puzzling thought as in Norway, that by teaching about different religions, not taking a stand between them, the school avoids influencing pupils towards a specific world view.

Liberal education is widely assumed to be the solution to the problems of indoctrination that particularly religiously based education comes up against. Part of the discussion has been about whether it is at all possible to have Christian education and upbringing without it amounting to indoctrination.[3] This debate looks a bit odd to people like me coming from the outside, knowing that the state school in Norway always has had a Christian basis and that Norwegians are not known to be more indoctrinated than other people, and also knowing that Christians do not seem to be, in general, less able to think for themselves than other people. The debate does not seem to take empirical evidence into account. The other side of the coin is all the children educated in secular schools, which in practice are atheistic, who seem to become indifferent atheists. The question of indoctrination here is hardly ever discussed.

Some liberals will also claim that even parents do not have the right to bring their children up within a particular religion, because it will not lead to autonomy and choice. Does this mean that a notion of, or belief in, absolute truth, is not compatible with rational autonomy? It seems to imply that if we do not bring them up within a religion, we bring them up within nothing. Or we bring them up within something that is not indoctrinatory and autonomy-preventing. What is this 'something' that non-religious parents and schools - or at least liberal ones - bring up and educate the children within? My argument is that it includes aspects of a secular world view, answering questions about human nature and the meaning of life.

1.2 Purposes for working on this topic

1.2.1 Reasons for belief in neutrality

My main purpose is to try to understand why it is so commonly thought or taken for granted that secular liberal education is neutral between world views or religions. Many have argued against this belief, but it does not seem to stop people from assuming that it is both possible and desirable.

To me it is obvious that this is not right, and I have difficulties understanding why it is not equally obvious to everybody. When I try to explain my view, I often fail to make people understand, let alone convince them. Therefore I want to try to find out more about underlying presuppositions in 'neutralists'' thinking. Hopefully both I and others later may be able to communicate better and - if possible - convince people that world view neutrality is impossible, that it is necessary to look to something else to get a good common school.

I am not trying to argue against those who claim that religiously based education is indoctrinatory. I would rather try to show that basic influence on children's outlook on life, their beliefs and faith, is present in any kind of education and upbringing. Differences in strength of influence depend more on how things are done, on the support at home and in society at large, than on the content of the world view in question.

I want to do this by trying to unwrap world view presuppositions in so-called world view neutral, or no-standpoint, education, and also by trying to understand why religiously based education is regarded as different and more harmful in this respect. To have something to compare the 'neutral' education with, to make the differences between them explicit, I shall use an account of religiously based education. But religions are very different, and discussing 'religiously based education' in general glosses over the differences between them. This makes it difficult to argue carefully and in detail and invites sweeping statements that might be true about some religions, but totally wrong for others. I have therefore chosen to focus on one version of one religion, namely Lutheran, Protestant Christianity.[4]

1.2.2 Alternatives to a neutral school

Another purpose is to discuss what kind of alternatives there are. This discussion is based on the case of the state school in Norway, but many aspects of it are relevant for the school in both England and other countries. If there is no neutral alternative, there is no alternative everybody will be pleased with. Therefore we need to know what the options are so that we can find one that suits a majority of parents, and, equally important, one that is clear enough for parents to *know* whether they want it or not. There is no point in getting rid of the present Christian basis for the school before we know what we might want instead. The present trend seems to be to go for something 'common', something so diffuse that everybody thinks it is what they want. As a result, nobody gets what they want. This way, I believe, everybody will lose in the end.

Is a Christian common school viable, or is a fully secular school the only possibility? My concern is not that the state school should necessarily be Christian, either in Norway or anywhere else. But we ought to know what we are doing and not fool both ourselves, teachers, parents, and pupils into believing that there is no influence in any particular direction. I want to discuss whether it is possible to take elements from one option and put into the other, primarily to try to keep everybody in the same school. It is making the options more explicit that is my primary purpose, although I want to argue that Christian education is the best option and that we therefore ought to keep as many aspects of it as possible. The basic question is, I believe, whether we want a God-centred or a human-centred upbringing and education in the state school. Then we can try to adjust the one chosen to make it an option also for those who want the other one.

1.3 Some concepts

1.3.1 World view

I have been using the notions 'world view' and 'world view presuppositions', examples of the latter being view of reality, view of human nature, purpose of life, etc. In Norwegian we use the concept 'livssyn', directly translated as life view, or view of life, and similarly in Swedish (livsåskådning) and German (Lebensanschauung). All these are fairly vague concepts, and it is difficult to tell whether they mean exactly the same or not. For my purpose here, dealing only with certain aspects of world views and not with 'world view' as such, they should be sufficiently similar to use 'world view' for 'livssyn'.

A world view would normally include beliefs about the nature of reality, the existence of a god, the nature of man, life after death, and ethics (Aadnanes 1992, 13-14). Religions are regarded as world views,[5] although they have other important aspects too, like worship. One way of describing a world view is as the way we 'see' the world, as an attempt 'to explain the whole range of human experience by reference to what is most ultimately real' (Holmes 1983, 52). Many people hold a view in accordance with a certain tradition (Christianity, Islam, Humanism, Marxism, etc.), others will have a watered down version or a more eclectic view. The way I use the concept, every person will have his or her own world view, however fragmented and unconsciously held.

B.J. Walsh and J.R. Middleton suggest that there are four questions that are important in a world view, or where the answers form the basis of a world view:

(1) *Who am I?* Or, what is the nature, task and purpose of human beings?
(2) *Where am I?* Or, what is the nature of the world and universe I live in?
(3) *What's wrong?* Or, what is the basic problem or obstacle that keeps me from attaining fulfillment? In other words, how do I understand evil? And
(4) *What is the remedy?* Or, how is it possible to overcome this hindrance to my fulfillment? In other words, how do I find salvation? (Walsh & Middleton 1984, 35)

World view, or view of life, is a relatively new concept, having basically come into use because of the secularization of western society, to include both religious and non-religious answers to the question about the ultimate meaning of life. P.M. Aadnanes says that research on world view questions is relatively new and to a large degree something that has been done in Scandinavia, particularly in Sweden (Aadnanes 1997, 61).[6]

Aadnanes talks about a world view's 'inside' and 'outside', arguing that it is important to include both. The 'inside' is the personal, subjective side, with emphasis on the individualistic aspect, on emotions and experiences. The 'outside' is 'the collective, socio-cultural, historic, and thus "objective" aspects' (ibid., 66).

To this 'outside' belong what he calls 'livssynsrammer' (world view framework), including social and cultural / cognitive aspects of our society that we are more or less aware of, but also more specific religious, philosophical and political traditions (ibid., 74-6).[7] So a person's world view is influenced by and depends on both traditional world views and the society he or she is a part of, but there is also room for personal variations and decisions.

Aadnanes discusses whether it is only the concept of world view that is new, or whether also the phenomenon it denotes is an expression of late or post-modernity. He argues for a view that draws on both standpoints. A world view is something that everybody had, also before this label was used, it is something basically human to ask questions about our life. But on the other hand, the notion of a personal world view is an expression of individualism. In collectivist cultures and epochs the frameworks and traditions would to a large degree decide people's views, but our secular, pluralist, and individualistic time leads to a focus on personal, subjective world views (ibid., 78-80).

This emphasis on the personal character of a world view also suggests that we ought to be cautious about talking about world views as something fixed and absolute. They are influenced by many factors, they change, they develop. The world view that can be read from our life is also not necessarily in accordance with the view we profess. People may even say that they have no world view, and that may be right, in theory. But in practice it is not, our life will always show what we think important, who we think we are, what we believe about God, etc. 'Whether we have spelled it out to ourselves or not, each one of us has a worldview, which forms a background to the lives we lead' (Smart 1983, 3-4). Neither our theoretical nor our practical world view is necessarily coherent, or even consistent.[8]

Based as they are on religious, philosophical or political traditions, it is clear that world views cannot be scientifically proved. They are beliefs. J. Nome calls them 'trosposisjoner', positions of belief, arguing that they consist of both rational and irrational aspects. The irrational aspects function as axioms that are self-evident, and these are central to our world view and create the basis for our rational reflection (Nome 1953, 78-80).

When Nome talks about positions of belief, he thinks in philosophical, epistemological categories, not religious ones. But, says A. Smith, a personal world view may also be belief (tro) in a different meaning, namely faith, a confidence or trust in something or somebody outside ourselves. Such trust is at the centre of a Christian world view. But it is also possible to talk about confidence in an ideology, in something that gives our life meaning and purpose (Smith 1985, 416-20).

A world view is thus not only a perspective for interpreting and explaining, it can also give a vision for life, a purpose. A.F. Holmes mentions four needs a world view can fulfil: it unifies thought and life, defines the good life and finds hope and meaning in life, guides thought, and guides action (Holmes 1983, 5).

The fact that people have different world views does not necessarily mean that there is no truth, only that some - or all - of us are wrong. Although postmodernism talks about different worlds, there could still be an objective world, which we have understood more or less of. We could possibly understand each other's view, at least to a large degree, and be able to change perspectives. As R. Trigg says in a slightly different context,

> Our concepts provide as it were a window on the world which may well distort it. This does not mean that we cannot recognise the possibility that we are mistaken and we may even be able to discover our mistake for ourselves. Other concepts may prove more adequate, as when someone is converted to a religion or adopts a new scientific theory.
>
> What in fact has been missing from so much recent controversy in religion, science and other fields, is the notion of objectivity - of things being the case whether people recognise them or not. (Trigg 1973, 168)

When it comes to education, I am not claiming that liberal or no-standpoint education is based on an explicit, complete world view, given in one particular tradition, only that it will be based on and transmit certain world view presuppositions. In my discussion I want to focus on a few aspects of world views, a few presuppositions that I regard as important in education: what reality is like, what it is to be a human being, a person, what the meaning of life is, and what therefore the aim of education is. A lot has been written about ethics and values in education lately, which is one of my reasons for not concentrating on it. Also, I believe that these other aspects are more basic and therefore more useful for looking into the differences between world views.

The world view influence of the school will have several aspects. It will partly consist of the society's framework, partly of the dominant traditions, and partly of the teachers' and textbook writers' subjective views (Aadnanes 1997, 74-6). Educators always convey their view to children who are forming their own or having it formed. It is, therefore, important for it to be coherent and the best one we can think of. All schools are, I would argue, world view schools, but of various degrees. In some schools world view will not be regarded as important and only be transmitted implicitly, in others it will be more explicit (Myhre 1970, 35). If the school has no written code that says that a certain world view should be transmitted, it will be fairly accidental which view has the strongest influence.

To form a world view is very close to the main task for upbringers: to give children a framework for understanding and interpreting the world they live in, to find meaning, purpose and direction for their lives. R.T. Allen suggests that 'the central task of education is to initiate the young in the meaning or meanings of life' (Allen 1991, 51). Liberal educators might want to say that they have no particular view on the purpose and meaning of life and that it is part of their philosophy that this should be left to the individual to decide. As far as I can see, this is a particular answer, the liberal answer, and one that a lot of people would disagree with.

1.3.2 Upbringing

The Norwegian language has no word equivalent to 'education'. The school's task has generally been talked about as 'oppdragelse og undervisning' - upbringing and teaching. These two are regarded as equally important tasks in school, tasks that are closely interrelated. Sometimes teaching is said to be included in upbringing, being the more cognitive side of what we do to help children become adults.

Upbringing is basically the process of helping youngsters to take over the responsibility for their own life, helping them to live. By living together with them, we necessarily recommend to them a way of life, we show them what it is to live as human beings, as persons. The German educationalist Klaus Mollenhauer says that an important aspect of upbringing is transmission, telling the children through our way of life what is important for us (Mollenhauer 1985/1996, 22). So even if teachers concentrate on teaching, because of their very presence they cannot avoid conveying something about the good life to those they teach.

That teachers always are role models seems to be more recognized in Norway than in England. In the general part of the new Norwegian National Curriculum, for instance, it is said that educators as role models should lead the way by their example (Læreplanverket 1996, 19; Core Curriculum 1993/1997, 9). Through relationships between teachers, other staff, and pupils, through the adults' behaviour, what they say and do not say, through the way the school is set up and run, through rules and syllabuses, the pupils are influenced in their view of what life is all about, what a person is, what is important, what is right and wrong, etc. Elements of what makes up a world view are conveyed.

It is this upbringing aspect of what happens in school that I am interested in. Not what the subjects and the subject content are, but what pupils will learn about truth, who they are, what the meaning of their life is, and which choices they have.

Because 'education' is the concept normally used in England about what happens in school, I shall use this concept too, but then in a wide meaning that includes and emphasizes upbringing. John White does the same (White 1982, 5 and 1990, 167), being concerned not only with what should be taught, but with how to bring up children.

Certainly, the most important influence in this respect comes from the home in the early years. But school gives a contribution, its importance depending, *inter alia*, on the pupils' age and the relationship between pupil and teacher. If coherent, the school's influence would probably mean more to pupils who have not got a very coherent view from home.

Talking so much about implicit influence and transmission, there is the question whether this is upbringing or socialization. Berger & Luckmann say about primary socialization that 'the individual not only takes on the roles and attitudes of others, but in the same process takes on their world' (Berger & Luckmann 1967, 132), implying that transmission of world view aspects is part of socialization. But it is also part of upbringing. The difference between upbringing and socialization is, in my view, a matter of intention. Socialization happens, all the time, through a lot of agents. Upbringing, on the other hand, is intentional, and it is done by people who have responsibility for children, either by being their parents or by delegation.

If parents and other upbringers and educators do not think about how they want the children to interpret the world and understand themselves and the purpose of their life, and do not think about how their own life transmits or could transmit this view, they are not doing their job properly. The children will be socialized into some world anyway, the educators' responsibility is to think about it and do it intentionally and with coherence.

1.4 Education in Norway, past and present

Most of the time since the second world war, the social democratic Labour party has been in power in Norway, with a strong emphasis on the common good, on solidarity and equality. It has been an aim to have one common school for all, this is also necessary because Norway is a very thinly populated country. Only about 1% of the children are not in the state school.[9]

Norway is sometimes used as an example of a nearly monocultural society (Tamir 1995, 163). Although it has changed over the last few decades, compared to other European countries this is still true, both ethnically and religiously. Only about 5% are immigrants, more than half of them from Europe. Nearly 90% of the population are members of the Lutheran state church,[10] although only about 10% are regular church goers (1993).[11]

School is in Norway primarily regarded as the parents' helping hand. The 1969 Education Act, in its first clause, expresses the purpose of state schools in the following way:

> The purpose of primary and lower secondary education shall be, in agreement and cooperation with the home, to help to give pupils a Christian and moral upbringing, to develop their mental and physical abilities, and to give them good general knowledge so that they may become useful and independent human beings at home and in the society.
>
> The school shall promote intellectual freedom and tolerance, and strive to create good forms of cooperation between teachers and pupils and between school and home. (Curriculum Guidelines 1987/1990, 17)[12]

The rationale behind the school giving Christian upbringing is not the state church, but that more than 80% of parents have their children baptized, promising to give them a Christian upbringing.[13] Both the previous and the new (1997) National Curriculum Guidelines emphasize that the school's basis is Christian and humanistic values. It has been argued, however, that the new Guidelines are more humanistic and less Christian, and also that they focus on the ethical and cultural side of Christianity and ignore the faith aspect. [14]

The new RE, Christianity with religion and world view[15], is compulsory for everybody, with the possibility to withdraw a child from certain activities only (like going to church, praying, etc.). It is very unclear what it will be like, the debate still goes on about both the epistemological basis for the subject and the rules for exemption.[16]

It is difficult to say what the school's Christian basis means in everyday school life. At least it should imply that the school's rules have to be in line with Christian ethics. Normally, there will be an end of term service in church. Apart from this, today it is very much up to the school and the individual teacher how much they want to make of it. There is no tradition for school assemblies, what happens of prayers and hymn singing happens in the classroom, at the beginning or end of the day. Nobody knows how common this practice is now, apart from it being assumed that it is more common in primary than in secondary schools. Some teachers will also say grace with their pupils before lunch.

1.5 Outline of argument

1.5.1 My perspective

In the process of working on chapter two I found myself writing about human beings that 'they are all created in God's image'. Why 'they'? Why not 'we'? Why did I try to write about Christianity from the outside, so to speak, when I definitely am on the inside and firmly believe that God has created us all in his image? Reflecting on this, I found that I was trying to be neutral, ending up writing as an atheist, as if God and Christianity are only one option among others. The liberal assumption that it is possible to step outside all views and look at them from a no-standpoint has deeply influenced our thinking, Christians as well as non-Christians. We find it in research as well as in education, and I found it in my own thinking and writing.

I try in this thesis to be explicitly Christian. I want to make explicit that I am writing from the inside, from the basic presuppositions that God is alive and the Bible true. Not only because that is what I am and believe, but also to use my own writing as an example of what I am writing about. I certainly also want to try to give an inside account of the views I do not share, but my discussion of them, and evaluation, will not be from a liberal perspective, so-called neutral, it will be from my Christian standpoint. This will underline a point I am arguing, that liberals in their discussion of Christian or religiously based education do not view it from a neutral viewpoint, a viewpoint that everybody would share, but from their very specific liberal perspective, with their liberal assumptions. And not only liberals themselves, but a lot of us are taking the same perspective, assuming that we are neutral, not seeing the implicit philosophical presuppositions. And if it is not possible to avoid the presuppositions in philosophical discussion, how do the liberals think they can avoid them in educating young children?

1.5.2 Outline

I start my argument in chapter two by giving a fairly detailed account of Christian education, on its own premises, looking into some world view questions, the purpose of education, and the relationship between upbringing and faith. This chapter shows how Christian faith, at least in certain versions, influences everything in education, that it cannot be confined to a religious area. One important function of the chapter is to give a frame of reference for analysing the neutrality of liberal education.

Chapter three is basically an analysis of two accounts of supposedly no-standpoint education, arguing that they both will transmit particular world view presuppositions, presuppositions that are incompatible with Christian ones and therefore not neutral between world views. First I focus on John White's theory, then I analyse Kenneth A. Strike's view of liberal education. I try to spell out their view of reality and human nature, meaning of life and purpose of education. Although I only analyse two accounts, I argue that I have demonstrated that education cannot be neutral between world views. Most attempts are human-centred, in practice atheistic, they are incompatible with Christianity in that they have no God-dimension.

In chapter four I list and analyse various reasons for thinking that religious or world view neutrality is possible and desirable. I argue that none of them is valid. A lot of them are based on a biased view of what religion is, at least in the case of Christianity. Also, they go wrong because they are concerned with religions rather than with world views in general, and because of their view of education and knowledge. When it comes to neutrality being desirable, a number of the arguments are about truth. The belief that claiming something as true does not go with autonomy is irrelevant, since all education claims truth, only in different ways. I argue that liberal education in many ways is more likely to indoctrinate than Christian education is.

Chapter five focuses on the writings of Terence H. McLaughlin, who argues that education can be both Christian and liberal at the same time, which I so far have argued is impossible. I analyse the presuppositions in the various forms of education he advocates and discuss how he comes to terms with including both Christian and liberal perspectives. He seems to work basically from a liberal point of view, with a liberal view of autonomy, trying to fit Christianity into this perspective. This, I claim, leads into contradictions when he tries to reconcile autonomy and faith. I argue that his notions of 'liberal' in 'liberal religious' and 'common liberal' education are different.

After having argued that no-standpoint, liberal education is no more neutral in relation to world views than Christian education, in chapter six I ask what this means for the common school. My primary claim is that common education ought to be explicit about its basis and built on what the parents want. The majority of parents in Norway - and probably in England too - are neither committed Christians nor committed atheists and may be uncertain as to what kind of upbringing they want the school to give their children. I argue that in principle, Christian education is the best option, and discuss how and to what extent it is possible to give Christian education in a state school with both pupils and teachers of many different faiths and convictions.

CHAPTER 2

Christian Education and its Purpose

In this chapter I want to discuss education based on, or within a framework of, Christianity. My point is not to engage in debate about various accounts of Christian education, but to outline an account that can serve as a background for and contrast to the liberal accounts discussed in the following chapters. This is also the version that will be my frame of reference when discussing Christian education in state schools (ch. six).

The natural choice for me is to work within the orthodox,[17] evangelical Lutheran tradition we find in the mainstream of the Norwegian Church. It will in many aspects be similar to other Christian accounts, and not too different from what is often called evangelical Anglicanism. The following account of Christian education is my own, based on writings by the internationally recognized Norwegian expert on Luther, I. Asheim, and other Norwegian theologians (T. Austad, B. Hareide, O. Øystese).[18] They differ in various ways in their view of Lutheran education, but they are broadly within the same tradition. In Norway most of the work on this topic is done by theologians, which makes it very fundamental, but also means that the perspective is theological, not educational.[19]

The reason why I have chosen the Lutheran tradition, apart from the obvious one, is that it has a very good way of coming to terms with faith and education. Luther's theology includes his model of the two governments, where he tries to hold together what the Bible says about God as creator and God as saviour. This model is helpful in education because it both emphasizes the limits to what people (e.g. teachers) can do to 'make' other people (e.g. pupils) Christians, and at the same time underlines the value and necessity of upbringing for life in this world.

Before I go into Luther's model, however, I want to outline what the world where upbringing and education take place, looks like from this perspective. This whole account will be given from the inside. That does not only mean that I shall try to present the view as it would present itself, it also means that it is my own view and in that respect is seen from the inside. It means that I see fewer basic problems with this view than with others, and also that this is where I get my perspective on education from. This is the view that - on the whole - determines what I regard as important and interesting aspects, both in the Lutheran view itself and also in other views. So in addition to giving an account of a specific Christian view of education and its purpose, it implicitly gives information about my own basic thinking within education.[20] When in the following I use the term 'Christian', I normally mean evangelical Lutheran Christianity (unless the context suggests otherwise).

2.1 Aspects of a Lutheran world view

There is no one Christian set of answers to world view questions, questions about reality and human nature, knowledge and ethics. First, the various denominations will differ in certain aspects. Secondly, Christianity is not a complete view, answering all questions, so it may for instance be combined with various philosophies, like existentialism or idealism. And thirdly, there will be personal variations.

Within traditional Christianity, certain aspects will always be part of the world view and determine the framework for education. There are, however, theological schools that are very different, and their educational consequences will also be others.[21] Most orthodox Christian traditions, however, will agree with the following account. Specific presuppositions about the world and the purpose of life will be included. Some such aspects are a living God who cares for everybody, objective ethics, linear understanding of time from creation to the day of judgement, and every person being of infinite value.Underlying all this is the belief that the Bible is a source of true knowledge about God and his relationship with human beings, that God in the Bible and in Jesus from Nazareth has revealed himself and knowledge that we could not otherwise find. This knowledge is not contrary to what we find out from nature, it is rather on a different level and in different areas, and it gives us the key to understanding the world and ourselves.

In relation to the three traditional categories of biblical hermeneutic - fundamentalist, conservative, and liberal - I would put myself in the middle category. Although this is a broad category, it is central to it that the Bible is God's authoritative revelation. It is a revelation in history, with its human side and with differences between the writers, but the Bible is still regarded as consistent, with Christ as the centre, and with one message.

2.1.1 View of reality

Any Christian view of reality will begin and end with God, a personal God, a God who created everything from nothing. His continued creation upholds the world, which has no life in itself. The German theologian E. Brunner says that God is the primary reality, everything else is secondary, dependent reality, called out of nothing, for as long as the creator will

(Brunner 1948, 18-19). 'God, then, according to Christian understanding, in a wholly objective, realist, sense, is the source and power of the world, of history, and of our own life as creatures and children of God.' (Hebblethwaite 1988, 6)

The world is not something that just happened to come into existence, it is made for a purpose, for God's glory. The world is both a material and a spiritual world. Not two worlds, as in Plato's philosophy. Not a material world here and now and a spiritual world to come, but one world with both material and spiritual aspects. It is a world created by a God who became flesh and is part of history, and where each person is a unity of body and soul.

A Christian perspective of the world is different from both a modern and a postmodern perspective. Modernity is characterized by the belief that the world can be known objectively by means of the scientific method. Reality is given, everybody lives in the same world, and beliefs are private additions that are all right as long as they have no socially public significance (Middleton &Walsh 1995, 43).

Postmodernism, on the other hand, denies universal truth, believing that we live in a reality we have constructed. Even if an 'objective' reality exists, we cannot learn anything about it, our access is always mediated by our own linguistic and conceptual constructions, our world view (ibid., 31-2). All worlds are therefore private. There is no metanarrative, no tradition, that can be shown to be universal, so we can only have small narratives, various cultural traditions, and the question of which one is true is irrelevant because there is no such thing (ibid., 76-7). Postmodernism favours 'Nietzschean perspectivism, which rejects the idea of the world in itself, of objective reality, as rooted in our longest lie: the belief in God' (Hollinger 1994, 177). What is important is that we find a story that is meaningful, a story which provides us with some way of interpreting our life, including religion or world view.

In Christianity, it is true that there is a 'world in itself', that there is universal truth and knowledge. But limited as we are, we cannot expect to grasp it, to understand it fully, and scientific method cannot tell us everything. God and the spiritual reality are as real as the physical reality. 'Postmodernism gently applied rightly questions the arrogance of modernism; postmodernism ruthlessly applied nurtures a new hubris and deifies agnosticism' (Carson 1996, 544).

D. Carson says we can approach truth 'asymptotically', i.e. getting towards it, but never knowing everything. This kind of truth is what Brunner calls world-truths. But there is another, singular Truth. If God is the primary reality, the Word of God is the primary Truth. Truth is God himself, the word (Logos), Christ. Knowing this Truth is not having knowledge about something, but a personal encounter. God does not reveal a number of truths, he reveals himself (Brunner 1948, 35-7).

The physical world is structured and runs along natural laws, but God rules also over the laws and can set them aside, for instance as an answer to prayer. They only limit our freedom, not God's (ibid., 23). Creation is not ours to rule over, we are God's stewards, we are responsible to him for how we look after it. This also means that nobody has a right to use the resources for their own good, it should always be for the good of everybody.

The world is no longer what it was meant to be, because people turned their backs on God and wanted to be their own god, to rule their own life. There is now an ongoing battle between good and evil, between God and the devil, and although God won the victory in Jesus' death and resurrection, the battle is still going on in every human being, both God and the devil wanting to win us over to their side.

Time in this world is linear. Just as God is the beginning of everything, he will also be the end. At the end of time, there will be the day of judgement, with God being the judge. He will create a new heaven and a new earth, where justice reigns and all evil will have disappeared. This is not reincarnation, with the soul being born into this same world but in a different body. It is the whole person, with soul and body, living in a new world.

The God-created and fallen world is the world both teachers and pupils live in. God is the centre, not an optional extra, an 'icing on the cake'. Such a God-centredness permeating a school is more important for its 'Christianness' than any single activity like an 'act of collective worship'. Whatever the pupils study, it is part of God's creation. Whatever senses or abilities they use, they are God's gifts. Whatever decisions are to be made, the purpose would be the glory of God and other people's good. All the time there is the struggle to do good and not evil, to let God be Lord. And there is the perspective of eternity, the knowledge that death is not the end, that there is a better life with God to come for everyone who wants it.

2.1.2 View of human nature

If I were coming from a liberal perspective, I might have focused an account of human nature on the difference between liberalism and communitarianism regarding the self as a self-created individual or as a product of community. And I might have tried to analyse a Christian view of human nature using these categories. But since I am coming from a Christian perspective, it will be the other way round, I shall in later chapters use a Christian view when analysing secular accounts.

A Christian view of reality begins with and focuses on God, and so does a Christian view of human nature (Sandsmark 1992, 114-15). According to the Bible, man[22] is 'a created and finite existence in both body and spirit' (Niebuhr 1941/1964, 12). A Christian view of human nature is God-centred, 'he is understood primarily from the standpoint of God, rather than the uniqueness of his rational faculties or his relation to nature' (ibid., 13).

Human beings are created in God's image, created to communicate with him, known and loved by him. God wants a personal relationship with everyone, he wants to be our Lord, but also our loving father, our faithful friend. He is a holy God who lives in the 'high and holy' (Isaiah 57:15), but he also lives in every person who welcomes him. We can listen to him, primarily in his word, the Bible, and we can talk to him in prayer.

The Bible also teaches that people have turned away from God and have become self-centred. Evil is not something peripheral, or something that has its roots in society, it is right at the centre of the human personality, in the will. We will be our own god, control our own life, be independent of our creator. This is what the Bible calls sin.

'Man is an individual but he is not self-sufficing. The law of his nature is love … This law is violated when man seeks to make himself the centre and source of his own life. His sin is therefore spiritual and not carnal' (Niebuhr 1941/1964, 16). This does not mean that everybody is selfish through and through, but that at the centre of our life is our own self. There is still in everybody a desire to love and do good to other people, but this desire always conflicts with the desire to do what I think is for my own good. Even the best desires are not completely free from selfishness. Therefore life will never be harmonious, it will always be a struggle.

Human beings are not free to turn to God by their own will, because our will is in this respect not free, it is self-centred. It is always God who takes the initiative, who asks people to give their life to him. In Jesus Christ he offers forgiveness for sins and eternal life. People are free to say no and continue their self-centred life, but real freedom is to be bound to God, the creator, and live according to his will (Asheim 1961, 202-24). Bound to God, we are free from being bound by our own self, by society or other people. There is a fixed point outside society and outside self to hold on to, to judge from, and from which to work for changes in self and society.

When people say yes to God in Christ, we get a new nature alongside the old one, a nature that wants to do God's will. But all the time this has to fight with the old, self-centred nature. Also for Christians life will be a struggle, a struggle to let God be God and not let the old self take over again.

God's norms for how we ought to live are from creation in people's hearts. This means that everybody is born with a sense of right and wrong, good and bad, a sense that conforms with biblical ethics, with love of neighbour. From this it follows that Christian ethics is not irrational, there are rational arguments for it that everybody can understand, even if they disagree.

But since people have become self-centred, reason too is influenced by self-centredness and therefore not a perfect guide. It thinks and acts as if it is itself God and the governor of life, not wanting to see what is revealed in nature and society (ibid., 100-107). Therefore God's revelation in the Bible is needed to show humankind what is really reasonable, what is in the interest of people. To get it right, reasoning must be based on the revelation in the Bible. This means that what is right and wrong has to be taught.

Christian ethics does not give us all the answers, we still have to think. 'Christians trying to discover what the will of God is put just as much of themselves into it as an agnostic does trying to discover what the right thing to do is.' (Ward 1986, 77) The rules in the Bible have to be understood in their context and then applied 'in the very different conditions of the modern world ... It requires sensitivity, experience and maturity' (ibid. 79).

Human beings are not free to turn to God, but they are relatively free to act in God's world in matters to do with other people, society, upbringing, etc., i.e. in all ethical matters. Therefore it is both possible and important to encourage other-concern and to restrain self-interest. It is also necessary to convey that doing good to others may involve struggling or even suffering. Every person is responsible to God for the way they lead their life, in relation to nature, other people, and to God.

A Christian view of human nature has implications for education. Every pupil has the same and infinite value, irrespective of how bright they are and what background they have, whether they are naughty or kind, noisy or quiet. Teachers can tell pupils - and show through their own lives - that God wants to be their friend, that he loves every one, even those who feel they are loved by no one. But it is up to them to respond, up to them whether they want to communicate or not. This is the choice everybody has, the decision they have to make: whether to face God, worship and serve him, or to turn their back on him and try to control their own life.

In the ethical area it is important that teachers encourage good and restrain evil. They should help pupils to see that they have desires to do both good and bad, and that it is possible to use one's will to do good. If we ask God, he will help us. Responsibility and forgiveness are important in personal relationships, both with God and with other people, and both dimensions should be part of the ethos of a Christian school.

2.1.3 Meaning of life and the aim of education

According to the Bible, there is a given meaning for everybody's life. God created us for a purpose, namely to give him glory, to worship and serve him. We are different and will do it in different ways, but this is why we are here. This gives meaning to every part of life, including education. To live in this close relationship with him is the good life. Outside it we are not fully human, not living the life we were created for. This does not mean that non-believers are inferior people. Everybody has the same worth, but the point is to what extent we live our life according to our purpose. In biblical thinking meaning is not in the person, but comes to us as a gift from God, as the revealed Word. We can only see this meaning by faith (Brunner 1948, 71-2).

The purpose of education, then, is to help children to understand what it means to worship and serve God and to equip them with what they need to do it. It is often said that education should have its end in itself, that to give it a purpose is to make it instrumental to something else.

In 'Ethics and Education', R.S. Peters distinguishes between extrinsic and intrinsic ends, between purposes and aims (Peters 1966, 27-9). An aim of education, according to him, is a specification of what the activity is, it focuses on the 'what', it tells what is worthwhile to achieve. This is intrinsic to education, to the activity of transmitting what is worthwhile. The extrinsic end is concerned with the 'why': why are we doing this, what is the purpose of it? According to Peters, '[t]hese are strange questions to ask about education itself, for as 'education' implies the transmission of what is of ultimate value, it would be like asking about the purpose of the good life' (ibid., 29). So we can talk of the aim of education, but not about its purpose.

As far as I can see, this way of thinking is closely linked to Peters' thoughts of what education is, and also to his view of the meaning of life, the good life. The following quotation may indicate that Peters does not believe in any ultimate meaning and purpose: 'Our basic predicament in life is to learn to live with its ultimate pointlessness ... the most important dimension of education is that in which we learn to come to terms with the pointlessness of life' (Peters, in Allen 1991, 54).

Peters seems to think that it is possible to discuss the aim of education independently of the meaning of life. I think he is wrong. It is his particular view of life and education that makes it natural for him to think like that. If life has no given, ultimate purpose, then it may seem arbitrary and instrumental to give education a purpose, an extrinsic aim. Education is an activity that is worthwhile in itself and should not be made instrumental to some other aspect of life, like getting a job, wealth, or power. But if life itself has an ultimate meaning, this means that both education, job, wealth, power, and any other aspect of life is seen in this perspective. Not one part being instrumental to another, but everything being part of a whole with a purpose.

So education does not only have a 'what', an aim, it also has a 'why', a purpose. God created us for a life in worship and service, and education is part of this life.

What does this mean? One of the questions often related to this is where faith comes into it. Is faith one of the things we need to be able to serve God? This is not a straight forward question with a straight forward answer, but it is one where Luther's model of the two governments is particularly helpful. I now turn to that model. I shall first give a short introduction to it, and then discuss each of the two governments and the educational implications.

2.2 The model of the two governments

Luther (1483-1546) was a theologian, not an educationalist, he did not work out an educational theory. But he did two important things for education: he worked very hard to encourage education for all (Asheim 1961, 21), and he outlined some important educational consequences of his theology. Hareide presents Luther's educational thoughts under two headlines: a) the necessity of upbringing, and b) the possibility of upbringing (Hareide 1955, 26). These two reflect Luther's concerns. He keeps telling parents and other people in authority that children need upbringing and teaching, but he also maintains that there are limits to what upbringing can achieve and that it is not a way to salvation.

Luther's model of the two governments is not a dogma, but an interpretation of how the New Testament presents the relationship between God as Creator and God as Saviour. It presupposes a theology that teaches that God reveals himself both in nature and history (general revelation) and in Christ (special revelation).

According to Luther, the Bible tells us that God governs the world in two different ways, or with two hands, namely his secular (weltlich) and his spiritual (geistlich) government (Regimente). God created the world, and upholds it because he wants to save it. What he does to uphold it is called his secular government, and what he does to save people is called his spiritual government.

The secular government is also called the government of reason. Our rationality, and our ability to know right from wrong, good from evil, are important in this government. He has also created structures for our relationships, some orders or stations (Ordnung, Stand), and each individual belongs to a variety of stations simultaneously. Ministry, family and secular authority are the three basic orders, and we have various stations related to the family, the ministry, and the secular authority (being children, parents, church members, clergy, citizens, judges, rulers, etc.) (Althaus 1965/1972, 36-7).

These 'Ordnungen' are where God hands out his good gifts, like love and justice, they are his tools for governing and upholding the world. These structures must remain if the world is to stand, although not necessarily in the shape they have in the present society (ibid.). Family, church and secular authority are God's means to restrain sin and the devil, and to make room for life and fellowship, to create order and justice. All ethical matters belong to God's secular government, Luther says, and since upbringing and education are moral enterprises, this is where they belong. They are part of

God's work to uphold the world as a good place to live, with good people and useful citizens, a world where the gospel can be preached.

Upbringing is necessary because human beings are sinful, we do not want to follow God's good will for our life. Also the devil works to prevent people from living according to God's will. We are too weak to withstand bad examples and suppress bad inclinations (Asheim 1961, 47). The purpose of upbringing is thus to lead people into God's structures and help them to be able to live there. The structures force us to live together and care for each other, but we need upbringing to learn to live in them. Upbringing can never make us perfect, but it can create good citizens, people who at least outwardly live according to God's creator will. The aim is *justitia civilis et moralis*, which is possible to attain (Hareide 1955, 62).[23]

On the other hand, what God does to save people, his work of salvation, is called his spiritual government, or the government of the gospel. God governs here as Saviour and Redeemer, he offers forgiveness for sins. In this government there is no way God can force people to comply with his will and his desires. In the secular government, parents have power over children, governments have power over citizens, and even the church has power structures. But there is no way of making people open their hearts and lives to God. The only means God has to influence people in the spiritual government is his word, the gospel, he can only invite people to receive faith as a gift.

God works through whoever preaches and teaches his word, whether clergy, teachers, parents, or whoever they are, even if they do not believe in him themselves. So when the Bible is taught in school, it gives the pupils an opportunity to learn more about God, and it gives God an opportunity to invite them to a life with him. It is a 'hear-government', where you hear the gospel and respond in faith or disbelief (Austad 1972, 3). Educators have no control over this response, what comes out of the teaching is a matter between the child and God.

It is perhaps natural to think that the distinction between the two governments is a distinction between institutions - church and secular authorities - or even between people - Christians and non-Christians. But it is not, nor is it a distinction between different things we do. Bible teaching can be in the secular government, and teaching geography may be used by God in his spiritual government. And that is the key - 'used by God'. The governments are two ways God deals with the world, or rather two purposes God has in what he does. He wants to uphold the world, and he wants to save people, to give them a new life.

The governments are different and must be distinguished, but we must not separate them (Øystese 1989, 300). They are both God's hands, working in and with his creation. But what is the point of this model if we cannot know which is which, if there is no way for us to know whether what we are doing is part of God's upholding or his saving work? There are two answers to that.

First, the model helps us to see that God has two different purposes. Although his ultimate purpose is to save everybody and create for us a new heaven and a new earth, he is also concerned with this world and our life together here. And although we have no control over his 'whats' and 'hows', the model makes clear that there are two different things we as educators can contribute to. In the secular government it is necessary for people to know what is right and wrong, good and bad, and to behave according to it, so that sets us some tasks. And in the spiritual government we know that the preaching of the gospel is necessary, so that has to be done.

Secondly, it highlights two important points for educators, and particularly for those interested in or involved in Christian education. The first is the value of good education for everybody, for making them good citizens, irrespective of their being or becoming Christians. The second is that pupils' faith is outside the control of the educator, that there is no possibility of indoctrinating anybody into Christian faith, even if we tried.

Parents' functions are mainly in the secular government, as upbringers, but they also have a task in the spiritual government, namely to teach their children the gospel, the word of God. The same is true for teachers. Their functions are basically in the secular government: they help parents with the upbringing, they teach secular subjects, they equip children for life in this world. But schools should also teach the Bible, Luther says, and in this aspect teachers are functioning within the spiritual government.[24]

2.2.1 The secular government

When Luther labels education a 'weltlich Ding', he means that it primarily belongs to the secular government, it has to do with God creating and upholding the world. It is important, though, to remember that it is *God's* secular government, not secular in the 'non-religious' meaning. Education happens in God's world, its being secular only means that its primary purpose is not salvation and eternal life.

God wants us to create and maintain a good society to live in - being good citizens, good politicians, good parents, good bus drivers, good teachers. To do our work in society is to fulfil God's calling. People need good education to govern homes, towns and countries in a wise way. Even if there were no soul and heaven or hell, Luther said, it would be necessary to have good schools - both for boys and for girls - and learned people. So education is for our life together here in this society (Asheim 1970, 126).

Luther is often attacked for having a too pessimistic view of human nature: we are sinners, with no free will, and with a useless rationality. This is only true within the spiritual government, regarding the question of salvation. In the secular government, in ethical questions, reason can guide us, and we have a relatively free will. There is in Luther an optimism concerning what upbringers can do to help children grow up to be morally good people. This is linked to his view of human nature, that people are both good and bad. Although God is the only person who can, through salvation, do anything radical about evil, upbringing can moderate it and also encourage the good. When Luther talks about young people behaving badly, he does not say it is because of their sinfulness, but he blames parents and teachers for not doing their job. Life is a battle between good and bad, God and the devil, in the secular as well as the spiritual government, and upbringing and education are God's 'weapons' (Asheim 1961, 23).

Luther even claimed that in ethical matters it is not necessary for educators to consult the Bible, because reason and tradition and natural parental love will tell them what is right. This reflects his theology, that people are created with a sense of right and wrong, given by God, and therefore consistent with what God tells us in the Bible. Sin, however, makes people liable to think reasonable what suits them best, so the Bible is needed as a corrective. Luther's society was permeated by Christian ethical norms, so tradition and reason and the Bible would tell people the same (ibid., 25-7).

So Luther is positive about the outcome of upbringing. It is possible to educate relatively good people, good citizens, where 'good' means people who live according to Christian ethics, at least outwardly. Education cannot change people's hearts, but it can restrain selfishness, encourage love and concern for others, build good habits, etc.

SERVICE AS THE PURPOSE OF EDUCATION

What then, within this framework, is the purpose of education? In the secular government the ultimate aim is 'zu Gottes dienst', for God's service (ibid., 58). This is not used as a specific, technical term, he does not discuss it, but mentions it as the obvious aim. It was important for Luther to make clear that we cannot serve God in the church only, by being priests or monks or nuns. No, we can all serve God in our various callings, in the stations, in 'Beruf und Stand' (ibid.), and we do it by serving our neighbours, by doing good to other people, both individually and as a society.

No particular actions are required, but to do what is good in our stations - to be a good parent, a good priest, a good teacher. So a child serves God by being obedient to parents and other authorities, and parents serve God by being good parents and not ignoring their children. Teachers serve God by being good teachers, by doing their job properly. As teachers, the 'neighbours' whom they are to love and serve, are their pupils (Pedersen 1996, 83).

Luther's phrase is 'to serve God in church and society'. M.J. Harran, writing about Luther's pedagogy, talks about serving 'God and society' (Harran 1990, 323). This blurs Luther's point that service in society is service for God as much as service in the church is. The point is that we can serve God in ordinary jobs, and as family members and citizens. These are all vocations, callings, and in all these positions God can and will use people in his upholding of the world.

What does it mean, then, to serve God? Service is a central concept in the Bible. Jesus talks about himself as a servant, and about all his followers being each others' servants (John 13:13-16). The greatest commandment is to love God and your neighbour, and this love is not primarily emotional, but practical (Luke 6:27-38, 1 John 3:18). It is a question of giving other people what they need, both as individuals and by influencing the society so it becomes a better place to live.

To give people what they need does not necessarily mean to give them what they ask for, or what is commonly assumed in society that everybody needs. No, 'need' must be interpreted within the biblical framework, from God's perspective. Christian ethics must guide the considerations about what people need. Some needs are obvious for everybody, like food and clothes, love and safety. Others depend on people's view of life and reality. According to the Bible, our most important need is salvation, forgiveness of sins - this is what we first of all should urge people to receive.

To serve God by serving other people is something active, creative. It means being alert to others' needs, taking into account that people may not necessarily need what they ask for, or ask for what they need. Jesus himself is the best example, he served people by giving them what he saw they needed, whether they asked for it (Luke 7:3-10) or not (Luke 7:12-15), and sometimes he gave them something different (Mark 2:3-12). We are not God, and it is easy to be paternalistic and impose on others what we think they ought to get, without enough knowledge and sensitivity and without asking for God's guidance. Service requires respect for those we want to serve. We offer them something, we do not force on them something they do not want.

Thus service is not an easy, straight forward lifestyle, it may require knowledge, wisdom, imagination, humility and love. But according to the Bible, this is the good life, the only good life. It is up to the individual to choose whether to live like this or not, but a life can only be good to the extent it is lived according to the Creator's purpose. The choice is between a God-centred life - the only true good life - and a self-centred life.

God wants everybody to develop their abilities and use them for the good and joy of others. It is a life focused on God and other people, away from oneself. Does this mean that we should totally neglect our own needs and interests? No, this is not the case. First, it is not possible, as Bishop Butler says, because 'we have a perception of our own interests, like conscious-ness of our own existence, which we always carry about with us' (Butler 1726/1964, 194). And secondly, we are responsible to God for looking after all that he has given us, like our health, physically and mentally, and our talents, so that we can make use of them. This is the good life, where joy comes from giving, not receiving, from serving, not being master.

The Creator made us people who depend on each other, we are relational and not self-sufficient individuals. The perspective on the good life in the Bible is primarily what is good for us together - and in the long run - , not what is good for *me*. Still, benevolence often leads to happiness, more often, says Butler, than pursuing other more self-centred affections like pride, revenge or sensual gratifications (ibid., 179). But doing good will nevertheless sometimes include sacrifice and self-denial. This is still the good life, because when we love God, the highest good is to do his will.

To live according to Christian ethics is not primarily to keep a set of rules, to avoid doing certain things. The rules - the commandments and other biblical norms - are there to stop us when in our selfishness we are about to harm others, or when, again in our selfishness, we try to persuade ourselves that something bad is good, or at least all right. A life according to Christian ethics is much more, it is positive and active, trying to find good things to do towards others. It is not guided by our own aims and desires, but by God and the needs we see around us.

But is not Christian ethics full of rules that are not other-concerned, rules about things that do not seem to harm anybody? It is often claimed, for instance, that there is nothing wrong with a homosexual relationship as long as the two adults involved want it. Is not Christian ethics here just an arbitrary rule to forbid something that does no harm?

There are at least two things to be said in response to this. The first one is that this is a very individualistic argument. We cannot just evaluate the two persons' lives, but must take into account the consequences for society. We know that there are cases where something that is good and enjoyable for individuals may ruin communities (e.g. pollution as a result of driving). In this particular question, as in so many others, there is no way we can know the consequences, we can only think in possibilities. This leads to the second response, which is that God sees further than us. We cannot see into the future and know what a certain lifestyle will lead to, but we can trust his word and know that it is better for us as a society, as a community, as humankind, to follow his commands, even if it may be less enjoyable for some of us individually. C.S. Lewis uses the expression that moral rules are directions for running the human machine.

> Every moral rule is there to prevent a breakdown, or a strain, or a friction, in the running of that machine. That is why these rules at first seem to be constantly interfering with our natural inclinations. When you are being taught how to use any machine, the instructor keeps on saying, 'No, don't do it like that', because, of course, there are all sorts of things that look all right and seem to you the natural way of treating the machine, but do not really work. (Lewis 1952/1977, 65)

He also uses a parable about morality as a fleet of ships in formation, where it is important that they keep the formation, that the ships are all in good order, and that they move towards their aim. To keep my own ship in order would mean to live according to God's will, and in the long run this is the only way both of living in good and right relationships with others, not hurting them, and doing my best to keep the whole fleet going in the right direction. Things are not prohibited just to be prohibited, there are reasons for it. Whatever I do - good or bad - will influence other people (ibid., 66-70).

EDUCATING SERVANTS

With the meaning of life being service, the aim of education is to help pupils to become servants. Since people are different, we will serve God and our neighbours in different ways. It is the school's task to help everybody to find their vocation, to find out about and develop their abilities and gifts, to help them to see where and how they can best serve - at home, at work, in society at large.

> [Luther's] emphasis on faith and grace allowed education to become the means to realize one's vocation in the world, an instrument whereby one comes to knowledge of one's gifts and abilities ... the Christian is by faith lord of all and at the same time through love the servant of all. Education is a crucial instrument in orienting the Christian toward service in the world. This is the realm where the Christian is able to exercise free will, even though he or she is fundamentally bound to the life of service ... (Harran 1990, 321)

According to Asheim, an evangelical Lutheran view of education would have two 'poles': faith and reality. It would be reality orientated and it would be rooted in faith (Asheim 1970, 167-8). The reality orientation means that it is important in education to know what reality really is like, to get to know the situation, the society where the pupils are to serve.

G. Haydon claims that the major danger of non-secular schools is that they may avoid exposure to particular moral views 'that are taken by many people within a secular viewpoint' or 'it may restrict genuine understanding of them' (Haydon 1994, 74). This should not be the case in a Lutheran school. Reality must come into schools as it is, not as we want it to be. The pupils must learn about it, learn to understand how people think, learn to evaluate it from a biblical perspective. There is no point in reading only Christian books, or concentrating on church history, or not learning about other religions. As a matter of fact, in our society it is necessary to learn about other religions and world views.

We always have to ask: what is the reality like that my pupils are living in, and will be living in? What do they need to be able to do good in *this* society? This means that the content of education will vary with the society where it takes place. It means that, in our society, they would for instance have to learn about occultism, because it is something everybody will meet. It should be taught in a way that would help the children to judge it and to see what it really is.

Choice of subjects and content within the subjects should be made with the criterion of being helpful in service. Some skills will obviously be necessary for all, like reading and writing. Some knowledge will also be necessary for all, for instance about nature and environment, and about how the society functions and how everybody can contribute to make it better. It is important to help pupils to be active in society in some way or another, to help the poor and weak, to promote justice. It is also important to learn about other faiths and world views, and to know that everybody, irrespective of faith, is created and loved by God and should be loved and served by us.

Also within each subject and focusing on the individual pupil, the criterion is service: How can we help those who are good at maths to use their maths for the good of society and individuals? How can we help those interested in history to do the same? Those going to be fathers, shop assistants, engineers and so on? And how can we help everybody to become good citizens? In a democracy, how can we best equip them to take active part in the democratic processes?

We must not, though, get a too narrow concept of usefulness, or think that usefulness is the only criterion for teaching something. Luther's theology made him enjoy the world and thank God for it, all good gifts being from God. He emphasized that learning is valuable in itself, it does not have to be useful. God has created us with a variety of gifts and talents to be developed. Playing an instrument, learning a language - they are all there as God's gifts, to give us a richer life. Even if the humanities were of no use in general, said Luther, and of no use for our salvation in particular (like making us able to read the Bible), they are still there as God's creation and gifts to give us joy and a richer life (Asheim 1970, 123-5).[25] But there is no contradiction between being useful and having value in itself. We get a richer life by using our gifts to give others joy and a better life.

All subjects have an inner structure and a relative autonomy which should be respected. They should not be 'christianized'. But neither should they be taught in a 'neutral' way that leaves God out completely and unconsciously conveys an atheistic view.[26] The framework of God's love and care for his world should always be there. Where other world views give rise to different interpretations of facts, this should be explained. A humble attitude towards the question of truth will prevent manipulation and intolerance. Although Christians believe that Christianity is the Truth, that does not mean that one person's understanding of it is absolutely correct (Myhre 1970, 30).

The world the pupils learn about is God's world, the world he created and upholds. This does not mean that it is necessary to talk about God all the time. But in our society, where God has been 'removed' from most areas, it may be necessary to make an effort to make sure that God is the centre, both in theory and in practice. Both what is taught and what is not taught, what is done and what is not done, contribute to the ethos of the school. R. Myhre claims that it is not right for instance to use lessons in biology or geology to argue for a Christian or anti-Christian view of the world, the pupils should only be presented with the facts and told that these can be part of various world views (ibid., 31-2). This is right as far as it goes, the point of most lessons is not to *argue for* a particular view. But Myhre ignores, or is not aware of, the fact that the lessons always will contribute to building up a particular world view, and this may easily be a secular one if we are not consciously trying to avoid it.

Serving God is not regarded as an aim for a particular Christian education for Christians only, but for education in general. In God's world, the meaning of life for everybody is to serve him, this does not depend on whether they believe in him or not. So true education is education within a biblical framework, seeking to help the pupils to serve God. Education is not primarily for their own benefit, but for other people and the society as a whole. And this applies to all children, whatever faith they have. They are all created by God to live according to his purpose, and even if they do not want to say yes to him, we ought to help them to live according to the content of Christian ethics, as they are created for.

Is it possible to have 'service for God' as the aim for educating children who do not believe? People without faith in God would obviously not want to serve him, but the meaning of this in the secular government, the serving of other people, could be the purpose of education for anybody. To do good to others is to serve God, whether the individual regards it as such or not. To do good to others is valuable whatever the motive is, and it is part of God's upholding the world also if the person does not think of it as such. God has given us the responsibility for helping every child to live according to his will, not only those who believe in him. So I would argue that service for God in the meaning it has in the secular government can be the aim of education for everybody. It is the *content* of 'service for God' that is significant, and not the *label*.

The label we use for it is, however, not irrelevant. If service is talked about *only* as doing good to others, without ever mentioning God, it is not a true, Christian education, although it has Christian elements in it. If, on the other hand, it is talked about *only* as service to God, pupils who do not believe or who later do not believe, may not regard it as a task or challenge for them. Both sides are important: to show the secular argument for the Christian notion of a good life, and to create an awareness of this secular world being God's world. But arguing and explaining is not the most important way of transmitting moral values and attitudes, it is more to do with the children imitating the adults. Other-concerned teachers will help the pupils to become the same.

Any education will transmit moral values and norms, in words and deeds, Christian education will transmit biblical ones. To bring up and educate children to serve other people, and even to want to serve other people, is that indoctrination? As far as I can see, it is no more - or no less - so than bringing them up to have a primary concern for their own well-being, or anything else that might be the purpose of education. All education will have some kind of purpose, linked to some view of the meaning of life. Unless we believe a particular purpose and meaning to be harmful, it will be the way the purpose is promoted that might cause indoctrination, not the purpose itself. And it would be difficult to argue that trying to do good to other people is harmful.

2.2.2 The spiritual government

'Spiritual' in Luther's spiritual government has a very different meaning from what it has in today's discussion about spiritual education and development. It is about the gospel, about God's work of salvation. He wants us to turn to him, to be saved, to receive from him forgiveness and eternal life. This is ultimately the good life - to live with him, here on earth and afterwards. But this life is not something to be forced on people, or implanted through education, it is a gift to be received or rejected. According to the Bible, God created people with freedom to reject him, to turn away and be our own god. What then can and ought upbringers and educators to do within the spiritual government? Are 'developing faith' and 'bringing them up as Christians' good expressions for what we are meant to do? Or is it all up to God, so we can do nothing?

In Norwegian there is only one word for faith and belief, namely 'tro'. But there is a difference between believing, on one hand, that Christianity presents a right or sensible world view and having this world view as basis for thinking (being a cultural Christian), and on the other hand having a personal relationship with God, having faith (Asheim 1991, 172, see also Habgood 1990, 110-11).

The first meaning of 'tro', belief, is nothing more than we find in all religions and world views. Everybody is brought up within a view of the world built on certain beliefs. It may be a world without a god, with a distant god, or with a god who matters in everyday life. It may be a world where death is seen as the end of life, the beginning of life, or the transformation into a different kind of life. It may be a world where the highest value is self realization, money, or unselfish love. It may be a world with universal, objective ethical norms, with relative, intersubjective norms, or with subjective norms. And so on. And children will, by and large, take over these beliefs and form habits consistent with them (go to church, strive for higher salary, eat without giving thanks to God, act according to their horoscope, not kill animals, etc.). At first they will do so unquestioningly, and a lot of the beliefs will remain unquestioned, particularly if they are widespread in society.

It is part of bringing up and educating children that we cannot avoid having this influence on them. And even more, we should not try to avoid it, because this is our task. Any education transmits a certain way of understanding the world, and this is always built on beliefs. Some of the beliefs, or presuppositions, are religious, some are not.

The other meaning of 'tro', faith, is in Lutheran theology regarded as a gift from God, as something a person can receive freely. For Luther, this is linked with his theology about sin. Sin is not 'Fehlern', wrongdoings, that people do and which we can, with God's help, stop doing, but it is rebellion against God (Asheim 1961, 116), turning one's back on him. To change this, people have to be born again, and that is an act of God. People can reject this gift, but never earn it. Christian life is thus something qualitatively new, something that God creates. He wants to set people free from our self-centredness, but we must freely accept his gift.

To have faith in God means to trust him, to have a personal relationship with him. This relationship is in the Bible characterized in various ways, one of the most common being that God is our father and we his children. It implies closeness, openness, trust, dependency. This must be kept in mind when we focus on another aspect of the relationship, namely being God's servants. Our master is not a distant one, trying to exploit us, but a loving and caring one. When we are in his service, we know that what he asks us to do is to the good for us and others.

According to Lutheran theology, God gives faith in baptism. The relationship between God and the person as father and child is created there, baptism is a new birth. This faith then needs to be nurtured, they need to learn what they are baptized into. They need knowledge, and they need to be part of a Christian fellowship to see what this means in practice, to give the biblical knowledge a framework for understanding.

Children who are not baptized also need knowledge about God and his work if they are to understand what Christianity is. Intellectual knowledge is not enough, they need to see it alive, to experience Christian love, to hear people talk about God and to him as a natural part of their life. It is important to help children to grow in their knowledge of God so that they know what they are doing when deciding whether this is a relationship they want to continue or not.

Thus, 'Christian' is not something people can be made by other people, and faith cannot be developed by educational means. Sometimes the expression that they should 'learn to be Christian' is used (Astley 1994, 9), or that they should 'develop Christian commitment' (Thiessen 1993, 29). These are ambiguous. They may only intend to say something about the content and methods of the upbringing, but sometimes they seem to be used for saying something about the purpose: to bring them up so they become Christians.

If we cannot and should not 'make' them Christians, what can and should we do as educators? The fact that faith never can be the result of our efforts, does not mean that there is nothing we can do towards it. The gospel needs to be proclaimed, people need to know what God has done. Without biblical knowledge, there is nothing for God to work from. It is important in Christian education to let the children meet the word of God as a unique revelation, as the Truth (Pedersen 1996, 79-80). This may be particularly important today, with 'spirituality' being topical, with an emphasis on people's inner life and a tendency to mix various religions and make one's own.

In the Lutheran tradition there is a cautiousness concerning upbringing and faith, a concern that we should not intrude on God's premises, but leave the spiritual side to him. Therefore the purpose or aim is commonly expressed as helping the children to understand and listen to God's word, the Bible. The focus is not on their response to the word, whether they become Christians or not, but on giving them the knowledge and understanding they need to respond. As they grow older, everybody has to make a decision themselves, whether to keep, receive or reject God's gift. Teachers can hope and pray, and teach as well as they can, that is their responsibility. Then the rest is up to God and the pupils.

The Norwegian theologian O. Øystese distinguishes between education *to* faith, *in* faith, and *for* faith. He claims that having 'education to faith' as an aim, i.e. education that leads to faith, is often linked with a theology where there is no room for faith as a new birth, where Christianity is only a way of life or a philosophical system (Øystese 1983, 93). It also blurs the distinction between what God can do and what we as educators can do. Therefore he prefers education *for* or *as basis for* faith, where the teacher's aim is to give the basic knowledge that God by his Holy Spirit can use for creating faith. If this takes place within a Christian setting, where the Bible is lived as well as taught, it may also be named education *in* or *from* faith (ibid., 95-9). Although the ultimate aim - what is hoped for - in all these three may be faith, something more limited should be specified as the educational aim.

It is important to distinguish between what teachers can do in this area and what only God can do, but that does not necessarily prevent us from talking about education *to* faith, having faith as an aim. C.H. Pedersen objects to Øystese's suggestions, arguing that we can talk about aims on different levels. When we think of the ultimate aim, the purpose for education, this should be the same as the purpose of life, even if we cannot reach it by educational means alone. It is possible - and often necessary - to have a direction, something we want to work towards, without it being completely in our power to get there. So the purpose for Christian education could, and should, be faith, argues Pedersen (Pedersen 1996, 85-6). Still, the focus is on the teachers and the ethos, not on what happens in the pupils.

The common distinction in English discussions between education and catechesis or nurture is interesting here. There seem to be two main differences between these conceptions. One is that in nurture you can take for granted that the pupils are Christians, in education you cannot. The other is the purpose in terms of what should happen to the pupils: in nurture you expect their faith to grow, you aim at changes in knowledge, attitudes, life, but in education you concentrate on knowledge only, and the purpose is that they should learn what Christianity is, critically.

Within an understanding where the purpose is focused on the teacher and not the pupils, this distinction is more or less irrelevant. The point is that Christianity should be presented for what it is, a relationship with God - with knowledge and life and all, including the critical element. The pupils' faith may make a difference in the way the teacher talks to them, but not in what he or she wants to transmit. We can never assume that all pupils are Christians anyway, even if they are in a Christian school and come from Christian homes, because they all have their own relationship with God, which develops and changes.

It may be argued that since Christianity with its truth claim conveys that non-Christians are wrong, this may be felt by the non-Christian pupils as if they are less worth. In this case it is crucial to distinguish between the believer and his or her beliefs. It is not only truth that is important in Christianity, love is important too. Whatever people believe, however wrong their beliefs are, they are to be loved. Whatever background the pupils come from, they are created and loved by God. Although Christian love includes telling people about God, telling them the truth, it also includes respect.

Øystese and Asheim often emphasize that faith cannot be an educational aim, because there is no methodology for being successful. The question is whether, or how, this is special for the spiritual government. Is there a methodology for being successful in other parts of education? Do teachers ever have control over the result?

We can have aims: that they should learn about Christianity, understand what the Bible says, even that they may remain or become Christians. But the personal response is out of our control. In a way this is the same in all subjects. We know that we cannot *make* them learn anything, but if they want to, we can help them to gain knowledge and understanding. We can help them to understand what the different subjects are about, or the different forms of knowledge as Hirst would have put it.

But then there is the personal response, the interest. We want them to like maths, to love poetry, to want to listen to music, to be passionate about history and biology. How do we do this? We do it by motivating them, by sharing with them our own interest, love and passion, hoping that something will catch. Music is a good example. If they are surrounded by love of music, if they are taught to play the piano from a very early age, they may grow up to love music, to want to play the piano to the extent that their whole life is taken over by it. But they may not, we have no methodology for being successful. This is the same in the spiritual government, we can only lead people towards something or somebody.

But if there are similarities, there are also differences. In Christianity, we are not concerned with love for a subject, but for a person, Jesus Christ. In Bollnow's terms, what we want is not a meeting with a subject, but with a person (Bollnow 1959/1969). And it is the most important meeting in people's life, with consequences for eternity. It is unique, because the other part in the meeting is the almighty God. And unlike a meeting with music, poetry, history, etc., it does not depend on a particular disposition or ability in the person.

The main difference, however, is that when it comes to faith, it is God who acts. We may help people to have spiritual or religious experiences, but faith is not produced, it is given. God chooses how and when to reveal himself, he addresses the individual in his own time with his 'follow me'. What happens in the relationship between God and a person is God's domain, not ours. Therefore we are in a completely different situation as educators in the spiritual government.

J. Fjelde, a Norwegian educationalist, says that the teachers' task is to present Christianity in the way it presents itself. They are not the guarantor for its truth, whether they are believers or not. They only have to present it in an open, genuine, honest way, teacher and pupils listening to the message together, taking it seriously (Fjelde 1970, 182-4).

But what does it mean to take it seriously? At least it must include taking a stand concerning its truth. To listen to and take seriously the Bible's claims about God, Jesus and ourselves mean that we have to respond with a 'yes' or a 'no' to Jesus Christ. It is not the teacher's task to push such a decision in the pupils - teachers have to show respect for other people's freedom. But if they want the pupils to take it seriously, they cannot ignore the challenge to themselves. This does not mean that the teachers have clear theological answers to all questions, but that they do not try to avoid the meeting with the person Jesus Christ.

The Bible tells the truth about God, the world and ourselves. It says that if we do not believe in Jesus Christ, our lives are failures. Life is not a question of choosing beliefs or a lifestyle that we find meaningful, or of promoting our well-being, it is a question of hitting or missing the Creator's purpose. The choice is between living a true life, facing God, or living on a fundamental lie, believing that we are in control of our own lives. What the true life leads to in terms of meaning and well-being is secondary. In fact, the whole notions of meaning and well-being take on new meanings when seen from a biblical perspective.

2.2.3 Autonomy

In my account of a Christian view of human nature, I did not mention anything about autonomy. This is not because autonomy is not important, but because the focus is not there. In the area of decision-making and choice, freedom and responsibility are more central concepts. In the spiritual government, it is God who addresses a person, who takes the initiative, who offers salvation and eternal life. But the individual has freedom to respond as he or she will. It has to be an autonomous decision, taking responsibility for one's own life. God addresses *me*, and the response has to be *mine*.

It is important, though, that the response does not have to be rational in the ordinary sense of the word, at least not in the first place, and maybe never. First, when Paul was stopped by Christ on the way to Damascus (Acts 9), he did not make a rational, autonomous decision to follow him there and then. The rational reflections came later. Second, not everybody has the same rational capacities. There are many, both children and adults, who are not able to 'think for themselves', to make up their mind about what to believe. Emphasizing autonomy, rationality and open-mindedness as much as liberalism does, easily makes these people second class. Not so in Christianity. Jesus talks about loving God with all our mind and all our heart - a 'heart-relationship' with God is no second best. Those who have got a bright mind are responsible for using it, also in their relationship with God, others too can come as they are.

Also in the secular government we are responsible to God for our lives. Here, too, those of us who are able to sort out difficult moral questions are responsible for helping those who are not, to live right. Rational capacity and autonomy are not necessary for leading a meaningful life, but we are all responsible for using what we have got. We are, in spite of sin, relatively free to do good in this world. But to serve society without being society's slave, we need an anchor outside society. Faith in God gives somebody outside self and society to hold on to (Asheim 1970, 172).

Haworth understands autonomy as ruling oneself and not being dominated by others and one's own impulses (Haworth 1986, 14). The negative part of this, not being dominated by others and one's own impulses, is certainly part of a Christian understanding of autonomy. The 'ruling oneself' part is more complicated, because the concept of autonomy must necessarily take on a different meaning within a Christian world view compared to a secular one.

In an atheistic world, it is a question of me governing my own life (autonomy), or other people doing it (heteronomy). In the biblical world there is another possibility: God, the creator. Christians do not *have* to obey

God, we *want* to. He knows us better than we do ourselves, he knows what is for our good, he knows the truth - he is the Truth. Living according to his will is nothing near being governed by other people who do not know us, who want their own good rather than ours, and who do not know the truth about the world. To regard God as part of the world I am autonomous in relation to is to make him into something smaller than God.

A Christian view of human nature says that we can never be completely autonomous, we will always depend on somebody or something. We will either be bound to the devil, to our own self-centredness, or to God, there is no freedom as such. According to the Bible (John 8: 31-36), we are only really free when we are bound to God, our creator. A self-centred life is no free life, it is not what we were created for, and sin and the consequences of sin will curb our freedom. The biblical scholar J.D.G. Dunn talks about 'the freedom of dependency on God'. We think that we can be free, independent, autonomous,

> [n]ever so! The human being can never escape from a state of dependency on things and relationships. The question then is simply whether it is a dependency which binds us closer to sin, flesh and death; or a dependency on a higher power, the power which makes it possible for us to be what we were made to be and which little by little moulds us into what we were made to be, the image of God in Christ. (Dunn 1993, 70)

And again:

> We can however speak of the freedom of self-knowledge, another ancient Greek ideal. We can do this so long as we realise that for Paul this means the freedom of knowing oneself to be a creature of the Creator, the freedom of human beings who know that they were not made to be independent, who acknowledge that the psychological and social reality of human beings is that they can never be truly independent, and who find their true freedom in a relation of dependence on God (ibid., 76).

To be autonomous in a biblical sense is to be bound to God and therefore free in relation to everybody and everything else. Freedom is something that cannot be imposed on people, nobody can choose this binding for anybody else. It is important for Christian educators to explain that it is up to the individual to decide who or what they will be dependent on. It is also important, on the basis of the Bible, to promote autonomous thinking, to avoid blind obedience to individuals and authorities.

To avoid indoctrination and manipulation taking the place of upbringing, our basic attitude to truth is important. Christians believe in the truth of the Bible, and this will show in our lives, just as anybody else will reveal their basic beliefs through the way they live. But we know, and must not conceal, that this is a belief, a conviction. I am convinced of the truth, but I cannot prove it, and there is always the possibility that I am wrong, that I have built my life on a falsity. Pupils should be given freedom also to question their faith. When we search for truth, no question is dangerous, because God is truth.

But can servants be free and autonomous? To serve does not mean being a doormat for everybody. We are God's servants, not other people's, and we are primarily responsible to God for our life, not to other people. Every servant is a person of infinite worth, loved by God the Almighty, this is the basis for our self-respect. All requests from individuals or from society at large should be judged by what God wants us to do.

To illustrate this, I would like to draw attention to Tom in Harriet Beecher Stowe's 'Uncle Tom's Cabin' (1851/1995). He helped other slaves to flee, but he himself would not. He served his masters faithfully, both the good and the bad ones, praying for their salvation. When his last master commanded him to flog a fellow slave, he refused. His master got angry, and cried that Tom was his property and had to obey. Tom's answer was that although the master owned his body, his soul belonged to God.

Tom was obviously used and abused in the most awful way, being a slave with no rights. But he was no doormat. He tried to use his place to serve others around him. And although his master could command him, Tom's real master was God, he did his work for God. When God told him that this he could not do, he disobeyed his earthly master. Although outwardly it was the master who was in control of his life, inwardly he was not.

This also illustrates that to be autonomous, it is not necessary to have many options. Very often in life we cannot do what we want, the circumstances do not allow it. And the possible actions are not many. Biblical autonomy does not lie in free choice between many options, but in our attitude, not in what we do but why we do it. Christians will always know that wherever we are and whatever brought us there, God is there with us and can turn the situation into something good. The point is that for Christians the aim of life - to serve God - does not depend on where we are or the circumstances under which we live. We can always find opportunities to show God's love to other people.

When talking about autonomous decisions and doing God's will, it is also important to remember that there are two different, although overlapping, kinds of decision. One is the moral questions where the Bible is fairly concrete, as in the ten commandments. God's will is to let him alone be God, to refrain from stealing, envy, etc. Although it may not always be straightforward to find out how we can best do it, at least we know from where to start our deliberations.

The other is decisions about our own future, like the choice of a job or a place to live. Here there is no direct guidance to get from the Bible. Basically Christians would do two things: think and pray. The thinking would be about 'common' aspects like abilities, family situation, desires, but also about how we could serve God in these jobs and places. The praying would be for God's guidance, for him to guide our thoughts and feelings and look after the whole situation, and some people would sometimes ask for more direct answers to particular questions.

This is not God deciding our jobs or homes for us, but helping us to see where he wants us, which is also where we ourselves want to be. But then we may, in our selfishness, decide to go for another option that looks more interesting to our 'old' self. This may be a conscious decision at the end of the process, or it may be that we do not really listen to God along the way because we have already set our minds on something particular. So sometimes our 'new' self 'wins' and we follow God's way, sometimes our 'old' self 'wins' and we do not. It would be strange to say that the latter is a more autonomous decision than the former.

Being led by God does not mean that there is always only one option that is right or good, an option that God in a way has to 'reveal' to us. Most of the time he works through our rationality, our emotions and desires, our knowledge about our abilities, etc. We may ask for guidance, both in moral questions and in other questions about how to lead our life, but the answer does not drop ready made into our head, we have to work things out ourselves. I would not ask God whether to take up swimming or tennis, I would work it out from what I would prefer to do and what was most practical to organize. But I would still know that God is there and that if he has some special purpose he will tell me or lead my thoughts in that direction.

2.2.4 A Lutheran school

Christian education is education based on and transmitting a biblical view of the world and of what it is to be a person. Its whole drive is towards equipping the pupils for serving others, and there is an explicit teaching of Christianity that should leave them with the challenge to respond to God. Underlying the whole life of the school is the presupposition that this is the true life. Øystese says that '[a] school is Christian to the extent that it makes it possible for the pupils to understand themselves and the world within the framework of a Christian view of reality' (Øystese 1985, 57, my translation). Christian education is for everybody, regardless of faith, it is concerned both with our life together in this world and with eternal life.

From what I have argued about Christian education, it should be obvious that the teachers must be Christians. Without believing in God it is difficult to convey, through life and teaching, that God is a living reality. Since Christianity is primarily a relationship, and not a set of beliefs, the pupils need to see such relationships in practice to understand what it is. Because it is a relationship between individuals, it cannot be put in a formula. You cannot give the teachers a method or some rules for how to make their education Christian, it will be their own personal life with God that will be reflected in how they relate to the pupils. The first stage in becoming a visible Christian teacher, says B.V. Hill, is 'to come into [Jesus'] presence, and never thereafter to leave it' (Hill 1982/1990, 102).

This does not mean that it is only the teachers' faith and life that determine the Christian ethos of a school. They must also be good teachers. Good colleagues, conscientious teachers, and good friends, says Hill (ibid., 103-4). Other things contribute too, like the faith and life of non-teaching staff. The school rules must reflect Christian ethics. This would include an emphasis on positive action to help others, not only a list of things to be done and not to be done.

The choice of subjects to be taught is important, and the content within the subjects. They should be chosen so as to develop the pupils' talents, and to help them understand and serve the society they are a part of. The text-books and other materials would need to reflect a Christian, God-centred view of reality and human nature. If we are concerned with Christian education in a largely secular society, it is even more important to make sure that life in school is explicitly God-centred, because society in general will be human-centred and implicitly promote the belief that God and religion belong to a separate area of life and have nothing to do with the rest of it.

In a Lutheran school Christianity must be taught so the pupils can meet the word of God. There will also be worship. This may be a problem if there are non-Christian pupils, because it is neither right nor possible to force people to pray to God. But on the other hand, it is impossible to understand what Christian faith is without the aspect of worship. Worship therefore has to be organized in a way that allows pupils to choose to be either onlookers or participants.

It is obvious that being brought up within such a framework gives a strong Christian influence. But it does not mean that all pupils in Christian schools are influenced by the same Christian world view, and even less that they end up with the same view. In addition to the influence from Christianity, there are both the social and cultural aspects of the society they live in, and the personal world views of the individual teachers (Aadnanes 1997, 74-6, see also above, p. 6). Also, the pupils are individuals who internalize different aspects, both unconsciously and consciously.

I want to argue that being brought up within a non-Christian framework, be it agnostic, pantheistic, or anything else, will give an equally strong influence, only different. S. Harbo did some interesting research among Norwegian student teachers, trying to find out how their upbringing had influenced their faith and beliefs. He found, not unexpectedly, that parents' faith had the strongest influence. The results show that for those brought up in Christian homes, 69.1% were Christians. For those brought up in secular homes, even more (87.2%) followed in their parents' footsteps. So, whatever the reasons are, this study seems to suggest that people are no more likely to stick to their parents' beliefs if the parents are Christians than if they are not (Harbo 1989, 129-30).

2.3 Other views of Christian education

Lutherans are far from the only ones to discuss Christian education, it is a topic within most churches - and also outside. Both education in general and the teaching of Christianity in particular are discussed. What is focused on and argued for seem at least to a certain degree to depend on theology. As far as I can judge, in most cases it is more a question of different perspectives and emphases than strong disagreements. Whatever the denomination, Christian education is an education where a Christian world view permeates everything.

The model of the two governments is particular to Lutheran Christianity, and it makes a difference in many areas of education. The differences are most clear compared to Baptist and Reformed traditions, in some areas also compared to Roman Catholics. Even in relation to Anglicans the government model seems to play a part. This is not the place to go into a thorough comparison between different views, but I would like to give a few examples from various non-Lutheran denominations to illustrate the differences.

In the teaching of Christianity the difference lies mainly in the cautiousness which Lutheran theology operates with when it comes to what education and upbringing can do towards faith. In other traditions the distinction between the work of the Holy Spirit and the teachers' work is more easily blurred, and we can get the impression that faith and salvation, and also sanctification - growing into the likeness of Christ - can be results of education. Sometimes the aim of Christian education is said to be to form a Christian person or personality (see for instance Jeffreys 1950, Andersen 1983, Beck 1964).

This forming of the personality does not agree with Lutheran Christianity, because the belief is that to be a Christian is not to have a certain personality, but to have a personal relationship with God. A person may live according to Christian ethics and display Christian virtues, but this does not make the person Christian (Asheim 1967, 135-6). And the other way round: a person may be a Christian, may have received Christ, but may not live the kind of virtuous and 'Christian' life we would expect. The point of education and upbringing is definitely not forming them into Christians. Not even in the secular government would 'forming' of the person be a natural Lutheran concept. The focus is not on being, but on doing: living the life God gives them in the society where they are.

J. Astley gives an interesting account of what he calls Christian religious education, meaning 'a confessional, churchly activity of evangelism, instruction and nurture' (Astley 1994, 9). He does not say which denomination he writes from, which is an interesting observation in itself, probably suggesting that he does not regard theological differences between the denominations as relevant for his philosophy.

He lists Christian attributes and argues that learning these is the aim of a Christian education in Christianity. He raises the question whether having Christian attributes is the same as being a Christian, and argues that although this may not be the case, Christian educators need such aims to be able to tell whether they are successful or not, 'an account that will enable us to *know* when someone is (more) Christian'. What he calls 'what it is *to be* in the right relationship with God, 'in Christ', redeemed, reconciled, re-created, etc.' cannot be observed. Therefore it cannot be taken into account 'in the practice - and therefore the theory - of Christian religious education' (ibid., 115).

Here again we have a blurred distinction between God's work and our work. Because it is difficult or impossible to measure what God does, Astley wants us to concentrate on what we can do. Fair enough. In a way it looks similar to Øystese's Lutheran argument about not interfering with what only God can do. But it is very different. It defines what it is to be a Christian in conceptions that *are* under teachers' control, something that *is* the purpose of education (although it has to be churchly education, not in secular schools - ibid., 9). It focuses on the results, even on measuring them to see 'how Christian' the pupils have become. Øystese, and even Pedersen - who disagrees with him over faith as an aim - would turn the focus to the teacher, to the helping of pupils to listen to the word of God, and not look for special attributes as signs of their success.

Astley's account makes it difficult to see the limits of the teacher's task in the spiritual government. His list of the attributes does not make it simpler. Among them are beliefs about God, faith and trust in God, moral virtues, awe, experiences of Christ, forgiveness, worship, Christian reflection (ibid., 112-13). How can faith and trust in God be taught and measured? Or worship, which is not singing and doing and feeling things, but our whole being before the living God? It seems to me that he may be in danger of ignoring altogether what God - and only God - can do. According to Øystese, this may be a result of unclear theological thinking, or of a theology where 'Christianity is only a way of life or a philosophical system' (Øystese 1983, 93).

The most obvious difference between Lutheran and non-Lutheran educational theory is in the emphasis on the secular government. This can be seen in a concern both for education for citizenship for Christians and for education for non-Christians. People who write about Christian education from a Baptist or Reformed perspective tend to focus on education for Christians, i.e. children from 'their own' Christian homes. The same is partly true about Catholics, although there is also a strong emphasis on education for the poor and underprivileged. When writing about Christian education, these groups often take for granted that the children are Christians, and the aim of the education is to nurture their faith (Weeks 1988, 7; Walsh 1983, 13). Christian schools exist 'to aid parents in their task of raising children in the fear of the Lord', says Weeks (ibid.).

In the US there is a strong Christian school movement, mainly consisting of Baptist schools. These are regarded as part of the church, they are normally for believers only. 'Christian schools often require proof that at least one of the parents is born again before children are permitted to enrol' (Reese 1985/1993, 280). They also seem to be very focused on the children's salvation, their spiritual life being the main concern (ibid., 278-9).

The Lutheran approach is different. Lutheran theology would acknowledge the importance of giving *everybody* a good education, regardless of their faith, because education is primarily for life in this world. This education is in many respects similar to a secular education, the important difference is that 'this world' is God's world, and our purpose here is to serve. Education is for the purpose of our neighbours and our society, it has a value in itself apart from also giving opportunities for pupils to learn about Jesus.[27]

In Reformed and Baptist schools, prayer and Bible reading are important and may take place in all subjects, the Bible being the most important textbook. Everything has to do not only with God, but with salvation. There seems to be no room given for studying God's creation and educating good citizens without linking it to salvation. The children's heart-relationship with God is at the centre of everything.

Their problem, from a Lutheran point of view, is the lack of the model of the two governments. This model underlines the biblical thought that to live and serve in God's world is important in itself. It is important to help everybody to become good citizens, whether they themselves regard this as serving God or not. This aspect seems to be lacking in many traditions.

When hardly anything is said about education of non-Christians, the impression can easily be given that there is nothing good to be said about such education from a Christian perspective. The implication may even be that only education where the Gospel is the power may be able to change people, like in the following:

> As *witness* Christian schooling testifies to the transforming, life-fulfilling power of the Gospel. We do not represent the human activity of schooling as a power to transform human life for good. As witness to the Gospel it points beyond the human activity to the transforming power of Christ who alone by his Spirit can transform human life for good. (Fowler 1990a, 47)

It is at least a very likely reading of this to regard it as saying that education that is not based on the Gospel cannot change human life for good.

This is indeed different from the Lutheran emphasis of upbringing as part of the government of reason, not the government of salvation.

The Anglican church has an approach that is more similar to the Lutheran, with a separate emphasis on educating for life in society. The Church of England schools were started with the dual purpose of serving the nation and providing Christian education for the church's children. In the nineteenth century the twin purposes were seen as two aspects of the same task, but today they are sometimes understood as alternatives (A Future in Partnership 1984, 40). The church schools today are part of the maintained system, but they are not to be similar to the state schools. They should be distinctively Christian, but not exclusive (Positive Partnership 1985, 24). Here too we find an emphasis on the school's Christian witness more than the resulting faith in the pupils. 'The church school ... has the responsibility to tell and live out the implications of [the Christian] message rather than to determine what people and pupils will make of it' (Brown 1992, 4).

The dual purpose may seem to have some similarities with the model of the two governments, but it is not easy to find out exactly what this 'service to the nation' means and why it is seen as a task for the church. At the start it was more obvious. The church wanted to contribute to 'enable the children of the nation, especially the poorer classes, to become literate and numerate and to develop skills which they required for work'. It also had 'a duty to provide education in the Christian religion' (A Future in Partnership 1984, 12). The latter would happen in all schools after the 1944 Education Act, and the state was by then responsible for giving everybody the basic education. Why then continue with church schools? And how do church schools serve the nation if their pupils are humanists, Muslims, and Hindus?

These questions have been debated a lot recently, including a debate at the Church of England's General synod in 1985. In the resulting document, 'Positive Partnership', it is said that the church should stimulate transformation of the world into becoming more like God's kingdom.[28] It is unclear what this means. Is this transformation the new life that God gives, or is it the result of good upbringing? Or both? In short: are they talking about what God does to uphold his world and what the church can do to make it a better place to live, or is the focus on the Gospel and its life-changing power? Trying to answer these questions may clarify the purpose of church schools, and I believe that the model of the two governments could be useful.

CHAPTER 3

Liberal, No-Standpoint Education

Many who argue against the Christianity based state school in Norway, claiming that it favours one view, want a school based on what they call common values, or humanistic values. They do not believe in a value neutral school, but they are convinced that there are values everybody would want instilled in their children and that they are sufficient as a basis for the school. Those who want a particular religious education for their children can deal with that outside school, primarily at home, religion being regarded as something in addition to the common moral values.

In England, the label for a common education acceptable to all has lately been 'liberal education'. Hirst said already in 1965 that the notion had become something of a slogan, usually meaning 'a form of education of which the author approves' (Hirst 1965, 113). Although the way this notion is used varies, there is now the widespread assumption that liberal education is the answer to the pluralistic situation in democratic societies. The primary reason for this is that liberal education focuses on autonomy and choice. The school's task in the area of religion is to develop children's autonomy, and to provide them with information about different religions so that they can make an autonomous choice as to which of these, if any, they want to adhere to. 'Liberalism requires neutrality with regard to ideas of the good life' (Feinberg 1995, 203), and both religions and secular world views have their own ideas of what the good life is. Although liberalism and liberal education have been met with a lot of criticism lately, the thoughts are still widespread.

So both in Norway and England, and in other countries too, we find this belief that it is both possible and desirable to have a school that gives information about various religions, in Norway also including secular world views, without influencing the pupils towards any one of them. It is this idea of 'no-standpoint' education that I want to focus on, more than the fact that it is called 'liberal'. In one respect, people who hold this belief are right about this kind of education being neutral between religions, since it treats them all from the outside, from the same secular point of view. But it is not a no-standpoint education. There are also non-religious world views, non-religious presuppositions about reality and human nature, and what then about neutrality?

Some people may believe that such an education does not influence the pupils towards particular non-religious presuppositions either, others may regard these as being less dangerous. Some seem to think that by removing any particular Christian influence from school and making it non-religious, or humanistic, or liberal, or just secular, we actually do not influence the children towards any particular set of beliefs, religious or not, but leave the choice totally with them.

One important reason for such a belief being alive may be that we talk about religions instead of world views, which makes non-religious beliefs more or less invisible. The important question, I would claim, is not whether you can avoid promoting Christianity or Buddhism or other religions, but whether you can avoid promoting any particular view of the world and the good life, be it religious or not. If the point is to avoid making the decision for the children about what to believe, transmitting Marxism or existentialism or atheism is no better than transmitting a religion.

It is certainly possible to abstain from transmitting any traditional world view and just leave the children to be influenced by whatever the individual teachers and the society around them convey. But even this is not neutral. Also, in its inconsistency it is not an upbringing that will give the children very much help in finding their feet in the world.

In this chapter I shall focus on two philosophers of education within the liberal tradition, John White and Kenneth A. Strike. They are different in many respects, but they both advocate an education that tries to be neutral in world view matters. My purpose is to show that there are world view presuppositions implicit in their views, and that these standpoints necessarily will be transmitted in the education they advocate. I want to highlight their underlying views of reality, human nature, and the meaning of life, and to argue that their no-standpoint education transmits particular standpoints that are incompatible with Christian education as outlined in chapter two.

3.1 Liberal education and pluralism

'Liberal education' is a fairly vague term, and so is 'liberalism', which is the basis for it. I do not want to go into what liberalism is, neither is it my task to discuss whether liberal education mirrors liberalism or whether it has its roots in a slightly biased view of liberalism.[29] Liberal education as such is not the focus for my work, therefore I am not dealing with the broad tradition from J. S. Mill, M. Arnold, Cardinal Newman and others. But the concept 'liberal education' is used by most of the writers I discuss in this and the following chapters, therefore I briefly want to look at certain aspects of it.

T.H. McLaughlin says that R.S. Peters, in all his three interpretations of liberal education, 'stresses the value placed on knowledge and understanding and on the removal of constraints on the free development of the mind' (McLaughlin 1991, 145).

When C. Bailey wrote about liberal education in his 'Beyond the Present and the Particular' (Bailey 1984), it was also primarily connected with reason and rationality, with search for knowledge. His conception is of liberal education as something different from, and opposed to, specialized and vocational education. It is not to be instrumental, not narrowly utilitarian, although it will definitely be useful in a broad sense, and it is to be concerned with the intrinsically worthwhile. It is aimed at liberating persons from the limitations of the present and the particular, widening their horizon, increasing their awareness of choice, and helping them to make rational choices instead of just react in a stimulus - response way (ibid., 19-28).

The aim of liberal education, according to Bailey, is also to understand what the world is like, to understand oneself, understand what it is to be a person in a world of persons and their practices, and to be a physical living organism among others (ibid., 31, 116, 128-9). Implicit here will be a view of reality ('what the world is like') and of human nature ('what it is to be a person'), and Bailey is aware of this. His reality is a secular humanistic one, he is not assuming that the education he advocates will be neutral. His concern is with knowledge and understanding and rationality, not with diversity and pluralism and choice.

To Bailey, knowledge is never absolutely certain, it is always a matter of having more or less evidence for our beliefs. Therefore he finds it confusing to talk about *true* beliefs, or true knowledge, he wants to claim that 'true' means 'ought to be believed because there are good reasons for believing it' (ibid., 60-62). It is not just a matter of choosing a view that you like, it makes sense for him to talk about evidence and reasons and objective knowledge.

P.H. Hirst, in his early writings, displays a very similar notion of liberal education to that of Bailey. It is the epistemological aspect that is in focus. Hirst wants liberal education to mean 'education based fairly and squarely on the nature of knowledge itself' (Hirst 1965, 113). It is all linked to the search for knowledge. And he wants to teach criteria for truth so that the pupils have a basis for their choices. Since there are no common criteria for truth in religion, we cannot agree on what is objective knowledge. Therefore we should only teach *about* religion, and not teach religion, pupils should be told that we know nothing in this area.

It seems to me, however, that 'liberal education' has got a slightly different focus or emphasis over the last few decades. What we have seen in writers like J. White and McLaughlin is that the need for liberal education is closely linked to society being democratic and pluralistic. White does not use the concept of liberal, McLaughlin suggests that he has 'no doubt avoided the term in his writings in order to prevent confusion with the narrow conception of Liberal Education developed by Hirst' (McLaughlin 1991, 152). But he is still within this tradition, very much emphasizing autonomy in children's choice of the good life, although he tries to get away from the extreme individualism.

Liberal education is now regarded not so much as a way of gaining knowledge and understanding as it is a way of making people autonomous so that they can make their own choices. 'Pluralism' and 'openness' are important concepts in this new context. Yes, rationality is still there, we hear about rational autonomy, but the emphasis is on choice rather than knowledge, on free choice rather than right choice.[30]

There may be many reasons for this change in which aspects of 'liberal education' that are emphasized. Pluralism is certainly one reason. When children from so many different backgrounds, so many different religions and world views, are taught together, it is difficult to teach them that one of the religions or world views is true. It may even be difficult to examine them critically, to see how they stand up to rational criteria, because they are so central to the identity of both pupils and parents.

D.A. Carson distinguishes between three types of pluralism; empirical, cherished and philosophical or hermeneutical (Carson 1996, 13-22). Empirical pluralism means that society is in fact plural, that there is a diversity of beliefs. By cherished pluralism he means pluralism that is regarded as something positive, something to celebrate.

In education we may see both attitudes. Sometimes pluralism is regarded as a somewhat unfortunate fact that creates problems for education. One particular view may still be regarded as true or right, or at least there may be a search for truth. In other instances the question of truth is ignored and diversity is seen as something to be promoted. Either the emphasis is on helping the pupils to understand and value their own tradition, or it is on teaching them about various views so that they can choose freely. We may also find the combination that pluralism is cherished because it gives freedom of thought and therefore room to search for truth. Cherished pluralism seems to be the attitude in liberal education.

Carson's third category - philosophical or hermeneutical pluralism - is that 'any notion that a particular ideological or religious claim is intrinsically superior to another is *necessarily* wrong. The only absolute creed is the creed of pluralism. No religion has the right to pronounce itself right or true, and the others false, or even (in the majority view) relatively inferior' (ibid., 19). This is postmodernism's creed, and postmodernism is another reason why the epistemological aspect of liberal education seems to be downplayed in favour of choice.

According to postmodernism, we construct the world we live in, and therefore we also construct all measures, all norms. This means that we can also change them, which again implies that there are not really any moral standards. We must choose, or construct. Since there are then no norms to say that one option is better than others, *what* we choose is not important. Then the act of choosing itself becomes central. Freedom of choice becomes important, and also keeping one's options open so that there is still freedom of choice (Middleton & Walsh 1995, 58-9). In a postmodern world there is no need for truth criteria or rational search for objective knowledge, because truth and universal knowledge do not exist. What is important is meaning for the individual. Gods are chosen to suit the individual, or even more, they are 'manufactured to foster human self-promotion' (Carson 1996, 32).

Educators in such a world would support every child in their belief, and teach them about various other beliefs so that they can choose the one they find most meaningful. Religions and world views have no given, objective meaning, the meaning is for the individual or within the community. Since people are different, what they find meaningful and helpful will differ. In this way postmodern philosophy gives a solution to the educational challenge of diversity of beliefs and supports liberal education's no-standpoint philosophy. This solution, however, presupposes agreement with postmodernism's view of truth. People who believe that they have found the Truth will object to their faith only being called meaningful.

3.2 'Liberal' as quality, basis, or alternative

It is not always easy to see to what degree and in which way writers believe that 'liberal' defines the education they want. Sometimes 'liberal' seems to be thought of as a quality that may be found to a greater or lesser degree in any kind of education, be it Christian, Muslim, humanistic, etc. At other times it is used as a label for a common education that could serve as a basis for all kinds of education, something 'neutral' that we can add various beliefs to. A third meaning is as an education that is an alternative to others, e.g. education is either liberal or Christian.

These three categories - quality, basis, and alternative - are not very distinct and they often overlap, and it is difficult to put particular writers or writings into one of them. They are still useful labels for analysis, and I want to use them in this and the following chapters for exploring various ways of thinking about liberal education.

QUALITY

If we can talk about both religious and secular liberal education, as some would, it would be natural to regard 'liberal' as a quality. In this case we could have liberal and non-liberal secular education, and liberal and non-liberal religiously based education. The world view presuppositions - whether the education is Buddhist, Marxist, Christian, materialistic, etc. - would be seen as more fundamental than the quality of being liberal.

This quality would basically have to do with autonomy, with being educated in a way that makes people able to choose and form their own life, without being limited (too much) by their tradition. Being liberal in this sense does not imply a particular content, it is more to do with methods and purpose. Whether the education is liberal or not, depends on whether it opens up other possibilities for the pupils, gives them real choice, or whether it tries to limit them within the tradition.

If 'liberal' is a quality that may be found in education based on any world view, truth claims cannot be ruled out. Christianity, for instance, must be allowed to claim that it tells the truth about the world, otherwise it will not be Christian education. Promoting autonomy cannot mean that it is necessary to tell pupils that all the options are equal, that no one is better or truer than the others. The basic view must be transmitted as the way the world is, it must be part of the ethos of the school. Autonomy must be promoted by allowing, or even encouraging, the pupils to examine this view alongside others, without trying to hide its unique position.

Another consequence of the world view being more basic than the liberal quality, is that autonomy and freedom must be interpreted within each world view. A God-centred and a human-centred view may have different understandings of what autonomy is.

BASIS

Another possibility is that liberal education is a kind of minimal education when it comes to values and beliefs, an education based on public values only, i.e. values that we can all agree on. Underlying this understanding seems to be the belief that world views, or at least religions, only influence parts of life, that there are areas which are 'neutral', or common in this respect. One such important area seems to be values that are necessary for public life, like justice and truth and tolerance.

Private values are either left completely to home and church, or they are discussed without the school taking a stand. Religious faith often seems to be included among the private values, faith is defined as a value, maybe even a moral value. In this way, by leaving out the areas where we disagree, the 'common basis' liberal education is the education for the common school. The additional moral and religious upbringing that some parents might like to give their children, can be given at home. This is, as far as I can see, a fairly common position.

ALTERNATIVE

The third way of understanding liberal education seems to be as fundamentally different from and an alternative to religiously based education, probably also to education based on particular secular world views. Then we could not talk about a Christian liberal school, or an atheist liberal school, but just a liberal school. 'Liberal' would be enough as label, nothing else, or more. Using a common distinction, the education would be based on comprehensive, not only political liberalism. 'Comprehensive liberalism offers not only political principles but also a conception of the good life, typically as a life of individuality or autonomy, that complements its political principles' (Gutman 1995, 558).

This implies that all the world view presuppositions underlying such upbringing and education must come from liberalism itself. There must be genuine, comprehensive liberal answers to the questions about meaning and purpose of life and education, how we are to understand the world we live in, and who we are. It would be a kind of 'liberal liberal education'. Then there must also be, in Ackerman's terms, a 'liberal liberal' primary culture, and, in Strike's terms, a 'liberal liberal' primary moral language. In other words, it must be possible also when the children are young to give them an upbringing that is basically liberal and does not need to get any input from another world view or religion.

Using the categories of quality, basis, and alternative in analysing what 'liberal education' could be, leads to the question whether 'liberal' is regarded as more or less fundamental than the presuppositions from religions or secular world views. This is a question that is rarely discussed. Many of the advocates of liberal education seem to assume that 'liberal' is more basic, that autonomy and rationality and public values are the same, whatever you believe about reality and human nature. J. White and K.A. Strike seem to think along these lines, and I want to argue that they are wrong. World view is the very basis of our understanding of the world and human nature, therefore world view is the very basis for education.

3.3 John White's view of education for all

White is probably the only one who has given a fairly detailed account of what the meaning and purpose of upbringing and education should be in today's England, his last and revised account to be found in 'Education and the Good Life' (1990).[31] I shall use this as the basis for my account of his theory, drawing also on recent articles and his inaugural lecture.

White writes about 'education', but says that he means upbringing (White 1990, 167 and 1982, 5), being concerned not only with what should be taught, but with how children ought to be brought up. His whole account in (1990) shows that his concern is with everything both parents and teachers do to the children, not only at school, and not only teaching. I take it therefore that White's 'education' and 'upbringing' are more or less equivalent to how I use the concepts.

The kind of education White advocates is one that he thinks suitable in liberal democracies like Britain. He argues that it is an education for all, a common education. He wants liberal values in education and a liberal curriculum (ibid., 11), but he also argues against certain aspects of liberalism, namely its extreme individualism and its division between choosing a life plan (well-being) and morality (other-concern) (White & White 1986). McLaughlin argues that White's later writings have tended 'to place far more emphasis on the shaping of dispositions, virtues and qualities of person-hood more generally' (McLaughlin 1991, 153). *Some* values have to be implanted, particularly some altruistic ones, but apart from that every person is the maker of his or her own life. White's education is certainly liberal in the meaning that concerns me here, pretending not to promote a particular world view or view of the good life.

That society is pluralistic seems to be implicit, he talks about a society where people hold different world views and where it is the school's task to work towards common goals without steering the pupils towards any determinate ideal of the good life (White 1990, 17). It is a secular education, although he normally does not name it as such. But in his inaugural lecture he speaks about a non-religious framework in a secular universe and about a secular education (White 1995, 3 and 19). This seems to be for children from non-religious homes, providing them with a secular cosmic frame-work, in the same way as religious children always have been provided with a cosmic framework within which to understand themselves. But the last sentence of his lecture says that he thinks of this framework as for *all* children, i.e. also religious ones (ibid., 19). This means, I assume, that he wants his secular education for all, at least for all who want an education for autonomy.

Autonomy seems to be the crux here. He wants an education that pres-ents different versions of the good life so the pupils can choose their own, and he acknowledges that this is not neutral, it is an education to autonomy (White 1990, 20-22). There may be other, non-autonomous ways of getting a good life , but in liberal democracies people have to make choices them-selves and therefore need to be autonomous (White 1989, 15). But apart from autonomy, the state should not take any stand in the question of the good life and well-being, people will then be free to 'practise their religion, express their ideas, control their own lives, and determine where they will live and what kind of work they will do' (White 1990, 22).

White's only alternative to an education that is neutral between world views or views of the good life seems to be that *the state* determines the aim of education, which view should be transmitted. Consequently, in a liberal, pluralistic society, he argues for autonomy as the only legitimate aim. He does not reflect on the possibility of letting the parents choose, having dif-ferent schools for pupils from different backgrounds.

3.3.1 Purpose of education and the good life

White suggests three aims for education that are self-evident or nearly so in a liberal democracy: personal well-being, others' well-being (altruism or morality), and personal autonomy. Although there are no necessary links between the three, he wants to show that for contemporary educators it makes sense to think of well-being as the overarching aim, including concern for others, and based on personal autonomy (ibid., 8-9). He takes for granted that everybody will agree that his three aims are important and obvious, and it may be difficult, at least at the first glance, to object to this. He does not, however, ask if there might be other candidates that might be obvious too, and maybe even more important. There are many problems with which to take issue in his account of the good life, I shall concentrate on the ones most central to my concern with world view.

WELL-BEING

A number of philosophers and philosophers of education focus on well-being, but they define it in different ways. White defines well-being in terms of satisfaction of our most important informed desires (ibid., 28-30).[32] Our desires are basically innate, part of our nature, but educators have an important task in forming them, in imposing second- and higher-order desires and helping to make a hierarchy of desires, building priorities between them. As the children grow up, they gradually take over the priority-making.

It is the culture we are brought up within that determines the forms of our desires and which desires are most important for us, and therefore what contributes to our well-being. The society as a whole will have its influence, and so will our particular upbringers. But when educators form desires and build new ones, they must have some guidelines - individually or from the society - as to how to do this. We obviously learn to desire what our upbringers think we ought to desire.

Where does this 'ought' come from? Not from objectively given values, White does not believe in such ones. Rather, 'there is a broad, taken-for-granted, agreement among (nearly all of) us about what desires are worth fostering' (White 1989, 11). This is probably based on long term experience, either universally or in a certain culture. If the empirical evidence changes, they change the form they try to give the innate desires and the hierarchy they build up.

There do not seem to be in White's account any desires that per se ought not to be there, he does not talk about bad desires and does not bring in the concept of evil.[33] What would he say about envy, then, or any selfish desire, like the desire to dominate others? He could not build on experience and say that these do not lead to well-being, because there is no other criterion for well-being than desire satisfaction. Neither could he say that they ruin other people's lives, because concern for others is for him not a necessary part of well-being, well-being can be built on purely selfish desires. So the only reason to rule out a desire is its being overruled by a more important one.

White writes about children being brought up disposed to promote their own well-being (ibid., 71). But he actually starts out with something different, saying that 'it would be widely, and almost truistically, accepted that school education, like education in general, should help pupils to flourish', should promote their well-being (White 1990, 8). Yes, teachers and other adults should be other-concerned, concerned with the pupils' well-being. But why then should not pupils learn to be the same, namely other-concerned, concerned primarily with promoting others' well-being, not their own? Helping pupils to flourish and helping pupils to be concerned with their own flourishing are not the same.

OTHER-CONCERN

In addition to well-being, White wants concern for other people, or being 'attentive to the needs of others' (ibid., 46) to be an aim for education. He does not like to talk about morality, he prefers the concept of altruism. The way he uses 'altruism' is not the only one, neither is the understanding he has of morality, so I shall use both, taking them to mean what both of us are concerned with, namely other-concern. White will not, unlike the ancient Greeks, say that it is a necessary part of well-being, but given that we want people to care for others, it must in some way be linked to their well-being, to their desires, otherwise there will be no motivation to be altruistic.

If this is so, it is important for the upbringer to implant altruistic desires in children. We must build value-commitments and priorities into them as firmly as possible (ibid., 49), the basic ones so firmly that they are never questioned. This obviously presupposes that some innate desires can be formed into or used as a starting-point for building other-concerned desires. It also seems to presuppose that these desires are so much part of human nature that building them in very firmly cannot be regarded as indoctrination and preventing children from becoming autonomous.

White gives a list of dispositions[34] that have to be inculcated in children if they are to be altruistic as part of their well-being. The list basically consists of dispositions to be attached to individuals and communities close to oneself and to have less warm but still good relationships with everybody else, and also dispositions to fulfil obligations and to protect and promote people's well-being (ibid., 47-8). He suggests that this list is nearly uncontroversial, and he may be right as long as we only look at the dispositions or desires included. More telling is to look at what is *not* included. Being disposed to put others before oneself, for instance, or to spread the Gospel, to pray.

For Christians, and probably for members of other religions, this list will not be right, because it leaves out indispensable dispositions. Faith in God is something that could and should permeate and give direction to all desires and dispositions, also concerning our relationship with others. Fellowship with God is essential in altruism. As an expression of White's understanding of altruism his list therefore tells us that belief in God is not part of it, the concept is in practice atheistic.

White advocates an intersubjective ethics. There are no given, objective values. 'We have indeed created [the values] and refashioned them - on a long time-scale, of course' (ibid., 119). But there are a number of altruistic dispositions with which '[m]ost people will agree that children should be brought up' (ibid., 48), so his ethics is not wholly subjective either.

The main concern for White here is to find a way of relating well-being (self-interest) to other-concern. He wants educators to teach children to live mainly by desires that are both self-interested and other-regarding, desires that bring good both to oneself and to others. Because we are social beings and often have shared ends, this will often be possible. To make the children attentive to others' needs, we instill in them a desire to do good, so that they get satisfaction from doing it.[35]

The upbringers play a crucial role in the children's view of their well-being and the place of other-concern in it. There are some desires or dispositions, White says, that are not negotiable (ibid., 92), these are to be accepted and not to be considered autonomously, because they are either part of our nature or necessary for society and everybody's well-being. This also applies to priorities to prevent anybody from *always* (my italics) giving higher priority to narrow self-interest. How often they do it will be up to the individual to decide as they grow up and become autonomous. If the educators fail in implanting altruistic desires and priorities, there does not seem to be any way of making the children do good to others. There is no 'ought' to tell them that certain things ought to be done or not to be done whether they desire so or not.

AUTONOMY

There is no necessary logical link between well-being and autonomy, says White, but in our kind of pluralistic society autonomy is a condition for well-being. There is no strong tradition to lean on, we have to make our own choices (ibid., 99). This is true also for children from minority communities where autonomy is not supported, because they live within a larger community and cannot be kept from learning about other views unless we indoctrinate them, indoctrination being defined as 'intentional prevention of reflection' (ibid., 104).

Autonomy is to choose our major aims ourselves rather than leaving it to 'tradition, religion or others' domination, all of which are social constraints' (ibid., 75). It gives us freedom to form our lives, it is 'opposed to a life of coerced choices. It contrasts with a life of no choices, or of drifting through life without ever exercising one's capacity to choose. Evidently the autonomous life calls for a certain degree of self-awareness' (Raz 1986/1988, 371).

In the strong sense of autonomy[36], which White advocates, there has to be critical reflection behind the choices. In a society like ours, where people have different major aims for their lives, White wants children to be brought up to be aware of this and to reflect critically on their own position. An example could be that if they are brought up within a secular, liberal humanism, they do not just continue building their life on this world view, but they reflect critically on it, and they decide whether to stick to it or to go for something else, like Buddhism.

To grow up to become autonomous, children first need firm dispositions and a firm desire-hierarchy. They should be 'shaped from birth onwards by their parents and other teachers and by the cultural values which inform their child-rearing' (White 1990, 82). The basic values should be 'imposed on them', but not 'in such a way that it is very difficult or impossible for them to reflect on them and thus be in a position to give them up' (ibid., 119). But some basic values and dispositions are not negotiable (ibid., 92), which I suppose means that they should be indoctrinated.

As children grow up, we teach them how to resolve conflicts between desires. They will start forming their own desire-hierarchy and take over responsibility for choices (ibid., 82). They will make their own version of the good life, of well-being, including the forming of new desires or getting rid of old ones. I suppose that for instance by getting to know other cultures, people might want to join one of them and thereby change a lot of their desire-hierarchy.

I cannot see that White says anything about what kind of criteria we should give children for finding out what would increase their well-being, or how to organize their desire-hierarchy. When we teach them how to solve conflicts, how do we tell them to judge the various desires they have, apart from getting all the information they need? It is difficult to see how they should know when to give priority to an altruistic desire. It might be right just to follow the strongest desire, or there might be other criteria. If there are none, it could be very arbitrary which desire gains the upper hand, it might to a large degree depend on the community they live in.

THE MEANING AND PURPOSE OF LIFE

As far as I can understand, White would not talk about The meaning of life, or The purpose of life, as something given, something coming from outside the individual. For there to be a given purpose, it must have been thought out by somebody, and there is no 'somebody' in his world who has the knowledge or authority to determine the purpose of other people's lives. The same seems to be true about meaning. Nobody in White's human-centred world can tell a child that 'this is the meaning of your life, this is why you live'. On the contrary, he says that 'autonomous thinkers come to see themselves as living in a world with no apparent meaning or purpose' (White 1995, 14). So the cosmic framework he wants to find for non-religious people does not give any answer to the question of *why* we live, unless the answer is 'for no purpose'.

It is not only religions that tell us that life has a purpose. Secular ideologies do as well. Like Marxism, where the purpose is to work towards revolution. But in White's view, this would be to take from people their autonomy. In his view, it is every individual's responsibility to choose their own meaning, their own purpose. But in one way he nevertheless operates with a given meaning, namely well-being. He takes it for granted that the good life - the meaningful life? - consists in well-being, and in well-being in his very particular way, namely as satisfaction of important, informed desires.

Children should be taught about various purposes people may have for their life so that they can choose what seems meaningful to them. If they think that working to protect the environment will give their life meaning and direction, then they decide that this is how they shall live. Or they may think that money is all that matters, or that serving the Christian god will make them happy, it is up to them to make an autonomous choice, seek meaning and give their life a purpose. Purpose is something they themselves give to their life, not something that is already there from the beginning.

3.3.2 World view presuppositions

HUMAN-CENTRED

Why does White have this view of well-being and the good life? If we take a closer look, a certain view of human nature and of reality as a whole will become more clear. What we see is a universe which consists of nature, including animals. There is no God, no eternity, nothing transcendent, and no built-in purpose. In most of White's writings this universe is presented as *the* universe, on the implicit assumption that the way he thinks about reality is how everybody thinks. Even when he explicitly calls it a secular view, he still seems to regard it as an understanding that can be the basis of education for all children who want an education for autonomy (ibid., 19).

Nevertheless he talks about 'our ordinary human world' (ibid., 8), or 'the world with which we are familiar' (White 1990, 32), as if 'our' and 'we' include everybody. But a lot of people are familiar with very different worlds from White's. Maybe he thinks that we all have a common world, 'the human world', and then Christians and other believers have a spiritual world in addition? As we saw in chapter two, this is not how it is. The 'ordinary human world' for Christians is a world where God is present, where people are dependent on and responsible to God, whether or not we want it or know it, and with a perspective beyond death.

Human beings, a particular kind of animal in White's world, are special, and their humanity makes them unique and gives them individual worth, independent of their health, intelligence, age, etc. They have developed higher-order desires whose fulfilment is not necessary for survival. They also have desires for others' desire-satisfaction. Since they are not governed by instincts, but reflect on their desires, they have to make choices. Because they are meaning-seeking animals, they often create a purpose for their life in this purpose-less world, each individual finding their own (ibid., 32).

White's account of the good life is not presented as neutral, but he still seems to take for granted that it would be acceptable to all, at least all who favour autonomy. But when we compare it with a Christian account, it becomes clear that its human-centredness permeates it all and makes it incompatible with a Christian education in general, not only for more or less fundamentalist minority groups. It is secular humanism, where Man is everything's measure, and where death is the end of life.

White's education could not possibly be God-centred. He might teach about Christianity, or about many religions, but there could be no knowledge of God's presence in the school, they would know no God to relate to. We see his view of religion also in how it is regarded as a social constraint like tradition and others' domination (ibid., 75), and how God is mentioned alongside social custom and peer group pressure as agents for ruling our life if we are not autonomous (White 1995, 13). These expressions are very clearly written from an immanent, human-centred view of the world, and there is no doubt that such a view will be implicitly - at least - conveyed in White's education.

Secular humanistic education might be less self-centred than White's, more other-centred, if a desire to do good to others were inculcated as the top of the hierarchy. But it would have to be human-centred, and this would not be questioned. As far as I can see, the whole set of world view presuppositions underlying his education will not be questioned. They may not be explicitly taught, but they will implicitly be transmitted: this is how it is. The human-centredness is even in the notion of the good life. If the focus had been on God, the aim of education and purpose of life would have be talked of in terms of God's glory. 'The good life' is not necessarily a self-centred notion, but here it is certainly *my* life that is in focus, my life as something I choose and I create.

WELL-BEING AND SELF-CENTREDNESS

White's account gives no criterion for evaluating which desires to give priority to. Not for the educators for deciding which dispositions to inculcate at the top of the hierarchy, nor for the children for deciding between all the other desires. It might be the strength of biological desires, or the culture of society, or both. As long as God is ignored, or only is presented as an option for my well-being, they see no outside criterion to judge from, and it may become fairly arbitrary which desires end up at the top.

Well-being is desire satisfaction, says White. 'Of two people, equally set on a life of philosophising, intimate relationships and watching rugby, the one who fails his philosophy degree, whose friends all drift away and who then goes blind is likely to lead a life of lesser well-being than someone who successfully achieves these aims' (White 1997, 240). All other things being equal, this is certainly right, since well-being is defined in terms of satisfaction of desires. But it definitely does not mean that the former is necessarily less happy than the latter, or leads a less good life. It is too simplistic to think there is a one-to-one connection between desire satisfaction and a good life. The successful person may not find happiness in his successes. And the other one may find happiness and meaning through his or her failures. This is true in a special way about people who believe in God, who can work out his purpose through failures as well as successes. Even if all our plans come to nothing, he has a future for us.

It is thought-provoking to notice some of the examples White gives of things that promote well-being: going to a selective school if you are clever (White 1990, 90), and getting a job that is well paid and pleasant (ibid., 86). Although there are other aspects, like the role of the arts, I find a flavour of materialism in his concept of the good life. Wealth and health - which he also mentions as important - are also to a very little degree under our control. The Bible's view of well-being is very different, it focuses on who we are as God's children, on attitudes, and on what we can do for others. This would give a very different ethos for education in general.

'The Bible's view of well-being', I said. The Bible does not use the concept, but is the idea there? That depends on how much content the concept carries with it. It certainly is not exclusively linked to a world view like White's. With different beliefs about what it is to be a person, different beliefs about well-being will follow. A Buddhist's belief about well-being will focus on self-purification. In Christianity, well-being would have to mean living the life you were created for, in fellowship with God, serving him, trying to help other people, giving God glory.[37]

However, the notion of well-being itself sounds very struggle-free and harmonious. It is therefore hardly suitable to convey a Christian view of the meaningful life, which includes a struggle against our selfishness that will not end until we die.

'Indeed, one may say, if being free, enjoying yourself, and satisfying wants are not among the conditions with reference to which the values of other things, conditions, and actions should be measured, then nothing is' (Haworth 1986, 183). This may just be possible to say within a Christian framework, but freedom, enjoyment and satisfaction would have completely different meanings from what they have in a humanistic context. The joy would be the joy God gives when we live according to his will, however full of struggle life is.

According to White, ethics has to be based on our nature, on desires and their satisfaction that are 'empirical features of our make-up' (White 1990, 32). In his view of human nature and reality, there could not be any instance outside human beings from where any values can come. This is what would be called naturalistic ethics, but in a broader sense than he uses it himself (ibid., 118). Although he may reject that his view is built on our biological nature only, it is certainly built on human nature, on 'deeply embedded features of our common life without which that life would be inconceivable' (ibid.).

His is also a pragmatic ethics: truth is what works. Experience and tradition tell us which desires and dispositions to inculcate in the next generation, more or less firmly. Empirical evidence is certainly important, although it may sometimes take generations before we learn about all the consequences of our desire-satisfaction. And empirical evidence can never this side of death settle the question about the ultimate purpose and meaning of life, what our *really* important desires should be and how we therefore ought to live.

There is no room in White's account for desires we ought to have even if experience tells us that the satisfaction of them might not lead to our well-being in the ordinary, self-centred meaning of that word. An example might be a desire to serve other people, even to a considerable cost for ourselves, or a desire to serve God, or to pray. Whether experience tells us that these are worth instilling in children, depends on which world we are experiencing; God's or our own.

White seems to think that we are not necessarily moral beings, since he claims that we can live the good life without any other-concerned desires, being wholly selfish. This too contrasts with the Christian view that we are created to do good, to love. But, he argues, nevertheless we ought to be brought up as other-concerned people. He starts out with altruism as something to balance the more self-interested well-being, but then he tries to merge them, arguing that most of the time people can be 'guided by desires which are self-interested and other-regarding at the same time' (ibid., 69).

This may be true to a certain degree, but the problem emerges when it is not. Having made everything into self-interest, children who are brought up like this would probably not have any notion of egoism, no awareness that they are more likely to do what is in their 'narrow' self-interest. How then can they fight their desire for self-centredness? I suppose that the way he tries to combine well-being and altruism is related to his view of reality and human nature, a view which does not allow for evil, let alone for the devil. There seems to be no room in his account for evil desires, for desires to hurt others, only for good - unfortunately sometimes conflicting - desires. From a Christian perspective it is necessary for children to understand that they will not be able to do good without struggle. Such an awareness will obviously not be part of White's education, the truth that will be transmitted to his pupils is that it is all a question of choosing among good desires.

AUTONOMY

For White, autonomy seems to be necessary for a good life only in pluralistic societies, where there are many versions of the good life to choose among. Christianity would probably have a stronger claim. The one traditional good life in a homogeneous society might be wrong, therefore also people in these societies have to think critically about how they ought to live. They ought to be autonomous, to do their own thinking and praying and listening to God and so make their own decisions.

White's focus is on autonomy, but in Christianity responsibility is more important. Every person is responsible to God for his or her life, no matter what kind of society they live in. There is no way we can get away from our responsibility by saying to God that 'I lived in a very homogeneously materialistic (i.e. tradition-directed) society and therefore had to spend most of my money on things for myself'.

To be autonomous means to make our own choices after critical reflection. White quotes from J. Gray that the autonomous person 'must also have distanced himself in some measure from the conventions of his social environment and from the influence of the people surrounding him' (ibid., 97). But White himself is not very distanced from his own conventions. One of his non-negotiable values is 'bodily desires' (ibid., 92), which would obviously not be on the non-negotiable list for a Buddhist. And could not a person even become, after critical reflection, a hermit - contrary to the disposition of enjoying others' company, which is also on his list (ibid., 70)? According to White, they could not. Thus some views are out of the question. Following White, people are actually brought up not to freely choose religion or world view. Why are these people still regarded as autonomous, while those who are for instance brought up not to reflect on and freely choose a job, are not regarded as autonomous?

Apart from inculcating the basic values, White seems to think that if children are to become autonomous, it is necessary for educators not to take a stand between various beliefs and values - various views of the good life. A couple of examples may highlight some of the problems with this thinking.

If for instance children are brought up by non-environmentalist parents in a non-environmentalist village, and then meet some environmentalists or learn that there is a group of people, a minority, who are very concerned about the environment and are campaigning for various ways of protecting it, where does their autonomous choice come in? Is it enough that they learn about environmentalism (a not very well defined term, I admit), that they meet arguments from both sides, and then are told that the choice is theirs?

We know how easy it will be for them to continue in their old belief, particularly since this will be supported by the majority, and we know that changing beliefs will require a change of lifestyle too. It is difficult to see that their choice can be free and autonomous to any large degree. The total influence is hardly neutral. Liberal educators probably ought to make an effort to make them value environmentalism, the minority view. The question is whether they should also claim that this is a morally better option than the other, or whether that would go against being liberal.

Also, what should the school do in practice? One thing is talking about for instance saving resources, another is what you do about it. What is the message if they are taught about the benefits of public transport, but all the teachers travel to school by car? If we really think it is an important issue, and one on which the pupils should take an autonomous stand, we must do what we teach. But if we do, there is no support for those with a different view.

Perhaps environmentalism is not a good example nowadays, because it seems to have become a public value, one the school is supposed to support and promote (although without very much support from society at large). Another example is children who are brought up in a vegetarian home, perhaps in a small community where everybody is vegetarian. They will soon learn that they are a minority. How can they make an autonomous choice, with so heavy an influence against what they are brought up within? It might be possible for a vegetarian liberal educator to say that eating meat is wrong, but it could also be regarded as taking the choice from the pupils.

And what about the school lunch? If it serves vegetarian food only, it tells the meat-eaters that they are wrong, or at least it does not give them any support. And the other way round. Serving both will not be equal treatment either, because as long as meat is served at all, the message is that the vegetarians are wrong (if it is regarded as a moral question, that is. If it it just seen as a question of taste or opinion, there really is no problem).

Which message comes across also depends on the reasons given. Most likely it would be argued that some people believe it is wrong to eat meat, others do not, and therefore we serve both so that everybody can do what they believe is right. This is meant to put vegetarianism into the private moral domain, but what it also does is to make morality in this area subjective or relative. It is of course also possible to say that one of the options must be wrong and the other right, but at the moment we do not know which one is wrong and therefore allow both. But by doing so we actually side with the non-vegetarians. We can show the vegetarians respect, but we still transmit to them that we think they are wrong. This influence is strengthened by being supported by society in general.

These examples show some of the problems in linking autonomy to educators not taking a stand. The children always start from somewhere, in all controversial questions, only it is easier to see it when they are in a minority. The influence from society at large is often so strong that it would require very strong educators and local communities to counteract it. And whatever we do, we favour some views and not others. This also relates to questions of religion and world view. Liberal educators would at least have to make sure that pupils from the majority become aware of their own beliefs and then do not assume that these are superior to other beliefs.

If children come from an atheist background, a silent assumption of atheism penetrating the whole school will give this alternative much more weight than others. So maybe, to counteract their early upbringing and give them some different experience, these children ought to be sent to a religious school, a school where God is more than an object for study in RE lessons. G. Haydon argues that in a secular society, non-secular schools may actually be in a better position to educate good citizens, because they can help the pupils to understand both secular and non-secular thinking (Haydon 1994, 72-4). That would probably be the real liberal education for them.

RELIGION AND RELIGIOUS UPBRINGING

With White's view of reality and human nature, there are only two options: autonomy or heteronomy. Either the individual makes the decisions her- or himself, or some other people make them for her or him. This view of autonomy would transmit to the children as a fact the belief that there is nobody above them. But this is secular humanism, and all their choices are *within* this world view, not between *different* 'major aims' for their life. They could easily be led to believe that they choose freely when actually education, or society in general, has made a very basic choice for them.

The reason for this view, as far as I can see, is that White does not come to terms with what it means to believe in God and follow him. He claims that if people are God-directed rather than self-directed, if they have their major goals 'decided by God', they are not autonomous (White 1995, 13). This seems to include all God-believers. But he also talks about 'many religious people', i.e. not all, for whom 'the ideal of self-determination is anathema, since one's task in life is to subjugate oneself to the will of God' (White 1990, 24). What does he mean?

In a footnote in (1990) he describes two groups of religious parents. One is those 'who bring their children up dogmatically to believe in the tenets of their faith' (ibid., 177). They do not encourage them to reflect critically on beliefs and values, on the contrary, they try to prevent them from being influenced by the values of the wider society (ibid., 104). This is indoctrination and ought not to happen in an autonomy-supporting society. He argues that '*all* children must be protected against true believers who wish to impose on them a non-autonomous conception of the good life' (ibid., 105). In Haworth's words:

> parents who indoctrinate their child in a particular religious point of view,
> so that on becoming an adult the child is not likely to be able to think

critically concerning the plausibility of that point of view, violate their child's right to an open future: such indoctrination makes it likely that an important aspect of the child's life as an adult will never come under his own control. (Haworth 1986, 127)

There are also the more liberal religious parents, parents who want their children to grow up to lead a self-determined life, i.e. to be autonomous. But these will, according to White, find a conflict between this and the 'precept of their religion that children must be brought up within the faith', they must be brought up as believers (White 1990, 177-8). The conflict is that the children will believe 'both that they must lead such and such a religious way of life, and that they should be self-determined' (ibid.). Such people should rather not have children.

I want to comment on three things here. First, his view of autonomy does not allow for a God who created people and is so different from us that he cannot be grouped with peer group and social custom. White makes the mistake of believing that his secular conception of autonomy is universal and categorizes religious parents according to his own secular categories. He seems to believe that either we have our choices made by God, or we make them ourselves. We either follow God's will blindly, or we follow our own.

Neither is right. The third version is that Christians want God's will to be their own. But because they have two natures, they also want to follow their own self-centred will. Life is therefore a struggle, a struggle that they have autonomously chosen, and continually choose, a struggle to let God's will more and more dominate their life because they know it is the best. It is autonomously putting their life in his hand, again and again giving up their own self-centred life, and getting a new, God-centred life that *also* is their own, following God's will that *also* is their own.

Second, he reveals a view of religion and religious upbringing that does not at all correspond with ordinary, orthodox Protestant Christianity. Christianity is life, a personal relationship with God, and not a particular religious way of life, not holding certain beliefs. The aim of parents is not that children should hold certain beliefs, but that they would want to continue their life with God.

His phrases 'bring up within the faith' and 'bring up as believers' are ambiguous. They might be understood as saying something about the result, namely that the upbringing necessarily leads to faith. From a Christian perspective, they should be understood as saying that the children will be brought up within a Christian understanding of life and reality, and not within any other world view. Because the parents are believers and everything in the home is understood from the perspective of believers, this will be the perspective of the children too. This does not say anything about the result, about what they will believe when they are grown up and have had to make their own decision.

Does White only see two groups of religious parents, those who indoctrinate and those who are liberal and autonomous in the way he understands this? It is unclear what he means by saying that all of us would subscribe to the ideal of autonomy, 'except those of us living in some strict religious community where we see our lives as directed by God's will rather than our own' (White 1997, 240). Does he define 'strict community' as any community where we see our lives as directed by God's will? Or could there be non-strict communities where this is the case? The kind of Christian education I described in chapter two does not fit any of his descriptions. His lack of clarity in this is probably again grounded in his misleading dichotomy between God's will and our own, in his liberal humanism where I am in control of God, not He of me.

Third, he writes as if only religious people bring up children as believers. He seems to imply that religious people have beliefs and values, secular people have values only, and even values that are common for all. As I have argued earlier, White's upbringing too includes a lot of beliefs, transmitted even without being made explicit. The question is which set of beliefs they take over from us, not whether they do it or not. And White has not said anything to show that Christian presuppositions are worse than liberal, secular humanistic ones as a basis for upbringing.

LIBERAL HUMANISM

In which way can we say that White's education is 'liberal' - as basis, alternative or quality? White's thoughts about education seem to be closest to the understanding of liberal as an alternative, only there are no other alternatives if we want to avoid indoctrination. It is clearly not thought of as a quality that we can find in education built on various world view presuppositions. He does not seem to regard world view as basic in education, rather as an optional addition. It may be possible to think of his understanding of 'liberal' as a basis, as a common education where world views can be added, where it is the individuals themselves who add the world view. But the basis is a fairly solid one, and some, probably many, world views will be incompatible with it and therefore impossible to add.

In many aspects White's humanism is similar to what Basil Mitchell calls liberal humanism (Mitchell 1980b). It is a combination of rational humanism, according to which human rationality gives an objective basis for morality, and romantic humanism, which regards morality as something completely subjective. According to the liberal version, there are *some* objective moral values, necessary for a stable society, and these reason can help us to find. Apart from these, the individuals find or choose their own morality, or their ideal form of life as P.F. Strawson calls it, and here diversity is to be encouraged.

Strawson uses different notions for this 'ideal form of life', and he does not seem to distinguish between personal ideals and ideals for people in general. He can for instance say that '[a]t one time it may seem to him that he should live - even that *a man* should live - in such-and-such a way' (Strawson 1961/1974, 26). Personal ideals and 'general descriptive statements about man and the world' (ibid., 28) are more or less the same. In this area there is no truth, only incompatible truths.

Mitchell argues that Strawson elevates his own presuppositions, his own personal ideal, to be *the* ideal, the truth for everybody.

> It is the ideal of imaginative sympathy with the ideals of others, no matter how alien these may be. It reflects a view of man as a being who, within the limits of his biological constitution, is free to become what he wills, whose 'existence precedes his essence'. If men are self-creations of this sort and if, as Strawson believes, there are no objective criteria by which to judge what they choose to make of themselves, one can help them, once their basic needs are satisfied, only by identifying oneself in imagination with their entire project of life, or their changing projects, and aiding their achievement; so long, that is, as they respect the basic social morality. It is characteristic of a being, such as man is on this view, that he expresses himself, among other ways, in the elaboration of religious and metaphysical systems which he is tempted to regard as true; and Strawson will sympathize with these, while recognizing this temptation for what it is, a delusive phantasy. (Mitchell 1980b, 53-4)

Liberal humanism, says Mitchell, defines people's beliefs about reality and human beings, their world views, as only individual ideals or preferences. White would probably give more weight to the common morality than Strawson, but he too seems to believe that his own account, where people choose their major aims, does justice to people's ideology or religion. This is not right, Mitchell argues,

> [n]either the Christian nor the Marxist, for example, can agree that his Christianity or his Marxism should occupy the status merely of a private preference with no authority over man's social life and no claim to objective truth. Christianity and Marxism are not 'personal ideals' or 'profound statements' which can fit happily into the niche that the liberal humanist is ready to provide for them; they are rival philosophies of life. (Ibid., 54)

The Norwegian philosopher Hans Skjervheim talks about 'the liberal dilemma': when the liberal principles are made absolute, they become anti-liberal (Skjervheim 1967/1996, 88). He mentions how in the French revolution, liberal principles led to the Jacobins killing their enemies. It is like saying: everybody ought to be free, but in *my* version of freedom, within *my* framework for understanding the world. One of Skjervheim's examples is about religious freedom. An interest in religion

> ought to be given full freedom as an *individual interest*. Usually we express this by saying that religion is a private concern. But how it is usually said - that religion is a private concern - is itself not a private concern, but a general principle. However, the extent to which religion is a private concern is not something external to religion, and for those who take religion most seriously, the liberal principle thus becomes coercive when implemented in practice. (Ibid., 91)

For those who regard their religion as the universal answer to the ultimate questions of life, making it a private concern is anti-liberal, the liberal state then represents coercion (ibid., 93). This is the danger White is in when he wants to prescribe a certain education for a certain good life for everybody who wants autonomy (White 1990). He even seems to believe that they all ought to be educated within his non-religious cosmic framework (White 1995, 19), believing that *his* version of autonomy and freedom are the only ones.

White's education does just what he says it does not: it steers the pupils towards a definite ideal of the good life. Not on a superficial level; it certainly gives room for different views of family life, career, hobbies, etc. But on a deeper level there is one view that is held to be the obvious one in our society, namely that it is the person him- or herself who fundamentally decides what the good life is for him- or herself. It is a human-centred view, there is no room in his thinking for a God who can tell us the deepest meaning of our lives. His theory may not build on one particular, comprehensive world view, but it is based on some world view presuppositions that conflict fundamentally with presuppositions in Christianity and probably in other religions too.

3.4 Kenneth A. Strike's view of liberal education

Even if White has failed to outline an education that would be acceptable to all, or even to all those who want autonomy, there might be other alternatives. To my knowledge nobody else has given such a detailed account, but many have suggested various solutions to the problem of 'common education' in a liberal democratic, pluralist society. One of them is K.A. Strike, who has discussed the problem in many articles, of which I am here using some fairly recent ones (1992-94). He admits that it is difficult to get education neutral between world views, or primary moral languages which is his term, but he still thinks it possible and desirable.[38]

Strike's concern is to outline an education that is acceptable to everybody, that does not transmit a perspective on life that is particular to one group. His basic category seems to be morality, and he uses the notion of 'language' for ethical outlooks. Different outlooks, or languages, 'are characterized by their distinctive vocabularies, their purposes, their standards of appraisal, the things it makes sense to say in them, and the inferential "moves" they permit' (Strike 1992, 226). Each community has its private or local language, and in addition liberal, pluralistic societies need a public or civic language that everybody understands.

Public language is what we need to talk together across local communities of various sorts. It has to be neutral between the various local ethical languages. It is a public ethics but without public grounding, where only arguments that are reasonable for everybody are valid. This common language does not end disagreement, but it facilitates 'conversation between those who otherwise lack a shared language. The alternatives are domination, coercion and violence' (ibid., 231). We may justify the arguments differently, but the justification should be kept out of the public language. Reasons distinctive to a particular faith should not be used, only public reasons, i.e. reasons 'that one can give to someone whose ethical outlook is rooted in a different local tradition than one's own' (ibid.).

The private, or local, language is thicker. It is a perspective for giving reasons for choices (Strike 1993b, 184), and it is necessary for people to understand their life and to express their view of the good life (Strike 1993a, 105). Such primary languages may be religious, ethnic, philosophical (Strike 1993b, 180). Here there is also room for God. These local languages, or perspectives, are important not only for the local communities, but also for the society at large, because that is where people's public reasons are rooted. The liberal common discourse is not enough for the society to survive, it is only a necessary tool in a pluralistic context, so the local languages should be left 'significantly in place' (Strike 1992, 227).

I find it puzzling that he talks about God and the good life in terms of morality, and that he seems to think that a person's basic outlook on life, what I would call a world view, basically is to do with morality (Strike 1993a, 105 and 1994, 24). The view we have of reality in general, what we think the world we live in is like, is more fundamental than ethics and determines to a large degree what we think in questions about how we ought to live. Strike is making a similar mistake to Mitchell's liberal humanism in making belief in God part of morality.

He is very clear that comprehensive liberalism is not neutral. Liberalism in itself contains many ethical standpoints and will conflict with other views, so he does not want this as the basis for society in general, nor for schools (Strike 1992, 228). What he wants as basis is an overlapping consensus which he calls pragmatic liberalism, which is also, he says, what Rawls writes about as political liberalism. The problem when it comes to education is that this pragmatic liberalism is not enough as a basis for a coherent education, hardly for any education at all. Such a school would have to be content with giving some instrumental goods (Strike 1994, 17). But he cannot see any alternative and argues that we have to do what we can within this framework.

The school must teach the children to use liberal, public speech, and this speech must itself be the language of the school. But the children must also get help with their local language (Strike 1993b, 178 and 185), the school cannot ignore it. As a means for this he suggests separate groups, using a principle 'that entitles groups meeting in public institutions to engage in conversations from which nonmembers are excluded or are spectators' (Strike 1994, 24-5). The liberal speech or discourse is not to be regarded as a competitor to the children's local language, they are both needed (Strike 1992, 233). Also, religions must be taught as well as secular philosophies, and 'students' expressions of their own spirituality' will have to be met with acceptance (Strike 1993b, 187).

What happens when children are taught to use a different language in public places, for instance at school? I would like to use an example to illustrate this, not from a school, but from a university lecture I attended (May 1997). The topic was instructional non-verbal communication and its effects on learning, and in the discussion afterwards the question was raised about things like eye contact, touch, etc. becoming instrumental, things we do to improve pupils' learning without really liking them or being interested in them, and how they might become counteractive if the pupils discover the truth. A few suggestions were made, and my own thoughts, which I kept to myself - for reasons that may become clear - ran along the following lines:

> The most important thing must be to love the pupils, to really care about them. Then we would not look at them or smile at them in order to improve their learning or in order to achieve anything else, but just because we love them. But if we do not love them, can we learn to? Yes, we certainly can, although we may never like them. An old teacher said that when he found some pupils difficult, he looked at them until he loved them. And we can pray for them, and ask God to give us his love for them.

A number of questions in my mind stopped me from giving my contribution to the discussion. The first group of them concerned 'love': will they understand what I mean by 'love', or are their conceptions very different? Do they have a conception of love as something that can be learnt? Will I have to give so long an explanation that we stray away from the main topic and they get annoyed? Or will they just ignore me? The rest of my questions were about prayer: how will they react if I bring in prayer as a means to loving my pupils (and thereby improve their learning)? Will they think it irrelevant since it is something that requires faith in God and therefore is not for everybody? Will they think that God and religion should not be mixed with education, at least not outside a Christian context? Will there be any possibility that this will be followed up, or will it be a dead end? If some other Christian follows it up, the others may feel left out, and if somebody else starts enquiring about God and prayers, we may get away from the main topic.

If I had been better prepared, I might have thrown my thoughts into the discussion, and then I would have known the reactions. But here it is not the reactions that are of interest, but my thoughts, and how they illuminate some problems that we could also find in common schools when trying to separate a public and a private language. The most obvious problem is how some pupils who know or feel that they are from a different background, probably from some kind of minority, may be silenced. Not willingly from the teachers' side, but because they are worried about not being understood, that their contribution will not be valued properly, or that what they say will seem irrelevant and not helpful to anybody else.

Another problem is the assumption that concepts (like love, or tolerance, justice, etc.) have or can have one and the same meaning independently of the background of those who use it. If Christian pupils, for instance, talked about love in a secular school, it might be assumed that they used it in a 'common', secular meaning, the same as everybody else, without their Christian framework having any influence on it. Do we really want people to have two different conceptions of the same concept, one public and one private? If we do, does that mean that what is part of their private language and most important to them, is not to be part of the discussion in the classroom? If this is so, and my - private - conception of love is necessarily linked to God's love, I would either have to not talk about love, or to talk about it in a way that I feel and believe is wrong. This could be a problem for adults who have got fairly internalized private values and conceptions, but even more so for children who have not, because the public language may interfere so much that they never get their private language fully developed.

An additional problem with such a liberal education is that it cannot be concerned with rationality or truth, says Strike (Strike 1992, 233-4 and 1994, 19). Because justifications for public reasons belong in the private sphere, and the overlapping consensus is concerned with consensus only and not with what is rational or right, there is no way we can or ought to judge the different views. Liberalism can be the basis for very little criticism. But more criticism is needed in education to achieve tolerance and autonomy. The children cannot be left 'captives of the moral convictions of their parents and community' (Strike 1993b, 183).

If we do not teach them to be critical about their own view, and others, they may end up in relativism, seeing the choice as arbitrary (ibid., 184). The only way to achieve this rational criticism is by schools being 'neutral facilitators of critical dialogue between diverse local traditions' (Strike

1992, 234). In this way the pupils can learn about and understand other views and get a chance to judge their own view critically ('hermeneutical dialogue'). This is Strike's theoretical solution, although he is not sure that it is possible in practice (ibid.).

Trying to evaluate Strike's view from my three categories, I think it is most like liberal as a basis. It is something that people with different world views can have in common, but where their own particular faith is for the main part kept outside (ibid.). It is not meant to be an alternative to education based on other views. It is different from John White's thoughts about education, with a much thinner basis or content. White believes that he has found a view of the good life that people would agree on, and he seems to think that his view of well-being is thick enough for a coherent education, without any additions from (other) world views. Strike's attempt to solve the problem is thus a criticism of White's theory.

Strike sees problems with his pragmatic liberal education, but he still thinks it is possible. 'One can at least imagine the possibility of a public education that is open to the exploration of various cultures, religions, and philosophies and that encourages meaningful dialogue between them, but which is at the same time impartial between their contending claims' (Strike 1994, 19). There will be several topics that cannot be taught, maybe not even discussed, for instance in sex education and moral education (ibid.).[39] He does not make it easy for himself to find a working account of education, but even so I still think he does not see all the problems.

The main objection to his education is that schools do not only teach, they also educate through values, attitudes and beliefs that permeate the school. This ethos is created primarily by the staff, but also by the rules, the buildings, the textbooks, the subjects and topics chosen. This is White's problem, and it is also Strike's. It is obvious in certain moral questions. Homosexuality, for instance, is one of the areas that Strike presumably would place in the private sphere because of public disagreement. But people live a large part of their lives in school and cannot do so in a neutral way. The school may not teach about homosexuality, or it may try to discuss it without taking a stand, but what do they do if there is an openly lesbian couple on the staff? Or if some parents want a gay teacher to be sacked? Whatever is said or done will support some views and go against others.

The ethos problem is even clearer when we focus on view of reality instead of particular moral questions. Since God is not part of the overlapping consensus, he will be absent in Strike's schools. Not necessarily absent in the sense of not being talked about, because he wants religions taught. But God will not be there as a living reality. He will not be worshipped. This means that for Christians, the most important part - or person - of their life will be ignored. It is not only a topic - 'God' - that they will miss, but everything will be out of perspective, the whole world will be different from what it is at home. Children from secular homes, on the other hand, will have their understanding of the world and their life strengthened.

Eternity is another example. Because life after death is not part of public speech, it will not be part of the school's perspective on life. Teachers and schools always convey something about the purpose of schooling, about why the pupils ought to learn this or that, about what is important in life (good exams, a good job, family, etc.). The Bible says that people's salvation and eternal life are more important than anything else. This should therefore be the ultimate perspective also for choosing a career. Ignoring this perspective in everyday life in school conveys that life after death is non-existent or at least unimportant. Actually, 'career' is not a neutral word either, it carries with it too much emphasis on success and ladder climbing. 'Service' is the biblical concept.

The same will be true when it comes to purpose of life. The school, says Strike, will not be able to give any strong influence here, no particular purpose will be conveyed (ibid., 17). It is hardly possible for schoolchildren to distinguish between not conveying a particular purpose and conveying that there is no particular purpose. Again, this conforms with liberal humanism: there is no particular purpose, people have different ones and it is up to the individual to choose his or her purpose in life autonomously. For Christians, or children from other backgrounds where life is believed to have a given purpose whether you see it as your own or not, this will be another discord.

God, and our relationship with God, is not something that can be confined to certain subjects, topics or discussions. Strike's liberal school may not convey a detailed and coherent world view or perspective on life, but it certainly conveys some secular humanistic presuppositions that are not neutral between the local languages. He calls it pragmatic liberalism, but in practice it cannot avoid being comprehensive liberalism. Although autonomy and individuality may not be taught, the attempt to stay neutral and not say anything about right or wrong, very likely leads to the understanding that it is up to the individual to decide.

The education will inevitably be thicker than he wants. Some of the children, particularly those from liberal humanistic homes, will have their local language strengthened, others will learn that their local language, their perspective on life, is not usable for any topic. For what do we transmit to children if we say that they cannot use God's good will as a reason for something being right or wrong if they talk to people who are not Christians? Does God's will only apply to those who believe in him? Is God not God for everybody?

This is the main problem with the pragmatic liberal education, apart from its failure to be real education. But there are others. One stems from the fact that children start school when they are so young that they have not learnt their local language properly. They live within a community and pick up its perspective, but a lot of things they still have not formulated for themselves when they go to school.

If the main language in schools is to be the public one, this means that a lot of children will get their thoughts and beliefs about a variety of topics first formulated in the public language, and the way we talk to a large degree determines what we think and believe (Strike 1993b, 179). They will learn to argue with public reasons only, they will get a secular structure and perspective on the topic and not be helped to see how this is part of a God-centred world. Some children also get very little help at home to find a coherent view of the world. The community's influence may be strong, but inconsistent. For many, school is the dominant educator. How are these children to get a robust morality, and world view, when they have 'weakened families and aimless schools' (ibid., 176)?

When he talks about ethical languages, Strike means the whole perspective or outlook, not only the words or concepts. But even the words often carry particular values with them (Strike 1992, 229). Take the word 'partner', which today is commonly used both for spouses and for unmarried people who live together. It is often assumed to be a neutral concept, inclusive and useful in legislation. But it blurs a very important distinction; it puts into one category two groups of people who, according to the Bible, are very different: the people in one group live according to God's will, the others do not. Secular humanists may think that partners are partners anyhow, but that is only *their* view. Again, this is important for children who are learning to understand reality partly through the language.

A last comment must be on Strike's use of 'evidence'. He argues that in the dialogue between different groups, which is also to take place in school, outcomes should depend on 'the open consideration of evidence' (Strike 1993b, 185). This seems to imply that the dialogue is not only for the purpose of learning about and from each other, but also for criticizing and looking for what is most rational. I would doubt that this is a task for schoolchildren with limited knowledge even about their own language. But even given that they could do this, who is to decide what is to count as evidence? Is God's good will irrelevant, for instance? Strike gets into a problem here because the different languages, the different world views, will have different criteria for what counts as evidence, and if only public criteria are to be used, this 'thin', liberal language will do exactly what he says it should not (Strike 1994, 19), namely evaluate the different local languages.

Strike admits that his vision for the state school would be difficult to put into practice. But even seeing this, he does not want separate schools. They are an inadequate solution because they exclude the possibility of dialogue (Strike 1993b, 178). They may give an education 'rooted in thick conceptions of a good life', which in itself is positive, but it is doubtful whether they could 'adequately nourish a suitable *civic* culture'. It is also possible, he claims, that they would give 'a highly indoctrinative education' (Strike 1994, 18). He talks here about possibilities and doubt, but has no real arguments against separate schools. It is remarkable that he is so negative to what seems to be the obvious and logical solution to his problems with the pragmatic liberal school.

Strike does not give such a detailed account of his common education as White does. It is therefore not so easy to see the world view presuppositions his education would transmit. But some of them are nevertheless very clear. It is to be a secular education, human-centred. And this is, at least from a Christian point of view, the crucial point and the most obvious sign that the education is not neutral between religions and world views. Also, conveying that it is up to the pupils to decide on the meaning of their life is a particular view, not compatible with any religion or non-religious world view that claims a given meaning to life. He tries to avoid the question of truth, which is likely to convey that it is not very important, probably irrelevant, and that the various primary or private moral languages contain their own, local truths.

The view that is conveyed may not be very detailed, but some aspects cannot but be conveyed. How strongly these will influence the children depends on a number of factors, not least on how thick and consistent their primary culture is. To me, the biggest paradox concerning this pragmatic liberal school is that it gives no help whatsoever to those children who really need help to find their feet in the world - those who get little help at home to form a consistent world view. Those from strong communities will cope with nearly everything and will have a frame of reference, a language, for interpreting the thin influence in such a school. But those who lack a robust morality, who have not been helped 'to form and articulate some sense of the point of their lives' (Strike 1993b, 180), will be left to themselves and the unintended influence.

The project of finding an education that does not take a stand between different religions and world views seems to be impossible. If upbringing and education are to be what they are meant to be - help for children and young people to find their feet in the world, then a coherent view of life should be conveyed. If we try to avoid this, various world view aspects are nevertheless conveyed. The central 'problem' in relation to Christian education is God, who will not be confined to a certain manageable area of life.[40] Education, like life in general, cannot be neutral towards God. If he is not there as the Creator and Saviour, he is not God, only a human-made means towards a life that is good in human-centred eyes.

CHAPTER 4

Arguments for No-standpoint Education

The background for the argument for liberal, no-standpoint education is normally that such education is regarded as necessary and desirable for common schools in pluralistic societies. For some, this education is regarded as fairly unproblematic. Others see problems, but cannot see alternative solutions. In this chapter I want to focus on why education that is neutral between world views is regarded as possible and even desirable, arguing that it is neither.

I want to analyse both arguments I have come across and other ones I can imagine may be used, and also more implicit presuppositions. There may certainly be arguments and presuppositions I have overlooked, but at least dealing with the ones I have found will take us a step further. Some of the arguments and presuppositions overlap, but they have different perspectives and are therefore treated separately.

In no way can this be an exhaustive list, because people may always come up with new arguments. Neither is there any strict logical system, but I have tried to organize it in four parts. First I look into various understandings of religion, understandings that may make it possible to think of education as being neutral between religions. Then I discuss arguments for the possibility and for the desirability of an education that is neutral between world views in general. Finally, I go into arguments about religion and autonomy, claims that religiously based education either makes autonomy impossible or at least makes it more difficult to attain than secular education.

Some writers very clearly write about religions, in others it is less clear whether they focus on religions or on world views in general, thus including secular 'faiths'. If a no-standpoint education is wanted, I cannot see that it is interesting at all only to focus on religions, because non-religious world views are not neutral either. So where nothing else is said, I shall assume that all kinds of world views are included. P. Gardner makes it clear that his arguments against religiously based education would be equally valid against atheistic education and also against at least some sorts of agnostic education. Atheism and agnosticism are not complete world views in themselves, but they are important aspects of many views. And I am not only concerned with education based on and transmitting a complete, consistent world view, but also with the transmission of certain aspects, like for instance atheism.

4.1 Presuppositions about religion in arguments for religiously neutral education

In spite of what was said above, secular world views will not be included in this section. It will focus on presuppositions that are particular to views about religion and its relation to life as a whole. Underlying any argument for religiously neutral education is always a particular view of religion in general or of the one religion in question. This view is sometimes explicit, but more often only implicitly assumed.

4.1.1 Religion is only or primarily a set of beliefs

This view focuses on religion as propositional beliefs. These are normally beliefs within a religious, separate area of knowledge, and they do not necessarily influence how we think in other areas. These sets of beliefs can be presented, on an equal basis, in RE, so that the pupils can choose between them.

P. Gardner seems to think of religion as primarily a set of beliefs and of religious upbringing as bringing up children to share the parents' religious beliefs (Gardner 1988 and 1991). A few places he includes religious practices ('to engage as believers in the religious practices and rituals of their parents', 1988, 89, see also p. 91), and he also mentions faith and framework for inquiries. Nevertheless, the overall impression is that religious upbringing is primarily to impose certain beliefs. These are propositional beliefs, 'believing *that* ...' he uses expressions like 'believing a proposition' and 'being open minded about a proposition' (ibid., 92), as well as talking about understanding beliefs.

In line with this, religious upbringing - at least of the strong kind he discusses with T. McLaughlin - is about inculcating 'a particular set of religious beliefs' (ibid., 96). Gardner argues that this makes it hard for children to become autonomous and to choose, or reflect about and assess, their beliefs (ibid., 90).

Now, Gardner seems to regard religion as primarily cognitive beliefs, but is this the reason why he thinks it possible for education (or even upbringing at home, which is what he writes about) to be neutral between religions? Or even more, does he indeed believe such neutrality possible? I find it difficult to be quite sure whether he thinks it possible to have an upbringing without imposing a set of beliefs at all, religious or not. A sentence like 'there is a danger in bringing up a child to believe a set of beliefs while encouraging him or her to be open minded about alternatives' (ibid., 93) may be interpreted as allowing for an upbringing without such inculcation. Also the general statement 'if one wants individuals to take the kind of reasoned decision about a host of competing views, we should avoid developing in them a commitment to a particular set of those views' (ibid., 96) tends to suggest the same.

He certainly thinks that a particular kind of agnostic upbringing is more likely to be liberal than either religious or atheistic upbringing, partly because it has fewer particular beliefs (ibid., 94, 97 and 105, note 47). But he sees tensions between the liberal ideal and agnostic upbringing too - the question is whether he thinks an upbringing exists that has no tensions in relation to the liberal ideal of autonomy, an upbringing that is neither religious, nor atheistic or agnostic, a kind of 'liberal liberal' education (see above, p. 50) that does not inculcate beliefs at all.

Also when he writes about agnostic education, Gardner focuses on the propositional beliefs, not on lived life. But one thing is what the parents say and teach, another is how they live. And they will, I presume, live as if God does not exist, or at least as if he is not relevant to their lives. Thus the influence, the view of reality that is actually transmitted, is in practice atheism, absence of God. The children may not be told dogmatically that he is not there, but as long as he does not seem to be there, he will not be part of their life.

Agnostic humanists may not express their dogmas very explicitly in education, but that does not mean they are not there. And it does not make them less likely to be indoctrinated, rather the opposite. It is easier for people, particularly for children, to relate - and object - to truth claims that are explicitly put to them, than to claims that are just assumed and lived by. If we talk about 'unshakeable beliefs', as Gardner does, there are non-religious ones as there are religious ones, only in a secular society they may be more difficult to spot and examine. Atheists may be clearer about their beliefs than agnostics, and this, I believe, makes it easier for children to relate to atheism. They may be more likely to think about it, to object to it, to try to find out about alternatives.

Christianity contains many propositional beliefs, but they are not the whole story, not even the centre of it. The centre in Christianity is the confession 'Jesus is Lord', and the relationship with God. 'God is not an intellectual construct. He is the one we worship and obey, who speaks to the heart, who is known only by faith and love and the one before whom all words fail' (Habgood 1990, 112).

Doctrines are not something separate from this relationship, they are not unconnected beliefs. They are condensed theses about who this Lord is and what he has given us: '... born of the virgin Mary, ... ascended into Heaven, ... life eternal' (creed of the Apostles). Or they are commandments to help us to live the good life according to his will for us. They are all connected in a way that makes sense if we regard it from the perspective of the living God making himself known to us. So at least regarding Christianity, religion is not primarily a set of beliefs and it cannot be confined to one area of life. Education cannot avoid being either Christian or non-Christian.

4.1.2 Religion is only or primarily a set of practices

This view focuses on what we can see, on the outward, formal aspects of religion. These may be institutionalized, like churchgoing and dietary requirements, or more private, like prayer. A 'practising Christian', for instance, may be perceived as one who does the right things, behaves in certain ways, where these are seen to be the constituting aspects.

In Lutheran Christianity, the practices are important, but not in themselves, only as part of a living relationship. God is not to be found in the church more than anywhere else, but we want to be together to meet him and worship him. Prayer is to talk with God. Baptism and communion are God's actions, visible signs of his presence. God works through them and through his word, but just 'going through the motions' without opening our heart to God makes nobody a Christian.

A school may try to avoid taking a stand here by not institutionalizing any practices, although individual pupils may be allowed to follow their own tradition. It may not always be easy to find out how to do this, as we have seen in the French state schools. Religious neutrality has there led to a ban on necklaces etc. formed as a cross, and on Muslim girls' headscarves. But such 'neutrality', again, is taking a stand, it is saying, in effect, that there is no need to worship God, it is not necessary to follow his commands. He is only important for those who have chosen him and they can leave him at home when they go to school.

4.1.3 Religion is about spirituality

In the present discussion in England about the spiritual side of education, it is often emphasized that it should not be linked to a specific religion, or to religion at all. M. Halstead says it 'must refer to the development of a particular dimension of the person' (Halstead 1996, 2). Spiritual education must be 'directed towards the development of fundamental human characteristics and capacities' (ibid.).

Although it is argued that spirituality should not be linked to religion, it is commonly assumed that religions are ways of being spiritual. They are about the inner world, about integrity and harmony, about emotions. We see the same in the discussion about worship, where it is the experience of worshipping that is important, not whom we worship.

One example of such an approach is found in B. Watson's article 'Children at school: a worshipping community?' (Watson 1988). In her account, it is not getting to know God that is important, but to understand what 'worship or meditation' is (ibid., 102). Therefore things can be presented in a 'neutral' way. She gives an example of an assembly:

> Introduce the singing of a hymn in some such way as this: Not everyone thinks that there is a God who made the world. You must try to think about this question for yourself. Let us do that by singing this song, and thinking about the words, whether you like them and whether your agree with them or not. (Ibid., 118)

The song to be sung is 'God ... Careth for me'. This way of introducing it should, Watson suggests, meet the worries of a parent who complained because her daughter was 'forcibly fed with a diet of "God loves me"', and it does so without evading the educational responsibility of helping people to be religiously literate' (ibid., 117).

This is an attempt to be religiously neutral. One day one god is worshipped, the next day another one, and the pupils should all the time make their own interpretations. The important thing seems to be that they have some 'worship', i.e. some quiet time to think about god and religion. But the question of truth is ignored. The important question is: is it true and therefore to be conveyed that God loves them, or is it not true and therefore not to be conveyed? Is worship something human-centred, something to give us good experiences, or is it a response to a living and holy God? Only the latter can be part of Christian education. As long as the school tries to be neutral, God 'disappears'.

The focus on 'religion' instead of particular religions gives the impression (which in Watson's case seems to be intentional) that religions are all about the same. The important thing is to have somebody to worship, it does not matter who. For Christians, and for other believers, this amounts to idolatry. According to the Bible it is irrelevant whether a person is religious or not, the all-important thing is whether he or she believes in Jesus Christ.[41]

Christianity is not a means towards becoming more spiritual, it is not about development, harmony and inner world, it is about how the Creator of the world tries to rescue the people he created and win us back from death and devil. He wants everybody, whether we are spiritually developed or not. The new life he offers will have a basic harmony because it will be the life we were created for, but there will also be a basic struggle between this new, God-centred life and the old, self-centred one. Feelings of harmony and spirituality will vary, for many people life is rather a struggle, but salvation is something objective, outside ourselves, which does not vary.

The way spirituality is often talked about avoids the question of truth. 'One possible reason why the "spirituality" approach is becoming popular is that it fits in with the rather common relativistic, do-it-yourself approach to religion' (Donley 1992, 184). For many, the question of truth is irrelevant,

they believe that the function of religion is 'to provide comfort and conso-
lation in face of the inescapable frustrations and constraints of human life'
(Mitchell 1979, 459). But Christianity is about objective truth, objective
reality, about life as a whole.

4.1.4 Religion is an optional extra

It seems that for some writers, rationality is regarded as being more basic
than our faith or world view. It is regarded as independent of our metaphysical beliefs, and religion is something that may be added to our life but
does not affect our thinking about knowledge and truth in other areas.
There is a basic, common rationality that is enough for understanding the
world and educating people to live in it. Religion is an optional addition,
icing on an otherwise common cake.

Paul Hirst is - or at least was - very clearly in this tradition, and he has
influenced many. According to him, religion consists of beliefs and practices that we can - and should - judge rationally one by one, and this rationality is independent of our beliefs. Whether there is a God or not has nothing
to say for what we think rational. He wants a 'fundamental commitment to
the progressive rational development of personal beliefs and practices
rather than uncritical adherence to, or determined defence of, any particular
set of beliefs and practices whatever their source' (Hirst 1985,13). Either
we take over traditional beliefs, or we are rational, but this rationality seems
to have no basis, the criticism comes from nowhere (ibid., 13-14).

Rational justification is also the only justification for moral rules (Hirst
1974, 12), and again, rationality is above God. It is his own or society's
rational thinking that determines whether a rule given by God is good or
not. We must use 'the canons of objectivity and reason, canons against
which Christian, Humanist and Buddhist beliefs must ... be assessed' (ibid.,
81).[42] We are not dependent on God in any way, rather the opposite: he
seems to be dependent on us for his relevance if not for his existence.

The kind of religious education Hirst thus advocates teaches only that
which is 'rationally defensible on objective grounds' (Hirst 1981/1993, 4).
If education is based on beliefs, it is not rational. 'The explicit or implicit
advocacy of any one set of beliefs as true ... must be seen as an illegitimate
objective for education in the sense I have been developing' (ibid., 7). The
stance of faith is for catechesis, not for education (ibid., 9).[43]

This traditional, Enlightenment view of rationality has been criticized
from many schools of thought, but it still seems to linger in discussions
about education and religion. E.J. Thiessen argues that it fails to take into
account 'recent discussions about epistemology as found in the philosophy
of science, philosophical hermeneutics, the sociology of knowledge, critical
theory, postmodernism, Marxist and neo-Marxist critiques of liberal defini-

tions of knowledge, and evolutionary and naturalistic epistemology' (Thiessen 1993, 105).

I would argue that Hirst gets it the wrong way round. World view is more basic than rationality. This is what MacIntyre argues in 'Whose Justice? Which Rationality?'. There is no rationality as such, only within different traditions.[44] 'Where the standpoint of a tradition involves an acknowledgment that fundamental debate is between competing and conflicting understandings of rationality, the standpoint of the forums of modern liberal culture presupposes the fiction of shared, even if unformulable, universal standards of rationality' (MacIntyre 1988, 400).

For Hirst, only the physical world seems to be real, but for Christians the invisible world is as real and as important and gives thereby a different perspective on the physical world. What is rational in a world where death is the end of life may be different from what rationality tells us where death is just the beginning. If by 'rationally defensible' (Hirst 1985, 13) he means a secular, God-less rationality, and the main Christian doctrines (e.g. Christ died to give us eternal life) are to be judged according to what is defensible for people who do not believe in God, then he is labelling most ordinary Christian people irrational. Hirst's understanding of the relationship between faith and reason is too simple.[45]

H. Blamires uses the conception 'the Christian mind' to show that Christianity makes a basic difference to the way we think. Among the marks that distinguish this mind from a secular mind are its 'supernatural orientation' and its 'conception of truth' (Blamires 1963).[46]

Reason is not neutral. It is logical, but always from a certain perspective.[47] Consequently, we cannot teach objectively if that means 'without any presuppositions about what counts as evidence and what makes sense' (Newbigin 1977/1982, 100). A Christian cannot leave God out of his or her rationality in any area and think as if he does not exist and care. Religion is not optional icing on a rational cake, it is a very basic ingredient in the cake. Different world views give different rationalities, and liberalism has its own.

> One can also understand all religions and ideologies from the point of view of ... a secular, liberal inhabitant of the Western capitalist post-Christian world. This point of view is naturally accepted by the majority of the inhabitants of this corner of the world as being simply 'how things really are'. This is the character of all myths. Those who inhabit them do not 'see' them, because they are the framework, the model by means of which they see. But this 'myth' is very recognizable by the inhabitants of other parts of the world as our particular cultural model. (Ibid.)

> The eighteenth century rationalist or the twentieth century humanist who claims to observe all the phenomena of religion impartially is also under

an obligation to expose for examination the fundamental axioms, the prior decisions about what is allowed to count as evidence, which underlie his way of understanding. (Ibid., 99)

4.1.5 Religion is a separate realm

Education that is based on the belief that rationality is neutral, will regard religion as a separate area that does not influence the rest of our rational thinking. The thought that religion is a separate realm may also be found without this philosophical backing. It is fairly common to think that religion is one compartment, science and mathematics and history are other, secular ones. G. Haydon reveals an understanding of religion as something that is not confined to RE, but could appear 'right across the life of the school' if not silenced (Haydon 1994, 71-2). But still he thinks that also religious schools will expose their pupils to some secular thinking, and he mentions mathematics and science as examples (ibid., 73).

The problem here is that 'secular' is an ambiguous concept.[48] Haydon takes it to mean that religious concepts and beliefs are not used. And there are certainly areas of many subjects that will be talked about, also in Christian schools, without involving Christian concepts or beliefs. But that does not mean that they are secular, non-religious compartments. According to Luther's model of the two governments, also the secular government is God's. Looked at from a Christian point of view, there is no 'secular' world in the atheistic meaning of the word, i.e. a world where God is irrelevant or absent.

Haydon seems to imply that the secular thinking in the secular school is the same as the secular thinking in the non-secular school, which may be true if we think of small, 'technical' areas, but which is not true if we look at how these bits are to be combined into a whole. He uses an example of a Christian scientist.

> Her thinking as a scientist, in doing experiments, writing up the results, reading articles, and (if she is an academic) teaching, may be qualitatively indistinguishable from that of an atheist. There will be other contexts during her life - during church services, for instance - in which her think- ing is radically different from the atheist's. There may, then, be a degree of compartmentalization in her life. (Ibid., 66)

This is too simple, and I would like to use my own thesis-writing as an example. To choose a topic and write a thesis might be regarded as a completely secular thing. No religious concepts and beliefs are needed in talking about it, it is all about reading and thinking and struggling to clarify things, finding a relevant topic and title, discussing things with my supervisor and others, wondering whether what I am doing could be useful, struggling to concentrate, etc. These are all 'secular' concepts, and an atheist could have said the same.

This is often how I talk about it, but it is not the whole truth about how I think. The basis of my thinking is that God wants me to work on this thesis, that it is his plan for me now. I talk to him about it, asking for help to keep the main focus and to write it in a way that would be helpful for people. When I feel miserable about not keeping up the speed I expected, or not feeling I can do the job well enough, I talk to him about that too. I certainly do not ask God how to write a bibliography, in a way that may be a completely 'secular' thing, but that is part of my work for God as well, it belongs in God's world.

This shows how impossible it is to separate Christianity from any part of life - and any part of education. If children are to get to know God, it is necessary for educators to talk like this, not only think. Not making God's presence and care explicit in all parts of school life will easily convey that religion is something separate, an extra that some people add to an otherwise common way of thinking and living.

But religion, or at least Christianity, is not an addition that can be separated from the rest of life. Neither is it something that only concerns a section of life - cognitive beliefs, practices, spirituality. It is a personal relationship with God that affects the whole outlook on life: how we think, who we think we are, what we believe the purpose of life is, how we perceive and act in the world in general. If arguments for world view neutral education are based on such a limited or one-sided view of Christianity, or of religion in general, they are not valid.

4.2 Presuppositions implicit in arguments for world view neutral education

It is sometimes argued and sometimes assumed that it is possible to educate without conveying particular beliefs about how life is to be understood. It seems more common to argue in terms of religions than world views in general, but the arguments I am discussing in this part also apply in case of secular world views.

Often the assumption seems to be that we all share some common values, or public values, and that these are enough as basis for education. In other instances the approach is that we can teach about various religions or world views without promoting one in particular. The last perspective I shall discuss, which is not found expressed very often but which is a possible stand, is that the school becomes neutral by the teachers' different views balancing each other.

4.2.1 There is enough common ground in public values

This is K. Strike's view, and also J. White's, although his basis of common values is thicker than Strike's. The thinking behind seems to be that we can separate the religious aspect or dimension from the moral values and that the values in this 'secular' or even 'secularized' version are common to all. Secular values can be public, but religious ones cannot - at least not in our society. It also seems to be a presupposition that moral values are the base line in education, it is moral values that are necessary and should be transmitted.

Enough should have been said already to show that this argument is not valid. Religion is not something to be added, it is something fundamental, basic. Moral values are not enough to form a basis for education, we need metaphysical beliefs too, and they cannot be both non-religious and religious in the same areas at the same time.

In his discussion with McLaughlin, E. Callan compares teaching with a strong religious influence with teaching with a strong political influence, using as an example a teacher whose influence is strongly communist (Callan 1985, 113-14). He seems to think that only very clear and explicit political and religious views, minority views, are likely to be indoctrinated. He does not see the very strong influence there will be from an implicit majority view as well. Those who have no communist teacher, who are not 'made' communists, what will they be 'made'? It should be evident that they will get a similarly strong politically biased education, only different, and that without being told. And those without a Christian or religious parent or teacher, will get a similarly strong secular influence. You cannot leave the child's commitments open, the influence is only more or less explicit.

Everybody gets a primary moral language with their primary culture, their beliefs and presuppositions, and norms and values will be understood and interpreted in this context. We cannot 'lift' the values out of their world view context and make them context-free. Even such a fundamental public value as justice may have different meanings for people from different primary cultures.

A Christian conception of justice, for instance, will start from how God reveals himself as just. 'Israel's fundamental experience, then is of *the righteous God who sets his people free*, not because they are mighty or worthy, but because he loves them and chooses them as his own' (Wren 1986, 45). Wren calls it loving justice: 'Thus, the Christian experience of God, in the cross and resurrection of Christ, is of a love that surpasses justice in the hope that justice can at last be created' (ibid., 51).[49] Justice is important, but love and mercy are more important.

This Christian understanding of justice cannot be expected to be society's understanding, but a humanist understanding is no less neutral although it may be more common in the sense of widespread. Although different conceptions will have much in common, the school will not be able to find a common, 'neutral' interpretation to use.

4.2.2 We can teach about world views without promoting a particular one

The basic assumption most often underpinning such a view is that education consists in teaching, in helping the pupils to get knowledge - objective knowledge that is not influenced by various beliefs. Upbringing within a particular faith belongs to the family. Hirst believed - and may still believe, despite the change in his theory[50] - that we can teach *about* religions and world views without teaching *from* one of them. In such education, we must teach 'the radically controversial character' of all religious claims (Hirst 1974, 81). Understanding of 'ways of life' can be taught (ibid., 84), but he does not seem to realize that the education itself, apart from what is explicitly taught, will convey aspects of a particular way of life. His rationality is in a way his 'nowhere', a place outside all particular views from where he claims to be able to judge them all.

Liberal education is independent of a particular view of reality (Hirst 1965, 126-7). The forms of knowledge are rooted in 'that common world of persons and things which we all share' (ibid., 137). I suppose this means that he believes that we can - and should - teach objective knowledge without conveying any view of reality at all, or that we all have the same view of reality. R.T. Allen argues against Hirst's metaphysically 'neutral' knowledge and education, saying that he 'needs that metaphysics of classical Realism with which he tries to dispense' (Allen 1989, 162). '[T]hat the cosmos has no intrinsic meaning or sets any Way for man', as Hirst claims, is a metaphysical assumption. The same applies to his claim 'that facts are, and can be only, mere facts, with no aspects of values and obligation, or that all real things are neutral and devoid of value-aspects or qualities' (ibid., 159).

Education is not only about knowledge, it also conveys a view of what it is to be a person. In a way Hirst agrees with this, saying that his education aims at 'a type of person' (Hirst 1974, 83). But the characteristics of this person are determined, he says, by something more fundamental than a religious faith or a philosophical belief system: the person 'is to have the dispositions, emotions, skills and so on appropriate to a life of reason with all the substantive commitments that must involve' (ibid.). That reason is more fundamental than faith is in itself a particular philosophical view. 'A life of reason' is too limited and limiting as a description of the kind of person God wants us to be, and will on its own promote a particular, non-neutral view.[51]

In an article about common and separate schooling, Callan writes as if there is no difference between teaching about religions and teaching from or on the basis of one of them. For those who want separate schools, 'the only "threat" that a common schooling dedicated to the aim of reasonableness could pose would be the sympathetic and open-minded exploration of rival convictions' (Callan 1995/1996, 281). If they want or allow such exploration, Callan cannot see that their school will be any different from the common one. The thought that the exploration will have to be done from a certain basis, a perspective, and that this might be different in the two schools, is absent in his discussion.[52]

If the separate schools are not to be like the common ones, the only alternative Callan seems to see is that the teachers require 'a dogmatic and contemptuous rejection of whoever rejects them' (ibid.). Either they are equally open to all views, or they contemptuously reject all who disagree with them. This is a very strange way of categorizing people. To believe that others are wrong does not necessarily mean to have any negative attitude towards them. It is no problem to reject a view without rejecting the person who holds it. Christian education may - and should - explore rival convictions, from a Christian basis, and in accord with Callan's requirement of equal respect and reasonableness.

One area where it might be relatively easy to see the non-neutrality of education, even for relatively old pupils, is in career education. Within liberal education the focus would be on the good life, on how to satisfy their desires and needs, be they altruistic or egoistic, and towards this end they should choose schools and jobs. They may certainly want to serve their country, the poor, or even God, but they may also want to earn as much as possible for spending on themselves. What their good life is, is up to them, as long as they do not hurt others or prevent them from living their own good life.

Within Christian education the perspective and focus are different. First, they will know that even if they never get a job, God has a purpose for their life and they can walk through life with him. Secondly, they know that whatever abilities they have are given to them by God for the purpose of his glory and helping to make other people's lives better. The important thing is their faithfulness, not whether their job or other tasks are important in other people's or society's eyes.

A lot of practical things will be the same within secular liberal and Christian education, and it may not always be possible to tell which is which from just visiting a lesson. But the overall perspective and purpose are completely different because of the knowledge or not of God's presence and love. We cannot convey both that reality is God-centred and that it is human-centred. We cannot both pray and not pray with the pupils over a particular situation. We may say: 'God created the world, but he does not explain in detail in the Bible how it came into being, that is what scientists are trying to find out.' Or we may say: 'Christians believe that God created the world, because that is what the Bible says. Scientists are trying to find out what happened, and Christians believe that whatever they find, this is how God did it.' These two ways of talking about God carry with them different realities, one where God is taken for granted, and one where he is somebody the Christians believe in. A lot of little things like this will contribute to the ethos, will convey something about reality.

Teaching about world views without promoting a particular one is not only impossible, it is also not good education. Education includes upbringing, helping children to understand and relate to the world. This ought to be done consciously, in a coherent way, so that the 'lot of little things' may contribute to a picture of the same reality.

4.2.3 Each child has got a basic understanding from home

The argument is that since every child has a primary culture, the school should work from there and not influence them in any other direction. They have a faith or a world view, like adults, so the school can leave them there and just give them more knowledge about their own and other views. This is a common view in the Norwegian discussion (e.g. NOU 1995:9).

In a way it is right that all pupils come to school with some kind of world view, but their reflection on it is limited and often inconsistent. The effect of the school's influence will certainly vary with the consistency and depth of the pupils' background, but this is the case with everything that happens in school and does not remove the school's responsibility for what they try to convey. The main argument against this view is, however, the same as in the previous sections: education and upbringing cannot possibly leave them where they are, influence is unavoidable.

If the point is that every child should be helped to work from their own background, this might be possible if teaching took place individually or in small groups, teaching only children from the same religious or world view background. Then the teachers might possibly enter into that background and teach from there, hiding their own beliefs.

One of the problems regarding liberal education is that the notion of 'liberal' is taken from political theory, where it has to do with adults in a society and how they can live together. This has led to theorizing about liberal education that regards children as adults in terms of values and world view. It seems to be taken for granted that when children come to school, they already have a world view like adults do. Thiessen, in a discussion of B. Ackerman's 'primary culture', suggests that 'the need for some coherence and stability continues even into adulthood' (Thiessen 1993, 227). For evidence he mentions U. Bronfenbrenner, K.-E. Nipkow and P. Berger, and he quotes Bronfenbrenner's reply to the question of the age of the child who needs stability and security: 'The matter is debatable, but I would suggest anyone under the age of, say, 89' (ibid., 293-4).

Arguing for the common, world view neutral school, Callan says that 'the exercise of reasonableness presupposes a deliberative setting in which citizens with conflicting values and interests can join together to create a morally grounded consensus on how to live together' (Callan 1995/1996, 279). But they first need to know what their 'values and interests' are. And I would argue that it is the adults' responsibility to 'create a morally grounded consensus on how to live together', not the schoolchildren's.

4.2.4 It is possible to neutralize the school's world view influence so that the choice is left with the pupils.

Neutralizing the influence could be done by asking the teachers to be as neutral as possible, to not display their particular views about the world and the meaning of life. Then the children would hopefully not pick up a particular view, but choose autonomously between them all, or stick to what was transmitted to them at home.

What would happen if the teachers should try to be neutral? This seems, in our society at least, to imply that anything to do with God is ruled out. Christian teachers, and believers within other theistic faiths, are supposed not to talk about God in a way that implies that he exists. They should not pray with the pupils. They should not talk as if moral norms and commandments are given. But what, then, should agnostic, liberal humanists try to say and avoid saying if they wanted to be neutral, not to reveal their own view? Speaking and behaving like an agnostic is not neutral either. If Christians have to speak like atheists or agnostics to be neutral, atheists and agnostics presumably ought to speak like Christians? But often secular people are regarded as being neutral in what they say and do, implying - again - that religion is an addition to something common.

So what should agnostics do, for instance regarding the question of giving thanks before meals? At least they could say that if they believed in God, they would have given thanks. Maybe they also should give the pupils a quiet moment so that those who do believe, may pray. Or say that it is up to the individual to decide. But it is unclear what they themselves should do, as role models. And when it comes to morality, it is also a question of which reasons they do *not* give for living according to certain norms, reasons that would have been given by Christians. It is all the way the problem of the zero-curriculum, the influence from what is left out, the picture we get of reality and importance by what is not taught.

B. Crittenden says that it is extremely difficult to defend 'the common secular, liberal-democratic values' without idealizing secular humanism (Crittenden 1988, 215-16). He is very sceptical to attempts to be neutral, and says that 'public schools will give support, in fact if not by intention, to various forms of a secular ideal of human life. Depending on the outlook of the particular teachers in a school and on other factors, the perspective from which knowledge is interpreted may vary from that of scientific rationalism to romantic relativism' (ibid., 217-18).

Teachers can try to be neutral, try to avoid expressing their beliefs and world view, but the danger is that they will end up conveying a different view. Also, being vague and trying to hide is not encouraging the pupils to think for themselves. '[T]he most likely result of the teacher's "shelving his own religious opinions" is not to stimulate the pupils' thinking but to suggest that religion is not worth feeling strongly about' (Jeffreys 1969, 8).

But even if the individual teacher cannot be neutral, maybe the various views can be balanced in the school as a whole? This could be done in different ways.

a) It could be the case that each teacher conveys his or her view, but that they more or less balance each other, or at least provide different examples, showing the pupils that there is more than one way to think about the world and themselves.

This is done by allowing - or even urging - the teachers to be clear role models, to live according to their beliefs, and thus provide different (at least in theory, they may be more similar in real life) ways of understanding the meaning of life and education. The teachers then also talk about it, they explain to the pupils that this is what they believe, and that the pupils have to make up their own mind. They make sure that the textbooks, the choice of subjects and topics, the school rules, etc., display the same variety of views. It may be along such lines Ackerman thinks when he says:

> While each child's *entire curriculum* will be organized on liberal lines, he will typically confront *particular educators* with the most diverse set of skills, passions, and beliefs. Indeed, many secondary educators will be confident that the lessons they teach, both in words and actions, represents *the* truth for humankind. Such intolerance (sic!) may often be pedagogically useful - so long as it is not permitted to envelop the child for too long a time, it will often be best for the child to assess a culture's strength when it is presented by its wholehearted enthusiasts. (Ackerman 1980, 159)

This variety would certainly be difficult to work out in practice, but at least it admits that the influence is there, it makes this clear to the pupils. If it were perfect, at least all the views among the pupils should be represented among the teachers, so they could all have one to identify with (but what if this one was an awfully bad teacher?) and others to contrast it with. The most difficult thing to make work might not be the teachers, but everything else, particularly things they would have to agree on across the school or between certain teachers: rules, subjects, topics, textbooks.

If at all, it would probably work better with the older pupils, and with those with a fairly clear view from home. For five or six year olds from homes with a blurred and inconsistent world view, it might not be of much help. But it is, I think, worth a try for those who see that education always conveys world view presuppositions and who also believe that we should avoid influence towards a particular view. If we believe this is important, and if we want children to search for truth, the most important thing seems to be that the teachers actually show in their lives and make clear in their words what they believe to be true and what is important to them.

I think I am saying that the only way of trying to be neutral as a school is to let all teachers be themselves and have their individual influence, and not to do anything to create or explain a whole. It will be very arbitrary which teacher influences the individual child most, it is not necessarily one with a coherent view or the faith or world view that the parents want the child to be brought up within. And the school will not give a consistent upbringing and education, there is no help given from the school as such to understand the world as a whole.

b) Another solution is that, regardless of the variety of views among the teachers, everybody makes explicit to the pupils all the time how their own view influences what they do in school, and say that they have no proof that it is true, so the pupils are urged to investigate and make autonomous choices. They also make clear the presuppositions in books, in choice of topics, etc.

This is fairly similar to a), but there is a difference in the emphasis on others' views being options as well. What I am trying to say in a) is that it is important to get across that the decisions, or choices, the teachers have made are actually basic for their life, it is crucial for them to believe what they believe. This b-option is a way of modifying it, more conveying that it is not all that crucial, it is one of these decisions you have to make. What I am concerned with again is truth, in this version truth is not central, it is more a question of meaning: we have all made our choice, you have to believe something, and you must find your way of living. This, however, is liberalism again, making the outcome of the decision less important than the decision itself and certainly less important than in Christianity.

4.3 Arguments for world view neutral education being desirable

Even if neutral education were possible, it might not be desirable. In this section I want to discuss arguments that have been used or could be used for the desirability of an education that is neutral between religions or world views in general. In most cases where these arguments are used, the writers seem to ignore the question of whether such an education is at all possible. They only argue that we ought to have a common, liberal school, a school where the pupils are not influenced in one particular direction when it comes to basic beliefs.

4.3.1 In a pluralistic society, it is not the school's task to
transmit one particular world view

This is probably the most common argument, and in a way it is right. It is not the school's task to choose one of many world views and transmit this to all the pupils, regardless of their background. The school - or the state, which would probably do the choosing - has no more access to the true view than anybody else. This is Strike's view, and he tries to solve the problem by suggesting a public values school. It is also S. Macedo's view, claiming that in common schools, 'the question of religious truth should simply be left aside' (Macedo 1995, 226). The problem is that this solution consists in exactly what they want to avoid, namely the transmission of some very particular world view presuppositions. If it is not the school's task to transmit one particular view, it is not its task to transmit liberal humanism either, so the problem is still there.

On the other hand I would argue that it *is* the school's task to transmit one particular world view. Given that it is impossible to be neutral, I would claim that transmitting one coherent view and being explicit about it is better than - deliberately or not - conveying a view that is not made explicit, or incoherent parts of different views. A number of children do not get very much help at home to form and be conscious about their world view, whether religious or secular. They do not get any specific help to understand the world around them. They are not shown that life has or may have a purpose or a meaning. Their parents may not have a very coherent, or even consistent, perspective on life, the unconnected beliefs they live by, more or less consciously, may even be harmful for themselves or the children.

Should the school still say: it is the home's task to give them the presuppositions to live by, to help to give them an identity, we will not do anything about it? If they come to school with an inconsistent world view, they can keep it, if they cannot see any meaning in life, that is not our problem? A. Gutman says, in a slightly different context, that 'children do not leave their souls behind when they go to school, and schools cannot escape looking after children's souls in many significant and subtle ways' (Gutman 1987, 53). The school is asked to educate in many areas where the home and society in general seem to fail - to do with mass media, alcohol, sexuality, and politeness could be mentioned from the last few years' debate in Norway. Many of these are world view topics. Why, then, should not school help in this most important area?

I would argue that particularly for these children, it would be better if the school tried to convey a particular view of life. In this way, those who get little help at home to sort out these questions, would get some help from school. Also, all parents would know what the school's influence was and could relate to that in whichever way they saw fit.

According to Strike, if the school is to try not to take a stand, it cannot say anything about the questions of rationality and truth (see above, p. 69). There may be a slight difference between 'not transmitting a particular view' and 'not to take a stand'. In either case, the school cannot say that one view is the true one, but the rationality question is different. If the school is not to take a stand at all, it cannot say that one view is, or some are, more rational than others. But if the point is that *one* view should not be transmitted, I suppose it would be possible to discuss the rationality of different views. A choice between the two might also depend on what the reason for the attempted neutrality is. A concern for parents' responsibility in this matter might lead to a different practice from what a concern for rationality and truth might lead to.

In an account of some Swedish research on children and world view questions, R. Skoglund says that one of the things they found is that children are very eager to find consistency, wholeness and meaning in life. Particularly ten to twelve year olds seem to be very concerned to find answers that are coherent, a view that works (Skoglund 1991, 41-2). An attempt not to take a stand may therefore easily lead to their regarding this neutrality as The answer, namely that none of the views is true, which is not a neutral answer.

4.3.2 The school's task is to go beyond their home background

This is C. Bailey's main argument. The pupils have got a world view at home, they have learnt certain beliefs. It is not the school's task to confirm these, but to help them reflect critically on both their own and other views. Education is about getting knowledge, about being rational and critical, about going 'beyond the present and particular' (Bailey 1984).

This also seems to be Ackerman's point, although he does not emphasize the critical reflection so much. Infants need some degree of cultural coherence if they are to find themselves, but the parents' control and guidance should diminish as the children get to school age. Liberal schools are not interested in 'weeding and pruning youngsters so that they will better accord to the parental design. In contrast, a liberal school has a different mission: to provide the child with access to the wide range of cultural materials that he may find useful in developing his own moral ideals and patterns of life' (Ackerman 1980, 155-6).

It is difficult to tell how fundamental Ackerman's notion of 'culture' is. In the above quote, which comes at the end of his discussion of this topic, he mentions moral ideals and patterns of life as areas where the children should develop their own. Sometimes his account gives the impression that he basically thinks of fairly limited parts of life, like in his example about a girl who wants to play with trucks where her parents want her to play with dolls (ibid., 151-4). There is no mention of basic world views, how a child's primary culture will give him or her a particular way of understanding him- or herself and the world as a whole. And in his account of liberal education he says nothing about the world view basis for it, only what should be taught.

Also, his contrast between the liberal and the non-liberal education is too categorical. There is a long way from, on one hand, deciding what kinds of toy children are allowed to play with and, on the other, conveying to them a coherent way of interpreting life, be it secular humanist, Hindu, Christian, or existentialist. World view is a different dimension from toys and other particular questions. Within each view, parents might either have a 'design' for their child, or they may want to 'provide the child with access to the wide range of cultural materials that he may find useful in developing his own moral ideals and patterns of life', although the evaluation of these 'cultural materials' will differ, depending on world view.

Both Bailey and Ackerman certainly have a point. School education should widen the horizon, should help the children to learn more and see things differently from what they do at home. I. Asheim uses the picture of school being a bridge between the small world of the home and the big world of the society (Asheim 1978, 109). They should, as they grow older, learn to understand how other people understand the world and themselves. This would help them to understand people from different backgrounds from their own, and also to understand their own background, because the contrast helps them to see their own identity. We might even have to put more effort into explaining other perspectives than their own, in order for them really to understand them.

Nevertheless, this is not all there is to it. They certainly need to have their own basis made explicit, taught, alongside other views, and they need to learn to evaluate all these views. But the question is where the criteria for the evaluation are to come from, because they cannot come from nowhere. There is nothing to say that secular humanistic, liberal criteria are better than others, or that it is better for them to be educated on a basis different from their home background.

It is also a question of age. A six year old thinks differently from a sixteen year old, and they can certainly not relate to their own background in the same way. A recent Norwegian discussion paper about RE in school was called 'Identitet og dialog' - (identity and dialogue) (NOU 1995:9), and this title points to a dilemma: RE, and school in general, should help to form children's identity, according to their parents' basic beliefs, and at the same time promote dialogue with people from other groups in a pluralistic society. In this lies also the possibility for children to learn about ways of life that they may prefer to the one they are brought up within and so even reject their background. At what stage they are old enough to be challenged about their own view is a difficult question to answer. When we consider the parents' responsibility and also think of where most people are in their identity formation in their mid-teens, it may not at all be a task for the compulsory school.

Another question is to what extent it is necessary for the school to actively challenge the pupils in this area. Sometimes people write as if children never think for themselves, that they never question things without being told to do so. This is not common experience, and I think that in a pluralistic society like ours, children cannot but discover that other people think and believe differently from themselves - maybe apart from liberals, that is. The latter may believe that everybody lives in a self-centred world, and that everybody has chosen their view because it seemed to be the good life, not for instance because they found themselves face to face with the living God. But even children from minority groups who are kept as separate as possible will, by the very fact that they are kept separate, understand that 'the others' are different. If views are made explicit and not just taken for granted, pupils will certainly start to compare and think and question without the teachers telling them to.

4.3.3 We do not know which view is true

This is not a relativistic standpoint, saying there is no truth. It simply says that we do not know the truth and therefore we should not educate pupils into one particular view. In this context, 'do not' normally implies 'cannot'. There is no way we can know which understanding is the right and true one, therefore we have no right to impose one on the children.

Many liberals today would argue against relativism, believing that there is objective truth, but this does not necessarily include religious truth. It might be possible to believe there is objective truth for instance in science, and even some basic ethical truth might be claimed, but religion and religious beliefs may still be regarded as something subjective, something to do with people's inner experiences rather than external, objective reality. As I have argued, Christian faith goes right to the heart of our understanding of what is objective reality, which makes it difficult to put religion and world view in a separate category when it comes to knowledge and truth.

It is important here to distinguish between basic, metaphysical truth and truth in specific, more limited areas, for instance in ethics. In questions of for instance tax paying, or of how we should treat animals, everybody will discuss from within an overarching view of reality and morality that is - at least at the time - taken for granted. In some of these specific questions it may be possible to avoid conveying a certain view through education in general, exactly because they are limited and only influence certain areas of life, areas that are not 'lived' within school.

These areas may, however, turn out not to be wholly theoretical after all. How we believe we should treat animals, for instance, leads to a view on vegetarianism, which, as we have seen, affects school meals and so is 'lived' in school.[53]

When we discuss such topics, it is possible to show how arguments and the whole discussion might differ, depending on the world views of those involved. We might for instance say that 'for people who do not believe in God, the whole question would look different. They would not take into account that human beings are created in the image of God'.

It is different if we are concerned with the basis itself, the perspective we have on life in general, the place we stand when we look at all the more detailed questions. This can also be made explicit and discussed, even compared to other basic outlooks on life, but we can never avoid building on it at the same time. We can discuss God-centredness and human-centredness, Christian belief and atheistic humanism, we can step outside our own conviction and look at it and we can step inside other beliefs and more or less understand them. But we cannot in our teaching and upbringing not convey something about what we believe to be the basic truth in these questions.

The sentence 'We do not know which view is true' raises big epistemological questions, some of which I can only just touch here. What does it mean to 'know' when it comes to our basic understanding of the world and the purpose (or lack of such) of our lives? What does it mean to 'know' that God exists and loves us? We have a tendency to think like Dewey, that the only way to knowledge is through science, that we can only know things if they are scientifically proved. To think that we could prove the existence or non-existence of our Creator through scientific research sounds quite foolish. The prophet Isaiah uses as a parallel a pot of clay examining its maker (Isaiah 45:9).

It is possible both to know and not to know at the same time. I do not know whether God exists, but I also know that he does, only not in the same way as I know that leaves are green or that Norway's constitution day is 17 May. I cannot prove that God exists, but I know that he does because I know him, because I have experienced him in my life. It is a knowledge that grows out of a personal relationship, like friendship, not something detached, scientific.[54] Nobody can know him without being involved, and I do not have the same knowledge of him as everybody else has. All who have met him, know that he exists, but because we are different, he meets us in different ways and we get slightly different pictures of him, just as we do of people.

It is also possible to give reasons for believing in God, for believing that the Bible gives the most convincing account of what is going on in the world and why. B. Hebblethwaite (1988) argues for what he calls objective theism - that belief in an objective God and in life after death is not only possible, but highly plausible. It is possible and necessary to evaluate the coherence and probability both of one's own world view and of others'.[55] Christianity is, among other things, a question of believing some historical accounts, believing that Jesus was the one he said he was. If Christianity is saying anything at all,

> it must be making claims about what is objectively the case. Since the fact that these claims may be true also means that they could be false, Christianity is put at risk in a way which is uncongenial to some. At the same time as it is clear that since its claims are of far-reaching significance and could be true, they cannot be ignored by anyone concerned, as rationality demands, with what is true. (Trigg 1973, 166-7)

'Faith is neither blind nor proven.'[56] But in the end all my knowledge is 'faith knowledge', and this is why it is impossible to convey the truth of Christianity without people getting personally involved. A Christian educator can say - with Job - to the children 'I know that my Redeemer lives' (Job 19:25), but only a personal encounter can convince them and make it living knowledge. That is what Jesus himself said when people asked him how they could know whether he was from God or not: Try! 'If anyone chooses to do God's will, he will find out ...' (John 7:17).

On the other hand, then, is it possible to know that God does not exist, or that life has no purpose? No, it is not. It is possible to believe it and to argue for it, but the scientific proof is not there either. And there is no experience similar to a relationship with God that could give any evidence for the belief.

Even if we do not know which world view is true, it is not a solution to try to inform the pupils without giving an answer. This is not a question of right or not to impose, but of responsibility to choose for them when they are too young to do it themselves, and then to explain reservations we have as they get older. We may say that we do not know the truth, but we also ought to be able to tell them what we - so far - have found to be the best answers to the basic questions in life and which we have based our life on.[57]

What about the indifferent teachers? Those who have not thought very much themselves about these basic questions, and who might have problems if asked about reality, the nature of human beings, the purpose of life? They will, like others, convey certain world view presuppositions, only they may do it unconsciously, and without trying to make their view explicit to the pupils. This may lead to indifferent pupils as well, pupils who do not really know what they believe, and who do not care. Some teachers may think that since they do not believe in God or do not belong to a certain religion or group, they do not really believe anything and do not influence the pupils in a particular direction. But *not* to believe in God also has a strong, particular influence.

4.3.4 There is no universal truth

This is a view I have not often seen argued, but one that sometimes seems to be assumed, probably often an influence from postmodernism.[58] 'Truth' gives way to 'meaning', the point is to find the values, beliefs, etc. that give meaning to my life. We can talk about truth within one narrative only, not universally across narratives.

When we talk about truth, it is important to distinguish between culture and faith, between multiculture and multifaith. Often the phrase 'religious or cultural tradition' or something similar is used, as if religions are traditions along the same lines as cultures. Culture is a difficult concept, fairly vague, and it has many aspects. Religious faith is often one of them. Traditions to do with dress, food, morality, etc. are often seen as closely connected with religion, but not seldom do they have other origins. An example is discrimination against women in Buddhism, which does not have any roots in their holy scriptures, but probably comes from cultures where early Buddhism flourished. Culture is not only religion, and religion is not only culture. Norway has a Christian culture, that is our tradition, but there are parts of our culture that has nothing to do with Christianity. Immigrants from Asia and Africa who are Christians are not thereby culturally Norwegian, they have their own cultures.

This is important when we talk about universal truth: to say that one world view, one religion, is true, is not to say that one culture is 'true', or the right or best one. When I say that Christianity is true, I do not mean the Norwegian version, with all its Norwegian culture attached, or the western version. I mean the personal truth, God himself, whichever culture he is understood within. Multiculturalism can be regarded as positive and exciting, but regarding multifaith as positive is from a Christian point of view to make religion relative and ignore the question of truth.

B. Mitchell distinguishes between four ways of thinking about religion and truth: 1) straightforward atheists who think that religions are partly false and partly consist of non-religious truths, 2) more liberal secular thinkers who think that there are religious truths, but where 'truth' is understood as what Strawson would call 'profound general statements about man and the universe' (see above, p. 65), 3) religious people who think more or less as in 2), but have a personal commitment to one of the truths, and 4) traditional believers who take for granted 'that what they believe about God is true in the straightforward sense that it describes the way things really are' (Mitchell 1979, 459-60).

People in groups two and three are the ones who would argue that there is no universal truth in religious and world view questions. Orthodox Christians, on the other hand, claim that the Bible tells the truth about what has happened and will happen.

R. Trigg claims that 'the main impetus to relativistic theories comes from the fact of human disagreement' (Trigg 1973, 123). The reasoning is that since we do not agree, there cannot be truth. But, he says, there may be truth even if we have not found it or do not agree about it. 'The fact ... that an argument may not convince someone does not necessarily reflect on its validity' (ibid., 124). He argues that if reasons can only be given within a theory or a structure, be it scientific, moral or religious, then there is no way we can even understand each other, let alone argue.[59]

In our pluralist societies, we will not agree on whether there is universal truth in world view questions. But if there were no such truth, or if neutrality were possible, non-neutrality would still be better in education. The best way of showing how a world view gives meaning to life (or tells you that there is no meaning, as the case may be) is to let the pupils see how it works in the life of adults close to them. If I were an atheist, I should be able to show how my atheism helps me to interpret the world and to find a purpose, whether given or created, or maybe to live in a purposeless world. If I were an agnostic, liberal humanist, I ought to be able to explain why I had chosen this view and how it affects my life and the purpose of what I do, and then say that I believe that they (i.e. the children) might as well be Buddhists, or Christians, if they find that more meaningful.

But to present them with various views from within a liberal framework, i.e. making it all a question of choice for giving them a good life, is not to present them with various views, but only to present them with liberalism. To be presented with Christianity, they must be presented with it as the truth about the world and themselves, not as a candidate among others that might give meaning and purpose to their life.

4.3.5 To present one view as true deprives the pupils of the possibility of making a rational autonomous choice

This is a claim I have come across very often, but I do not think I have seen any argument for it. To me, the claim does not seem obvious. The first problem is what it means to 'present one view as true'. Does it mean that this truth is explicitly stated, or does it also include that it is implicitly assumed?

Of course, if children only get to know about one view, they may not think that it is possible to see things differently. If they never hear about a life after death, not from anybody, I suppose we would say that they are presented with as true the view that death is the end of life, and they will therefore not be able to make an autonomous choice in this matter. But also if all the people they know live as if death is the end of life, and eternity or reincarnation is just something they hear about in a few RE lessons, they are presented with one view as true, and therefore, according to the claim I am discussing, with no possibility of a rational autonomous choice.

What comes through in our lives is likely to be understood as truth. For instance if teachers talk about God in a way that makes him sound part of reality and important for their life, he will be conceived as being real and important, i.e. the proposition 'God is real and important' is regarded as true. I suppose the use of the notion 'truth' is part of the problem here, because we normally use it about propositions, and education, particularly transmission of world view, is not so much about propositions. It is about lived life, about presuppositions. So if teachers never talk about God apart from in RE lessons, and then as somebody religious people believe in, encouraging the pupils to think whether they would like to believe in him, God will, I suppose, be conceived as probably existing, but relatively unimportant, and definitely not necessary for life. The proposition 'God may exist, I may believe in him if I want to, but it is not crucial' may be regarded as true.

So some truth will be conveyed through ordinary school life, and what is explicitly said will be understood in this framework. This does not mean, at least not in Christian education, that this truth cannot be questioned. B. Mitchell claims that faith and criticism are false alternatives. They are 'two sides of one coin'. Wholehearted faith does not exclude criticism, and criticism does not make faith 'merely tentative and provisional ... Without faith in an established tradition criticism has nothing to fasten on; without criticism the tradition ceases in the end to have any purchase on reality' (Mitchell 1996, 271).

Belief is belief, not seeing. Faith gives a certainty that is different from certainty by seeing. This is not a problem in relation to autonomy. 'Autonomy provides for a holding to certain views more firmly than others and also even for holding them in the face of criticism up to a point, what Benson terms "balance between a supple mind and a stiff neck" ' (Shortt 1986, 111). You can believe it is true, base your life on it - and may have to die for it - , and still the thought may be there: I may be wrong.

Anybody who is honest, whether we are Christians, Hindus, existentialists, agnostics, liberals, - any honest person will have to say that the foundation for our life is belief, or faith, that we have no proof. We may have experiental knowledge, we may have good arguments, but none of us can prove our perspective right. For some it may not matter if they are right, maybe it does not even give meaning to talk about being right, what they are concerned with is living the good life. White will probably not say that he is right, he might say that it does not make sense to talk about the right perspective, that everybody has to choose the meaning of their own life. But would he claim that he is right in saying this? Would he say that for instance Christians, who claim that Christianity is true, are wrong? Or may he admit that he may be wrong in his belief that it is up to everybody to give fundamental meaning to their life? These are questions that he, as far as I can see, has not addressed.

The second and main problem with the claim I am discussing in this section, is that it says that we cannot make autonomous choices if we are told that one option is true. Why is this? I suppose the problem must be that if something is presented as true, the pupils may believe that they have no options, there is no decision or choice for them to make.

Given the setting of a pluralistic society, imagine pupils from Christian homes in a Christian school, with only Christian teachers. Ideally, both implicitly and explicitly the truth of Christianity will be conveyed, at least this will be the intention. But the pupils cannot but know that other people believe and think differently. They do not only know about them, they meet them outside school, and they know their thinking from media. If their education is good, they get help to sort out what the differences between various views are. Part of their knowledge of Christianity will be that they have to make a decision - or repeated decisions - themselves whether they want to follow Christ or not.

Given the same pluralistic society, imagine pupils from secular humanistic homes in a fairly secular humanistic state school, with only secular humanistic teachers. At least implicitly the truth of secular humanism will be conveyed. The more explicit transmission may vary, but if it is a liberal school, what should be taught is that secular humanism, Marxism, Buddhism, Christianity, etc. are all equally valid views of life, or at least we do not know which one is better, so they have to make their own choice. The pupils cannot but know that there are people who belong to these various traditions, but they may nevertheless believe that they have all chosen them as from a list of possible options of the good life. But if they know some people who are Christians, for instance, they may know that this is not the case. If their education is good, the secular humanistic basis for the school is made explicit to them, and they get help to sort out the differences between this and other world views.

What about autonomy - will either of these educations prevent the pupils from making a rational autonomous choice? The concept of choice is difficult in this context in general, but it is too big a topic to go into here.[60] We do not choose a world view.[61] We grow into it, and maybe out of it, sometimes unconsciously, but often by making smaller or bigger decisions. But whether we think in terms of choice or decision(s), the relationship between truth and autonomy is not straightforward. Here are some examples:

a) we know only one option and tell them this (e.g. apples fall down)
b) we know more than one option, but we only tell them one, they have no chance of finding out (e.g. the earth is round)
c) we know more than one option, but we only tell them one, they will certainly find out about others (e.g. nuclear plants are not dangerous)
d) we know more than one option and tell them about all, saying that one is the truth (e.g. people believe different things about evil spirits, but there are no spirits)

e) we know more than one option and tell them about all, saying that we do
not know the truth, or there is no truth (e.g. there are different models for
organizing society)

When our concern is with religions and world views in pluralistic societies, a) and b) are certainly out of question. c) is not good education. In a
Christian school d) would be the model, in a secular, liberal school e)
would be the explicit model, but implicitly it would be d) there too. This
combination of d) and e) could easily amount to indoctrination and make it
impossible for the pupils to make an autonomous choice or decision. I can
see no reason why d) on its own would do the same.

I would argue that the school's influence on the pupils' choices or decisions to a large extent would depend on the teachers' lives, whether there is
harmony between what they say and do, and whether the pupils like what
they see. However strongly we tell the children that Christianity is the truth,
they will not believe it unless our life says the same and they get to know
Christ themselves. Using threats and force may make some conform, but
that is not education, and conforming is not faith.

Haworth seems to think that there is a necessary link between wanting
autonomy and belief in subjective values (Haworth 1986, 191-3). One of
the main reasons for valuing autonomy so highly, he says, is that we have
no reason to impose on children our own, subjective conception of the
good. 'The autonomous position presupposes pluralism', he claims (ibid.,
193). This is too simple. If he only means that you need options to be able
to choose and therefore pluralism is necessary, it is not interesting. If, on
the other hand, he thinks of 'philosophical pluralism' (see above, p. 47),
implying that it is wrong to believe that one religion or world view is superior, I would argue that he is wrong. Autonomy can be regarded as necessary and highly valuable also for people who believe that there is one right
conception of the good, one right view of life and the world.

Trigg discusses Hare's emphasis on our freedom to form our own moral
opinions and how he believes that this freedom is restricted if reasons for
choice of moral principles can be said to be good or bad. Trigg disagrees,
arguing that we are free to be both illogical, irrational and inconsistent.
Presumably, he says, 'if we are sane, we will do none of these things
knowingly, but it by no means follows from the fact that something is the
case that everyone will recognise it to be so. Indeed, we are not forced to
accept anything as a fact in the first place' (Trigg 1973, 133).

No reason can have any influence until it is recognised by someone to be a
reason. *If* there are reasons which have some kind of objective validity,
their presence does nothing to reduce human freedom. Men would still be
free to assess such reasons as they wish and to ignore or reject what are in
fact perfectly good reasons for believing or doing something ... It is an

undoubted fact that our personal decisions about what we shall commit
ourselves to are *our* decisions ... No-one else can commit us to a religion,
a morality or anything else of the kind. (Ibid., 134 and 131)

In some ways, Christianity has an even more radical view of autonomy
than liberalism. It claims that there is one true world, one given purpose to
life, one true God to love and follow, and that all other world views and
theories of the good are fundamentally wrong, although they are certainly
not wrong in all details. Fundamentally, there is one right way and some
wrong ways.

Even so, Christian educators not only want children to become autonomous, they regard it as highly important that they lead their own lives and
make their own decisions to as high a degree as possible. Parents and
teachers should not 'build a wall around their child, keep him in the nest'
(Haworth 1986, 190) and try to make him or her live *their* life. The children
are not *theirs*, they are persons in their own right and have to learn to take
responsibility for their own life, whether it will make life easier for them or
not, and - more important - whether they will choose the right path or not.

It is not, as in liberalism, a question of the pupils choosing between different theories of the good life, none of which can be said to be the right
one. Neither is it only a question of living morally right, of loving your
neighbour, but of life and death, of choosing the relationship that they are
created for and that will give them eternal life. So when Christians help
children to take responsibility for their own life, the result may be that they
walk away from God. But that is how it is, nobody can be forced to live
with him. They have to face God, they have to decide how much they will
let him influence their life. The educators can only show them the way by
walking it themselves. It is implicit in a Christian view of life and of human
nature that people are responsible and autonomous. As M.V.C. Jeffreys
says, 'Jesus' teaching is a perfect example of the reconciliation of positive
declaration of the truth with concern for the freedom and authenticity of the
response - a reconciliation which, as we have seen, some modern authorities on education invite us to think impossible' (Jeffreys 1969, 23).

4.4 Arguments for secular education being better for autonomy

In some cases the argument for secular education is not that it is neutral, but
that it is less harmful for autonomy than religiously based education. This
seems to make secular education 'more neutral' than the latter. Since
autonomy normally is the main reason for wanting world view neutral education, such arguments will be analysed here.

4.4.1 Religions are full of detailed beliefs

The argument here is that religions are complete systems which give little freedom for autonomous thought. Compared to non-religious world views, they are more detailed, more of a system of beliefs that form a whole, you have to take it or leave it without any possibility to put together your own view.

This is the kind of argument P. Gardner uses. He says that the main reason for religious upbringing being more detrimental to autonomy is that religions provide frameworks for assessing moral and social issues, they have particular positions on such issues and are therefore more influential and pervasive. If influence and pervasiveness are accepted as criteria for the importance of beliefs, as he believes they should, religious beliefs may be regarded as more important and therefore more persistent, more likely to stick, and therefore more likely to make autonomy difficult (Gardner 1988, 97).

It is far from obvious that details and particular positions necessarily make a system of beliefs more pervasive. More important, I would argue, than the details is the fundamental beliefs that govern all thoughts and actions. In this respect atheism is as pervasive as theism is, and comprehensive liberalism as influential as Christianity. Moreover, in our society liberalism is more common and therefore probably more difficult to see and assess and be critical about. Having few specific beliefs increases this difficulty. 'Truth is something the individual decides for her- or himself' is not a detailed belief, but it is certainly a particular and pervasive belief. According to McLaughlin, religions may be more substantial in their beliefs, but whether this makes them more pervasive or not is an empirical matter (McLaughlin 1990, 112).[62]

Gardner's examples of issues where religions often have certain positions are 'abortion, adultery, sex before marriage, the roles of men and women, the upbringing of children, what is not to be eaten or how one should spend certain days' (Gardner 1988, 97). It ought to be taken into account that religions are very different in how particular their positions are (McLaughlin 1990, 112), so we should look at one religion at a time, not 'religion' in general. Also, there are many different atheistic world views, and these too may have specific positions, some of them fairly detailed, at least in certain areas (like Marxism).

It is obvious - unless people do not believe in God - that the Creator of all is the final authority for how we, the created, ought to live our lives to make them as good as possible. God's commands are not limits for our flourishing, they are guidelines for a good life. To follow them is for Christians not a burden, it is the new nature's desire.

In some areas the Bible gives concrete rules for how to love our neighbour, in others not. In either case it is possible to give reasons for the positions, reasons that can be understood also outside a Christian framework. But if we have the perspective of God's love for us and his desire to make our lives good and meaningful, Christian ethics is logical. If life is a gift from God, why should we end it? If God gives us a day of rest every week, why should we not keep it, knowing that he wants the best for us? And if God wants marriage to be the framework for living out our sexuality, why should we think it better for us to live otherwise?

If we try to imagine a homogeneous Christian society, where traditional Christian positions are held, we may be able to see that it is the odd secular liberalist who has 'particular positions'. Instead of reasoning from the basis of God's love for people, taking into account his own and other people's egoism, he actually argues that he has the right to do what he wants, as long as he has thought it through himself and thinks it is good for him, and it does not harm others. He does not even take God the creator into account. Is it not very strange not to listen to God?

The centre of the beliefs in Christianity is the relationship with God, the knowledge of God. The beliefs are not a system to be learned and believed in a vacuum, so to speak. To the believer, they do not appear detailed or specific, they are just logical consequences of how we are created. The relationship with God does not continue automatically, it is not static, we have to work on it and consciously renew it. If the relationship dies, the specific beliefs lose their meaning. Liberal humanism, with its centre in man, leads to a similar, but smaller, set of beliefs, although not always articulated. But being articulated should not make them more harmful for autonomy, rather the opposite.

4.4.2 Religions claim to be true

As we have seen already, the truth claims often seem to be the crucial point. The focus in this section is on whether there is any difference between religions and secular world views in this respect. One difference might be that religions seem to be exclusive, they claim that all other views are wrong and that they only have found the whole truth. This is right about Christianity.

But this is also right about some secular world views, and it is right about liberal humanism as Mitchell describes it (see above, pp. 64-5). Liberal humanism claims that Christianity is wrong in being exclusive, but this makes liberalism itself exclusive: 'you may believe what you want as long as you do not claim that your view is the only right one. You must believe (here is the exclusivism) that any other faith is as good as yours.'[63]

It is also important to look at how this truth is claimed. One thing is that specific beliefs are said to be true, that may happen more often in more substantive views, whether religious or not. More important in education, however, is the implicit truth claim in the understanding of the world that is the basis for everything. Miracles for instance, which seem incredible within an atheistic framework, are no problem at all if the basis is the God who created everything from nothing.

Education built on liberal humanism will also have implicit truth claims, with liberal humanistic values and beliefs running through the whole school. The person, or the individual, is the centre of his or her world. There is no God who has any claim on the pupils, who has created them for a purpose. There is no given meaning to life, the purpose of education is to give them knowledge so that they can make informed choices about what they want their life to be like, what meaning they want to give to it. It is a very individualistic system of beliefs, with little room for concern for society. Basically everything is here for them.

Imagine a pupil asking: 'Is it true that there is no meaning to life, that I have to find one myself?' What would the liberal answer be? Probably something like 'Religions and ideologies present you with their answer, you will have to choose'. This is a 'yes' to the pupil's question; there is no given meaning, you are right. What else might they say? 'This is the privilege of being a person, that you may create your own life.' Again a truth claim.

Or what is the difference between what a Christian and a liberal humanist would answer about God's existence? It certainly depends on the age of the pupils and other circumstances, but here are some suggestions:

Christian: 'Some people believe there is a God, others do not. I believe in him. I cannot prove his existence, and I may be wrong, but I have based my life on him.' Not 'you have to make up your own mind', that tastes too much of 'it is up to you whether he is there or not', of it just being another topic where everybody believes what they find best.

Liberal humanist: 'Some people believe there is, some (or I) do not. It is impossible to know. You have to make up your own mind.' Not 'I have based my life on the belief that there is no God, at least not one that is relevant to my life', because that seems to give the matter too much weight, as if everything depends on getting the answer to this question right, and according to liberal humanism, it does not.

According to Gardner, those agnostics who think that their agnosticism is right, that it is impossible to find out whether there is a God or not, come into the same category as theists and atheists in relation to truth claims. But there may be agnostics who 'teach their children to be on the look out for new arguments, new evidence and the like' (Gardner 1988, 94). If this is the belief they are taught, and if early beliefs persist, the children should continue to look for new evidence about God's existence.

The question is what counts as evidence, what kind of arguments they learn are valid. Because in such an upbringing, the children obviously have to be taught the arguments for and against God's existence and what kind of evidence they are to look for. And what is it? According to the Bible, no more evidence will and can be given this side of death, apart from the experience of everybody who receives Christ. But this is evidence that appears *after* 'the leap of faith', not beforehand. So from this point of view, the only thing that parents and teachers can do is to encourage the children to try, to start building a relationship with God - then they will find whether he is there or not. But if they teach the children to look for a kind of scientific evidence, they have effectively closed the children's eyes.

The difference in influence on the pupils probably lies, not so much in what is said, truth claims or not, but in the importance the matter is given. In Christian education, God's existence and relevance is a key point, our response to God is the most important decision in our life. God is a constant reality which we have to relate to in some way or another, even if it is by ignoring him, deciding that he is not there, or that we do not want to have anything to do with him. In liberal humanism, this is one question among others, and the starting point is within a framework where he is irrelevant.

4.4.3 Religious practices create habits it is difficult to get out of

It might be argued that religious believers are forced to do certain things and that this prevents them from making autonomous choices. These might be church going, fasting, praying, giving, etc., practices that non-religious world views would not have. And there certainly are such habits that Christian and other religious upbringers and educators try to get children into. They are practices to do with worshipping God, and moral habits. The question is whether these are more difficult to leave behind than non-religious habits.

For Christians, these habits or practices will be part of life. They will not be dead habits, something we have to do, but part of our life with God. Church services and prayers are places to meet God, things that the new God-given nature wants to do. They are good, life-sustaining habits, like eating breakfast and keeping your body fit. If this new life dies away, if we lose our faith, the worship has no meaning anymore and disappears. Some outer 'motions' might continue, but we all, religious or not, have a lot of habits that we just have not got rid of because they do not do any harm and we hardly notice they are there.

From the outside, religious practices may be described as lifestyle habits. And non-religious world views may include lifestyle habits as well. Materialism, for instance, with all its shopping. Is going to church at a set time every week any worse than going to the supermarket or the shoppingcentre at a set time every week, often with a number of rituals surrounding it? And which of them might be hardest to stop doing? Would liberal education be as concerned with the habit of shoppingcentre-visits as with church-visits?

Religious practices are either part of life or they are dead, meaningless habits alongside non-religious meaningless habits. When it comes to moral habits, the only reason why they may be regarded as more difficult to get out of than non-religious people's moral habits, is that they are linked to faith and therefore have a different reason for being stuck to. But again it is important to remember that we are talking about two different world views, and Christians do not behave in certain ways because they have to, but because they want to. And actually, in a Christian's life there is not very much room for set habits in the way we relate to other people. God created us different and he treats us differently, that is what we should do to each other as well, in love and with creativity.

4.4.4 Religion imposes faith and worship, which are not only unnecessary, but also irrational

If faith and worship are called irrational, that is because they are viewed from a materialistic or atheistic perspective, a view of the world where there is no room for God. Then the beliefs would be irrational as well. Writing about indoctrination and Catholic schools, P. Walsh suggests that '[s]ome-body who is convinced that the main Christian beliefs are irrational, incredible and irrelevant to anything that matters is going to remain suspicious of us no matter how open and honest our R.E. methods seem. For how else, he wonders, can you account for so many people being wedded to crazy beliefs if not by indoctrination?' (Walsh 1983, 13).

If science is made the judge for deciding what is real or not, which I would claim is a very limiting view, faith and worship become irrational. But this is to turn things upside down. It is not rationality that determines what is real, but reality that determines what is rational. In one of C.S. Lewis' books about Narnia, Uncle Andrew and the children heard wonderful singing. But when Uncle Andrew realized that it was a lion singing,

> he tried his hardest to make himself believe that it wasn't singing and never had been singing - only roaring ... 'Who ever heard of a lion sing-ing?' And the longer and more beautifully the Lion sang, the harder Uncle Andrew tried to make himself believe that he could hear nothing but roaring (Lewis 1955/1968, 117).

And he succeeded, so when the Lion later spoke - and everybody else heard and understood the words - Uncle Andrew only heard a snarl. In our world, it might be irrational to believe that a lion is singing and speaking, but in Narnia it was not. Uncle Andrew was obviously irrational in trying to shut his ears to reality. In a similar way, worshipping God is only irrational if there is no God to worship. In a world created and upheld by a loving God, with this God wanting to be everybody's master and friend, it is irrational to try to ignore him, to want to be one's own master. The only rational thing to do is to bow down and ask for mercy. In God's world, it is humanists and atheists and liberals who are irrational.

4.4.5 If God is the ruler and master, people cannot be autonomous

Gardner thinks that beliefs 'founded on divine revelation' are problematic for autonomy. If God creates faith, and if it is God who chooses man, not man who chooses God, there may not be any role to play for human autonomy. There may be no room for doubt, for challenging the beliefs, for 'questioning and examining in an independent and critically open way' (Gardner 1991, 74). A secular upbringing may thus be better, because there is no transcendent authority to diminish people's autonomy.

But if God is there, there is no point in closing our eyes to his existence because we want to be autonomous. Behind this thinking might lie the belief that faith in God means being guided or 'controlled' by him, not being our own master, but always being told what to do and mean. Such a life is not compatible with autonomy in the ordinary secular sense. Or maybe the point is that if we bring up children within Christianity, with faith in God, they are so 'controlled' that there is no way they can get out of it, they cannot think for themselves. J. White seems to say that no Christian can be autonomous, because they always have to do what God tells them (White 1995,13).

If the point is to say that since God chooses people, there is no way people can decide whether to believe in him or not, this is not right. It is true that God creates faith, that he gives faith as a gift. But he does not do this automatically, without the person willingly receiving this gift. It is also true that God chooses persons, but that does not mean that we are just 'acted on', that we have no choice. If God did not choose us, call us, we would never even think of approaching him, but when he does, he leaves the decision to the individual. He wants disciples, friends, and these are positions we cannot be forced into, we must want to.

In the same way, there is freedom to leave. Faith is not static, but a living relationship, and if not kept and developed and worked on, it will die. According to the Bible, this is also because of the continuous battle between good and evil, between God and Satan, where Satan wants people to turn away from God, and he has an ally in people's desire to be their own god. The Bible nourishes faith, and it requires commitment to continue to read it and take part in worship.

Within Christianity there is plenty of room for questioning and doubting, the Bible shows how people have come to God with all kinds of thoughts and questions and never have been turned away. There is also plenty of room within the church for questioning and examining - that is what theology is all about. That there are limits to what churches would regard as

Christianity does not mean that there are limits to what people can think and believe, only that they cannot require their own beliefs to be accepted within the church.

When it comes to what Christians can decide or not decide to do, there certainly is no difference from non-Christians or non-religious people, everybody may do what they want. The difference is that Christians know somebody who knows what is best for them and for their neighbours, therefore they ask him.

People are not like puppets in God's hand. He does not give ready cut solutions to all problems, he does not lay out our life in detail in front of us. It might be as difficult for a Christian as for a non-Christian to know what to do in a specific situation, taking all aspects into account, weighing all the arguments. Often people wish that the Bible was more detailed and gave more explicit answers, but Christians, as other people, have to exercise their autonomy and find solutions for every individual situation. The Bible does not give us the answers in ethical questions, it gives us guidelines and insight.

The thought of God being a ruler who does not allow his subjects to think for themselves is a fairly crude picture of God, nothing like the Bible's picture of him. Obviously, being a Christian does mean not being your own master, it does mean that God is Lord, but God is not a tyrant. Christians know God as a loving God and have basically given their life into his hand. They do this again and again, struggling with the old desire to be their own god and take their life in their own hand. Richard Harries says that '[f]or an agnostic, being mature means simply standing on one's own feet. But for a Christian, being mature means taking responsibility for your life before God and under God' (in Ward 1986, 77).

But what does it actually mean to be our own authority, our own master? Can people who do not believe in God be more autonomous than believers? The basics in our thinking come from outside ourselves anyway, and if not from God, most likely from the society we are a part of. We can be more or less aware of them, and as we get aware of them, more or less conforming. But our own master? Nobody is autonomous understood as wholly independent of others, we always depend more or less on individuals and groups. We agree with them or disagree with them, depending, *inter alia*, on the degree to which we know them and trust them. It is difficult to see that it should be more autonomous to make decisions about following the society's norms than to make decisions about following the norms and will of a loving God.

Gardner writes as if questioning and examining in 'an independent and critically open way' is an unproblematic phrase (Gardner 1991, 74). But independent of what, and criticism based on what? Since we are never wholly independent, with our thinking and rationality formed by our culture, our criticism will always be criticism from a certain perspective. There will be presuppositions implicit in the perspective that may decide the result, or at least limit the possible outcomes. If we, like Gardner - or at least the liberals he writes about - start our 'open' criticism from a position that does not allow for a God who is bigger than our little rational mind and whose thoughts are higher than our thoughts (Isaiah 55:9), then it is not very 'open' and 'independent'.

4.4.6 Faith is so important to religious people that they will use all means to make the pupils believers

Religious people are thought to regard their faith as so important that they want to inculcate it without leaving the children any choice. There is no room for critical thought, the children will be formed as believers. This may be right for some religions, and it may also be right for some non-religious world views.

As for Christianity, it is both right and wrong. Right about the importance of faith, wrong about the inculcation and forming. Faith *is* important to Christians, it is a question of life and death. And if you know that you have got something that can give the children eternal life, you certainly want to give it to them, and you use all available means.

But even if we want to inculcate faith, it is not possible. And it is not biblical. Some separate propositional beliefs might be inculcated, but for a Christian it is the faith that is crucial, faith in Christ the Truth. We cannot form Christians, because Christians do not have a particular form, they have a particular relationship, a relationship that requires a free, personal response to an invitation. Believing that God is the creator of all truth and is himself the Truth, critical thought which is searching for truth can only lead closer to God.[64]

Sometimes autonomy and choice seem to be as important for liberals as faith is for Christians. We might say, paraphrasing the title of this section, that 'Autonomy is so important to liberals that they will use all means to make the pupils autonomous'. Because it is in the children's 'real interest', autonomy ought to be the aim of education, even if the parents object (McLaughlin 1991, 142).

4.4.7 The influence in religiously based education will be very one-sided

Many seem to think that it is only fairly extreme religious people, perhaps called fundamentalists, who want an education based on their own faith. From this should follow that they also want a limited content and limited beliefs to be taught, limited by what is true in their own eyes. Both White and Macedo (see above, p. 62 and p. 169, note 52) seem to be in this category. My argument so far should show that this is not true. As for content, there does not need to be any difference between a religious and a secular school. As for perspective and purpose, both kinds of school will have their own, and as long as these are made explicit, the one- or many-sidedness may be the same.

The problem is when secular liberal education pretends to be neutral and only teach *about* different world views. Then the influence will in effect be more one-sided because the pupils will not get any outside perspective on it. And, as W.B. Ball claims, the result of such teaching may well be that they end up not choosing at all.

> The range of choices is very broad; the pupil is a child. Practically, only one choice may be available: to make no choice. His teacher - quite central in his consciousness - cannot affirm; that, too, is a teaching. His teacher may offer religions or religious ideas for comparison - objectively, we hope. The one thing the child is not really able to do is to compare them. (Ball 1967, 157)

Not only children may have such reactions. A. Baier writes about undergraduate students doing courses in comparative ethical theory. She claims that these courses, like courses in comparative religion, result in the students losing faith in any of the alternatives. 'We produce relativists and moral skeptics', she says, 'persons who have been convinced by our teaching that whatever they do in some difficult situation, some moral theory will condone it, another will condemn it'. This leads to them turning to self-interest or mere convenience (Baier 1985, 207-8).

Gardner is worried that parents may restrict the information a child gets by choosing a school that continues the restrictions from home (Gardner 1991, 78). He thinks of religiously based upbringing and education. I would think that in our society, children of atheistic and agnostic parents are more likely to have this problem. State schools commonly transmit an understanding of the world that is similar to their home background and which is also reinforced by society in general. Religious schools will normally have teachers with the same faith, but it is difficult to see this as a problem in a pluralistic society where the pupils cannot avoid meeting people of different faiths outside school and most definitely through media.

4.4.8 Separate schools may not nourish a suitable civic culture

This argument is one Strike uses when arguing for the 'public values school' (see above, p. 72). Often an argument for a common school and against separate schools is taken also to be an argument for a neutral school. This is not necessarily so, which my own argument shows. But because these are often so closely linked, I want to include this argument against separate schools, an argument that has some implicit assumptions about religiously based schools, not being as good as 'neutral' ones.

Strike does not explain what the separate schools' problem related to the civic culture is, but it is likely that he means - at least - that separate schools are inadequate because they rule out dialogue between children from different backgrounds. A civic culture in a pluralistic society needs a pluralistic school.

Callan is more explicit in his argument against separate schools, arguing that developing the aim of equal respect requires a school with 'diverse ethical voices' (Callan 1995/1996, 280). Dialogue may be simulated in separate schools, but that is not really good enough. It is the same argument that is used in the consultation paper 'Identitet og dialog' (NOU 1995:9): it is necessary for children to learn tolerance and respect for people from different backgrounds, the only way this can happen is by going to school together.

Two assumptions seem to be implicit here, neither of which can be justified. One is that a religiously based school is for children from this background only (Callan 1995/1996, 280). This may be true for certain groups, but not for all. Many church schools welcome children from other backgrounds, and at least in a Lutheran context this is how it ought to be. Separate schools ought to be open to anybody who wants the kind of education the school gives.

A *de facto* common school, Callan says, welcomes all children, it offers 'a learning environment that is genuinely hospitable to the credal and cultural diversity the society exhibits' (ibid., 268). In Callan's context, this seems to imply that the school does not take a stand between them. Not only are the pupils equally respected, but their beliefs and cultures are also regarded as equal. The consequence of this is that a school which is open to all must be based on liberal humanism.

What are the pupils taught about truth in this *de facto* common school? Disagreements about faith would probably be experienced as no more fundamental than disagreements about choice of a job would be in a Christian school. People's faith is not taken seriously, which implies a lack of respect. Respect does not require that we believe others' choice equally reasonable. Teachers in a common school, who cannot say that one view is better than others, lose the basis for respect. Children need to learn about respect from their own home perspective.

The other assumption is that to learn tolerance and respect, dialogue with people with different values is necessary. This is not a philosophical, but an empirical matter. The deduction from being a pluralistic society to the necessity of a pluralistic school is often taken for granted. But as far as I know, there is no evidence that it is correct.

Northern Ireland is sometimes used as an example of a society where separate schools for Protestants and Catholics contribute to continuing the division. I would argue that Northern Ireland is not a good example of a democratic, pluralistic society. There may be different motives for separate schools, and it is important to distinguish between schools that are there to build walls between communities, and those whose main raison d'être is to give the children a good and coherent basis in a confusing world. In the latter case, the school may actively work to instil tolerance and respect for others in the pupils. Separate schools do not have to be hostile to others. Tolerance and respect may be learnt even better in a separate school, because the pupils' own world view can in a more explicit way be used as motivation.

The separate schools do not have the obvious constant possibility for dialogue, but opportunities for dialogue may be created. Some of the schools may have children from different backgrounds. But even if not, there will be differences on a more superficial level, and this is a good starting point for teaching young children respect. Callan uses 'teaching, scholarship, and familial intimacy' as an example of the good life, on this level there can certainly be multitudes of views of the good life within a Christian framework.

We do not know how important world view dialogue in school is for 'a suitable civic culture', for helping us to create a good society for all. Separate education is not necessarily linked with prejudices towards others, and a common school will not necessarily instil respect. We see this in the case of integration of children with special needs into the mainstream school. Sometimes they are met with respect and care, sometimes they are ignored, or even bullied. Dialogue and respect have to be worked on, in any kind of school.

A Christian school would teach that everybody is to be loved and respected, whatever their values and beliefs, whether we know them or not. God loves everybody and wants to serve them, and he will help us to do the same.

CHAPTER 5

Liberal Christian Education?

In the previous chapter I discussed reasons for believing that world view neutral education is both possible and desirable, or at least that secular education comes closer to this ideal than religiously based education does. I have argued that Christian faith will have a more pervasive influence on all aspects of education than most of the 'neutralists' seem to be aware of. One reason for this may be that so-called Christian education has not always been Christian, it has just been 'ordinary', secular education with some Christian 'icing' in the form of acts of worship and periods of Christian RE. On the other hand, I have also argued that the liberal, no-standpoint education has equally pervasive world view standpoints built in, and thus the two are incompatible.

Nevertheless, various attempts have been made to give an account of an education that is both liberal and religious, or liberal and Christian. E.J. Thiessen argues that if we get philosophically defensible notions of rationality, autonomy and open-mindedness, Christian nurture and education can be liberal (Thiessen 1993). R.S. Laura & M. Leahy argue that it is possible for religious upbringing to be compatible with the liberal ideal of rational autonomy (Laura & Leahy 1989). The Norwegian consultation paper 'Identitet og dialog' tries to outline a religious education that both is fundamentally Christian and leaves the choice between religions and world views to the individual pupil (NOU 1995:9). The most thorough discussion of the question is probably T.H. McLaughlin's argument for a liberal, religious education as an alternative to the common liberal school (McLaughlin 1991).

Have these writers seen things I have overlooked, so that my argument is shown to be invalid? Or have they got a different conception of 'religious', 'Christian', or 'liberal', and if so, what are the basic presuppositions in the education they are arguing for? I want in this chapter to focus on McLaughlin's writings. His argument for liberal, religious education is made even more interesting by some of his other writings that are about the two kinds of education that the liberal religious version 'consists' of, namely liberal common education and Catholic education. I shall look at his view of these three kinds of education in turn, discussing them in relation to the arguments and presuppositions analysed in chapter four. Comparing and contrasting the three accounts casts light on what his liberal religious education actually is, to what extent it is religious and to what extent liberal.

5.1 Terence H. McLaughlin's view of liberal religious education

5.1.1 Common values education

When he writes about the common school in a democratic, pluralist society, McLaughlin makes clear that he is arguing from within a liberal perspective, without saying that he shares this perspective. His main emphasis is on the distinction between public and private values - or non-public as he calls them in his more recent writings. An education for all cannot be based on and convey a particular view of life and of what it is to be a person, it must contend itself with transmitting public or common values. 'Public values are those which, by virtue of their fundamentality or inescapability, are seen as binding on all persons ... Private values are those which go beyond what can be insisted upon for all members of a society'. This distinction is, he says, the liberal version of the distinction between basic, non-negotiable values and 'those which are open to plurality and diversity' (McLaughlin 1994, 462).

In a pluralistic, liberal democratic society the common school therefore should have a twofold influence. In common values it should have a strong, substantial influence, but in non-public values, in matters where there is strong disagreement,[65] the school should seek 'principled forebearance', it should either be silent or encourage the pupils to 'come to their own reflective decisions about them' (McLaughlin 1996b, 146).

Liberal education is thus non-neutral in common values, but neutral in controversial matters. Central in liberalism is a lack of certainty about what the good life consists in (McLaughlin 1992, 109). A particular philosophy of life or view of human nature therefore cannot be presupposed or taught. In religion and morality the only influence can be in the common value domain (McLaughlin 1996b, 146). One religion cannot be taught as if it were true, because the education should not aim at 'producing religious persons' (McLaughlin 1992, 108).

Autonomy seems to be the aim that is most emphasized in McLaughlin's writings. He defines liberal education as involving '(i) the aim of developing a form of autonomy, (ii) an emphasis on fundamental and general knowledge, (iii) an aversion to mere instrumentality in determining what is to be learnt, and (iv) a concern for the development of critical reason' (ibid., 107).

In his thesis, he argues within what he calls a fairly strong form of liberalism, involving the following assumptions that are relevant here:

a) that the development of personal and moral autonomy is a fundamental value and parents should have this as a major aim in the upbringing of their children;
c) that no one set of religious beliefs can be shown to be objectively true. (McLaughlin 1991, 11-12)[66]

It is interesting to notice that he only includes religious beliefs, not non-religious world view beliefs.

McLaughlin's account of common liberal education seems to be fairly similar to K.A. Strike's, probably intended to be thinner than J. White's. He obviously wants and believes it is possible to have an education that is neutral between world views. His understanding of 'liberal' is closest to that of a common basis (see above, p. 49).

Where does this leave him in relation to my list of arguments and pre-suppositions in chapter four? It is difficult to say anything with certainty because so little is made explicit, but he seems to assume that it is possible both to base education on common values only (4.2.1), and to teach *about* various religions and world views without teaching *from* any of them (4.2.2).

According to McLaughlin, upbringing at home needs a basis or a frame-work, and he borrows Ackerman's conception of 'primary culture'. He argues for the possibility of a religious primary culture leading to auto-nomy, also in schools. But education obviously does not in his view have to have a primary culture, at least not a thick one, it is possible to teach on a thin basis of public values only.[67]

There is a certain ambiguity in the notions of 'thin' and 'thick' applied to the basis of a school. The most adequate way of interpreting both McLaughlin and most others who use the concepts is probably in terms of sufficiency. A thick basis is then a comprehensive one, one that is sufficient for upbringing and education, giving answers to the basic questions about reality, human nature, the purpose of life, etc. A thin one, on the other hand, would consist of public values only, depending on some other person or institution to provide the thick basis, trying to avoid answering these kinds of question itself.

Sometimes, however, it seems as if this distinction between thick and thin is mixed with the number of beliefs presupposed and taught, and how detailed they are. We then get something along the lines of P. Gardner's argument, where he claims that a secular upbringing is better for autonomy because it involves fewer beliefs and therefore has a weaker influence. But the 'thickness', or the comprehensiveness, of a basis or culture does not depend on the number of detailed beliefs, but on whether or not it gives answers to the important world view questions. That it is up to the individ-ual to find their own answer, is also an answer, and many such answers will contribute to a thick basis. Even an education that is based on and transmits comprehensive liberalism will be thick, although it has relatively few explicit beliefs.

It is probably helpful to distinguish between a school's basis and its ethos. The basic values or world view is what is intended to be transmitted, but the ethos or culture is what is actually conveyed, the character or spirit of the school (Williams 1998, 48). It seems likely that, at least for some groups of children, the thin basis of a liberal, common school will be perceived as a thick ethos. Silence or attempts to be neutral may function as answers. This is related to B. Mitchell's argument about liberal humanism, but it is also partly a psychological point that requires some empirical research.

McLaughlin believes that it is possible to teach from a thin basis of public values only. But he also quotes and seems to agree with the claim that 'every form of education teaches implicitly or explicitly a philosophy of man' (McLaughlin 1996b, 141). This is what I argued in 4.2.1, implying that more than public values will be conveyed. He seems to contradict himself.

Then again he says that 'in contexts where there is a *homogeneity* of values ... a particularly distinctive kind of person is being produced (sic!)' (McLaughlin 1991, 324, my emphasis). If the above argument is valid, also contexts of 'value diversity and controversiality' (ibid.) will 'produce' a distinctive kind of person, because the context, the ethos, will be perceived as more homogenous than it is intended to be.

It is, however, important to distinguish not only between basis and ethos, but also between these two and result. A school may intend to be neutral, it may in effect convey liberal humanism, but the pupils' resulting world view depends on many other influences too, most particularly family background. For the many children from secular homes, at least, with little awareness of these matters, the school's influence may lead to liberal humanism. They may perceive and believe that pluralism is a value in itself, that it is up to them to create a purpose for their life, and that religion is something private.

That McLaughlin regards public values as enough to base education on is also a bit puzzling since he says that they have 'a broadly procedural feel to them' (McLaughlin 1992, 113), i.e. not much substance. But he also talks about strong, substantial influence in common values (McLaughlin 1996b, 146), where then does the substance come from? He knows that values are not, at least not always, neutral between world views,

> any suggestion that religious views of morality involve merely adding another dimension to independently existing secular values must be rejected as obviously crude. In many cases the value itself is significantly shaped by the religious or secular aspect under which it is viewed. Often the value does not have an independent character and life of its own, even where

there is considerable overlap between religious and secular invocations of it. (McLaughlin 1991, 99)

Freedom and autonomy, for instance, have different meanings. There are particular Catholic meanings (McLaughlin 1996b, 144), which implies that the public or common meanings are not the only ones. Different meanings may even contradict each other. J. Haldane says that 'no account of values can begin to be adequate unless it has at its heart the recognition that mankind has an eternal destiny ... we exist for the sake of God's glory' (Haldane 1996, 134-5). This is a Catholic view of values, including public values. If they are not understood in this way, they are understood in a different way, which is also a particular, 'thick' way. In McLaughlin's common school it may be explained how values are understood from different perspectives, but the life of the school will give them a secular context, with no reference to God's glory. This will be incompatible with the Catholic view and therefore not neutral.

In a number of his writings, McLaughlin voices some doubt about the common, liberal education being neutral. But mostly he seems to think that these are practical problems that may be overcome. 'There may well be practical difficulties facing the common school in avoiding the transmission of general secularist and relativist views. However, liberal educational values confront the common school with a principled obligation to address and resolve them' (McLaughlin 1992, 114). This can be done by ensuring 'that the child is exposed not merely to possibly disjointed elements of knowledge, but also to the various general "interpretative attitudes of the world" which lie at the root of different "world views" '. They must learn about different ways of understanding the whole world, it being their own task to 'make a coherent whole of their educational experience' (ibid., 115).

Despite some doubt, McLaughlin seems to believe that education does not inevitably convey a world view, but that it can give knowledge about various views and encourage the pupils to choose. In some of his latest writings, however, the doubt becomes more clearly expressed. He seems to think that maybe a comprehensive liberalism is unavoidable after all (McLaughlin 1995b, 252). And he asks: 'Is the attempt to confine the value basis of the common school to values which are in some sense not "significantly controversial" counter-intuitive and damaging? Is the influence of the common school as a result undesirably thin?' (McLaughlin 1996a, 17). It may be too thin, or as I argued above, it may get a particular, liberal thickness that was not intended and maybe not even desired.

McLaughlin's opinions about the world view neutrality of the liberal common school seem somewhat ambiguous and contradictory, unless there is some deeper understanding that unites them all which I have failed to see. His doubts seem to grow stronger, but he continues to argue for the same kind of education. If I am right, the most likely explanation of this is that he cannot see a better solution for a common school in pluralist societies. Most important for him is the development of autonomy and critical reason, and he seems to take for granted, like so many others, that the no-standpoint school is an obvious solution to this, although not the only one. This may be because he believes that presenting one view as true deprives pupils of the possibility of making an autonomous choice (4.3.5). But since he also argues for liberal religious education, it is probably more likely that his reason simply is that pluralism should stop us from transmitting one particular world view in common schools (4.3.1).

Another presupposition that might be underlying his argument for the neutral common school is that we do not agree on which world view is true (4.3.3), or 'no one set of religious beliefs can be shown to be objectively true' (McLaughlin 1991, 12). They are controversial, they require assessment by individuals - they are non-public.

If there is no true answer, if there are no rights and wrongs outside the public area, choosing easily becomes more important than the answer. Everybody must find a theory of the good that gives meaning to their life, and it does not matter which one. But then this becomes the true answer. If, on the other hand, we believe that there is a right or true way of understanding the world (relativism being one option), according to McLaughlin the school should not take a stand because people cannot agree on what it is. He does not want the common school to be silent on such matters. He wants it to take non-public values and standpoints into account where relevant. But he seems to be hesitant to criticize such views, they are, after all, the beliefs of the pupils' parents. The aim of the work of the school is to illuminate the various views (McLaughlin 1995b, 251).

Why is it so important to present all reasonable options without taking a stand? What are teachers to answer if pupils ask why we are silent about truth and falsity? It is strange that the pupils are to do all the assessing themselves in this important matter if there is a truth we want them to find. We should at least go through the options with them, helping them to evaluate, giving them criteria for evaluation, sorting out what we regard as the most likely candidates for truth. And if we want them to understand that it is important that they find the right answer, must we not then show them that we have done some serious thinking in our own life?

The notion of public values is linked to the liberal conception of 'theory of the good'. McLaughlin uses ''comprehensive' theories of the good' as more or less synonymous with world view, or 'overall views of life as a whole' (McLaughlin 1996b, 145). The conception is slightly confusing in this context. Kantian liberals draw a distinction between the 'right' and the 'good', 'between a framework of basic rights and liberties, and the conceptions of the good that people may choose to pursue within the framework' (Sandel 1984, 3). The rights are the public values (McLaughlin 1996a, 14) that are said to be basic and binding for all. Then people have different theories of the good in addition to this, and there is an 'alleged independence' between them (McLaughlin 1995a, 26-7). This very easily leads to the thought that the public values are the most basic, the fundamental, the objective, and that the good therefore is less fundamental, less objective. This may be right when the question is about making a society function, but it is not necessarily so in the individual's life.

A world view, or view of life, or religion, consists of both public and non-public values, and in addition both metaphysical and epistemological beliefs, and what is most fundamental will vary. In some world views, particularly in humanism, ethical values are often regarded as most basic, but in Christianity, belief in God and in Jesus Christ is much more fundamental. Not only basic, but it permeates everything, so that not even the public values are independent of this 'theory of the good'.[68]

To call belief and trust in God a theory of the good makes it something less fundamental and important than it is, it is seen through the glasses of comprehensive liberalism. It makes service for God and neighbours one option among others as purpose for my life, not *the* purpose I am created for. It makes Christianity something I can choose because I find it would give me a good life, instead of a challenge from the almighty God to choose between life and death.

McLaughlin takes as an example of a non-public value remarriage after divorce (McLaughlin 1996a, 14). Some claim it is wrong, others not, therefore society cannot enforce one view by law. In the same way, he says, education in common schools cannot be based on a 'thick' theory of the good. Leaving on one side the problem of actually making the laws neutral, the bigger problem is the deduction from law to education.

In society, all adults have their view of remarriage, it is for them part of their overall ethical view, in its turn part of a world view - all more or less coherent and stable, and to a large degree a result of their upbringing. How they argue for or against will depend on this view, and will differ. They may appeal to God's laws, universal natural laws, the good of society, solidarity, the individual's freedom - they may claim that there is a right answer to the question that is binding for all (this not necessarily implying that they will enforce it by law), or that it is up to the individual.

But children are not adults and do not have the adults' responsibility for their life and their beliefs. In a much more fundamental way than adults, they are in the process of forming their values and their world view. What liberal education will do is to teach them that there are different answers to this moral question, and that it is up to them to decide, judged from what they think will lead to a good life. The criteria for what a good life is, will also be individual. If they are not otherwise influenced outside school, they may then be inculcated into believing that nobody can tell them the right answer to this question - there is no right answer.

They may be told that for instance Catholics believe that remarriage after divorce is wrong, but that this is only something that is true for Catholics, who are people who get their 'answer' from God, or maybe from the Church.[69] This, regarded as a 'neutral' presentation of various views, will become The View. If this happens in many areas, they may all go out into society with the same overall view, not making it pluralistic, but very homogeneously liberal in a comprehensive way.

5.1.2 Catholic education

We have seen that McLaughlin's view of liberal education is very much like the view I have argued to be incompatible with Christian education. What then about his view of religiously based education? Is it so different from my account of a Lutheran education that all my arguments in the preceding chapters would not apply?

McLaughlin argues that there are forms of Christian education that are compatible with liberal principles. He discusses briefly an account given by the British Council of Churches and argues that it may be understood to want as an aim autonomy in his liberal sense (McLaughlin 1991, 246-50). About Catholic education he seems to be slightly less certain. According to recent official Catholic statements, the aim of 'religious upbringing is to produce a person who autonomously and freely accepts faith' (ibid., 252). So the Roman Catholic Church wants autonomy, but the conception is not necessarily a liberal one, it is sometimes written about rather negatively 'as an expression of "immaturity" ' when it questions faith (ibid., 253). K. Williams, however, refers to a Vatican document that asks 'that critical thinking be encouraged in young people' (Williams 1998, 51).

I want to look at McLaughlin's account of Catholic education to see whether differences between this account and my own account of Lutheran education can explain some of the differences in our thinking about liberal religious education. Would he for instance argue that there are no basic differences between his common liberal education and his Catholic education, only the latter is thicker and gives substance and non-neutrality to the former?

McLaughlin's account of Catholic education is very different from how he presents common education. A certain view of life and human nature is to be promoted, the aim is to form persons of a particular kind. Catholic schools are based on and seek to promote an understanding of the world, of reality, with Jesus Christ at the centre and related to him in all aspects. This seems to be in harmony with what G.A. Beck says in his account of aims in Neo-Thomist education: 'Only when we know what man is can we say how he should be educated' (Beck 1964, 109). The aim is an integral formation, a synthesis of culture, faith and life, in the light of the Gospel (McLaughlin 1996b, 141).

This makes clear that Catholic education is Christ-centred, that the very basis for education is a view of reality and human nature that is related to Christ and concerned with salvation and faith. McLaughlin quotes P. Walsh who claims that the Gospel is the yeast in the cake, permeating everything, not an icing added afterwards (ibid.). He also quotes a Vatican declaration saying that 'the knowledge which the pupils acquire of the world, of life and of men is illumined by faith' (ibid.).

The notion of formation of believers is frequently used, both by McLaughlin and by other writers on Catholic education. 'The formation of Catholic believers' is mentioned as a possible purpose for education (McLaughlin 1996b, 138), another aim is 'to produce a person who ...' (McLaughlin 1991, 252). He also talks of moral formation as 'the shaping of religious and moral personhood and character', and the aim is to be helped to 'know and love God more perfectly' (McLaughlin 1996b, 143[70]).

The Lutheran emphasis on the personal relationship side of faith makes it less important to form a certain kind of person and more important that the Christ-relationship should influence her or him into becoming more fully the unique person they were meant to be. The focus for the teacher is on telling them who God is, not on forming them. In the moral area the emphasis is not so much on acquiring certain virtues as on getting them into good habits that will help them to do good also when they do not want to. I am not claiming that there is a contradiction between a Lutheran and a Catholic understanding, only that a difference in focus and emphasis in the theology of faith is reflected in the theory and aim of education.

It is underlined by McLaughlin that faith is proclaimed or offered, not imposed, and that faith is a fruit of grace and freedom (McLaughlin 1996b, 144). Again he quotes Walsh who says that 'real faith is always a personal and free response to God' (Walsh 1983, 14). But still he uses the formulation 'to form religious faith' and says that the school seeks 'a total commitment to the Person of Christ' (McLaughlin 1996b, 143).

There seems to be an emphasis on the development of faith as an aim for Catholic education. P. Walsh holds that 'such schools should make quite explicit their commitment to the development of faith as their primary rationale' (McLaughlin 1991, 217). This is different from Lutheran thinking, where the primary rationale for schools is to give good education for life in this world, but where the world is understood in a Christian way and where knowledge about God and his salvation is essential. A formulation like 'strive to bring forth a response from the heart' (ibid., 74[71]) would not be used in a Lutheran context, where the focus is on what the teacher can teach them in words and life, not on the children's response.

As far as I can see, there is no mention of autonomy or critical rationality in McLaughlin's account of Catholic education. That obviously does not mean that it cannot lead to these qualities, but it might suggest that they are not the most central aims or topics. McLaughlin's other writings show that he regards them as important. And it is possible, he argues, to aim at both faith and autonomy. The long-term aim may be autonomy, the short-term faith. Parents and teachers may hope for faith in the long term too, but cannot require it (McLaughlin 1984, 79).

Without going too deeply into theology, I want to suggest that there may be a difference in the Lutheran and the Catholic notion of faith that is important in the discussion about autonomy and indoctrination. To put it very briefly, McLaughlin's Catholic conception of faith seems to have an emphasis on rational beliefs, religious practices and a personality formed in a certain way. The Lutheran conception, on the other hand, focuses on the personal relationship with God.

The emphasis on rational beliefs is seen in many places. In the discussion about 'fixed beliefs' in the sense of 'stable' or 'unshakeable' (McLaughlin 1991, 21), the notion of religion as a set of beliefs is very strong. Faith is something people accept or adhere to (McLaughlin 1996b, 144), as if it is something complete that is there outside them, for them to consider rationally. The emphasis on rationality is also seen in an argument like 'what is demanded is autonomous religious faith based on appropriate reasoning and evaluation, not mere lip-service or conditioning' (McLaughlin 1984, 79).

This understanding of faith as very much something intellectual, something to do with rationality, is also implicit in Bryk, Lee and Holland's description of a profound change in Catholic catechesis that came about with Vatican II. 'The concept of faith as a free choice made over time by an informed, educated conscience replaced the spirit of indoctrination into the mind of the Church' (quoted from Groome 1996, 124). To put it crudely: before, you were not allowed to think, the right meanings were just put into your mind, but now you are informed and educated so you can make your own choice.

Sometimes McLaughlin argues as if religion - in general, not only Catholicism - is 'a particular set of beliefs' (e.g. McLaughlin 1984, 80), but then he mentions practices, attitudes, rituals, etc. (ibid., 81), suggesting that it is more than propositions. When he writes about Catholic education, the general impression is that 'faith' to a large degree is acceptance of certain doctrines (4.1.1), combined with certain practices (4.1.2). If this is right, maybe one reason why he thinks neutral common education is possible is that religion consists mainly in beliefs and practices that can be added to the rest of people's lives.

If this emphasis on the intellectual and the practical (using the sacraments, going to mass), combined with formation of the personality, is right - or at least used to be so, it makes more sense that there have been accusations of indoctrination and that McLaughlin is concerned to show that it is possible for religiously based education to promote autonomy.

If, on the other hand, the emphasis is on knowing and trusting God, indoctrinated dogmas are of no use, and there has to be a personal, autonomous response. In Lutheran thinking, faith is primarily regarded as a living relationship, as something personal, something changing. In that case faith is not so much a rational matter, it is not something that people adhere to or not, it is not something that might be put into their minds by indoctrination. There certainly is a rational aspect to it, like there is to friendship and marriage and all close relationships, and there are practices, but we do not catch the nature of faith by focusing on propositional beliefs and certain rituals.

There are, however, claims in McLaughlin's writings that contradict such an understanding of religion. Beliefs are not sufficient, there is a need for 'the child to *be* religious - to begin to actually *practise* his or her faith' (McLaughlin 1991, 74). And he quotes from a Catholic source that catechesis 'should not be satisfied with external expressions only, however useful they may be, but ... should strive to bring forth a response from the heart and a taste for prayer'. This involves learning how to take part in the practices, but more than that. It also implies learning to want to be religious, with 'a stress on such notions as "developing a love for God and His will", a "hatred of sin", feelings of thanksgiving, repentance and so on' (ibid., 74-75). Still, this seems to be formation of virtues more than developing the relationship with God, the getting to know God that is the source of all these other things.

What, then, about the compatibility between Catholic education and liberal, common education? Could Catholic pupils go to the common school without getting any influence that is contradicting their Catholic upbringing? McLaughlin seems to think so. In liberalism's language, Catholicism is a theory of the good. According to his account, common education can be based on public values only and so, although with difficulty, be neutral between such theories. Common education should therefore be compatible with Catholic education, only thinner, leaving out the 'theory of the good'-aspects.

This requires religion, in this case Catholicism, to be something separate, a religious area or domain that can be added without changing the basis. But this does not fit with what he says about religiously based upbringing and education in general and about Catholic education in particular. 'It would be tempting', he suggests, 'to see a religious upbringing as one which (merely) *goes beyond* a basic general upbringing ... But there are problems in seeing a religious dimension to upbringing too crudely as an *addition* to a separately characterisable base. The religious dimension is bound, to some extent, to affect and impinge upon, that base' (ibid., 73).

When he writes about Catholic education, there is no saying that religion is 'an optional extra' (4.1.3). The Catholic faith and world view permeates everything. If Christ is to be the heart of all understanding, this is not a matter that the school can be silent on or discuss in certain lessons, it is a matter that is either there throughout, or it is not. 'Every education teaches a philosophy', says G.K. Chesterton, 'if not by dogma then by suggestion, by implication, by atmosphere. Every part of that education has a connection with every other part. If it does not all combine to convey some general view of life it is not education at all' (in Haldane 1996, 126).

A characteristic of Catholic education, according to T.H. Groome, is sacramentality - to see God in all things. 'A "sacramental consciousness" means being aware of the presence of God as the backdrop and foreground of life', to 'look through' reality to see God in all things (Groome 1996, 112). This is what the world is like, according to Catholic faith. A reality without Christ, without God, is not neutral. If knowledge is not illumined by faith (McLaughlin 1996b, 141), the whole of education is totally different. Different, and not neutral, but - from a Catholic perspective - wrong.

But then McLaughlin is not right about the compatibility of Catholic and no-standpoint, common education. The moral teaching will be different, the whole interpretation of reality and life will be different, the purpose of education will be different. The Catholic education will have its world view influence, and so will the liberal, common one.

McLaughlin mentions that from a communitarian perspective, liberal education is criticized for leading to individualism and choice based on self-interest (ibid., 147). Although this is discussed in an article about Catholic education, he does not go into the problems this implicit influence may cause relating to such education. On the contrary, he claims that Catholic education can be compatible with liberal educational principles (ibid.). But it is difficult to see how an influence towards individualism and self-interest can be compatible with the view of human nature and morality that is to be conveyed in Catholic education.

There are many differences between Catholic and Lutheran education, but they are similar in their all-pervasive character. I find it hard to understand why McLaughlin argues as he does about the world view neutrality of the common school. It is one thing to want it to be neutral because a common school for all is positive in many ways, quite another to think it possible. The only explanation I may suggest is that in his writings about the common school he is so much influenced by the liberal way of thinking and the liberal conceptions that he does not really see it from a Catholic or religious perspective.

5.1.3 Liberal religious education

McLaughlin's liberal religious education cannot simply be a combination of the common liberal education he describes and the kind of religiously based education that he outlines in Catholic education, they are incompatible. So either 'liberal' means something different in this context, or he thinks of a different sort of religion.

Why does he want to argue for this kind of education? He wants to show that religiously based education is not necessarily indoctrination, and that religious parents have the right to choose a religious upbringing and education for their children, as long as autonomy is the aim. Therefore he argues that there are other forms of liberal education than the common values one and that it is possible to have liberal education in religious schools. He does not claim that all religious faiths are compatible with autonomy, only that there are some that are. '[C]ertain religious faiths, including a significant proportion of the Christian tradition, can, at least in principle, accept a concern for autonomy in a significant sense as compatible with, and even demanded by, its central tenets' (McLaughlin 1991, 70).

When discussing the common liberal school, McLaughlin uses 'liberal' in the sense of 'basis', a public values education, an education with a minimal basis that everybody can agree on. When he argues for a religious liberal education, he uses 'liberal' as a quality, as certain characteristics that you might find in education, whatever it is based on. The specific religion is the basis, and as long as it allows for autonomy, critical reasoning, etc., the education is liberal. His view of religion here seems to be the same as when he writes about Catholic education. So it is the interpretation of 'liberal' as quality that makes his liberal religious education possible.

In which ways and to what extent is his liberal religious education liberal then? Autonomy seems to be the crux of the argument. The point is not that he wants a non-neutral liberal education, but that he wants to show that religiously based education can promote autonomy. It is autonomy that is the focus, not neutrality.

The problem is that when he - and others - discuss the common school, neutrality between world views, or theories of the good, seems to be a condition for autonomy. '[A] broad introduction to the religious domain is required, not merely the teaching of one religion, and certainly not as if it were true' (ibid., 154). And the liberal view is that 'children's autonomy is best facilitated by a form of education ("Liberal Education") which systematically and objectively exposes the children in an appropriate way to the range of values, beliefs, ways of life and life ideals which ought to be considered by them, and in relation to which their autonomy can be developed and exercised' (ibid., 142).

On the other hand, in the kind of liberal religious school he advocates, 'the truth of a particular religion is presupposed and taught' (ibid., 194). This does not mean, I suppose, that other religions are not taught, but that one is taught 'as if it were true'.

Thus, either he thinks that the religious neutrality is not, after all, a precondition for promoting autonomy, or he thinks that we can both presuppose and teach the truth of one religion and at the same time, or at least in the same school but possibly later, teach all religions objectively, without taking a stand between them. To teach that 'no one set of religious beliefs can be shown to be objectively true' (ibid., 12), as is one of the assumptions in liberalism, is no problem in any case, because it does not in itself require that we refrain from basing education on a particular religion, as long as we make clear that it is a matter of faith, not facts.

It is a little unclear to me what McLaughlin actually thinks about what is to be conveyed as truth in liberal religious education. Two other topics contribute to this slight confusion. One is his reference to the Swann report, 'Education for All' (1985). He says that the liberal religious school should provide

> a form of nurture which is capable of acting as a basis for the kind of open, phenomenological approach to religion which Swann recommends. Thus such a school would not eschew the phenomenological approach and the breadth and diversity associated with it, but would introduce it to its pupils at an appropriate point as part of its efforts to develop their auto-nomy in religion from the basis of a particular religious tradition. (McLaughlin 1991, 205)

In the Swann report's approach, the curriculum 'must be permeated by a genuinely pluralist perspective' (ibid., 197). What does this mean?

It is fairly clear that McLaughlin's school is meant to start from a basis that is taken for granted, that is conveyed as truth. But when other religions are brought in for the pupils' autonomous choice, then there will be a phenomenological approach and a genuinely pluralist perspective. According to the Swann report, the phenomenological or undogmatic approach 'does not seek to promote any one religious viewpoint' (Education for All 1985, 470).

The report's concept of pluralism 'implies seeing the very diversity of such a society, in terms for example of the range of religious experience and the variety of languages and language forms, as an enrichment of the experience of all those within it' (ibid., 5). This notion of pluralism seems to be at least pluralism as something valuable, maybe also meaning that no religion is regarded as superior (Carson's second or third meaning, see above, p. 47). Is this the attitude McLaughlin wants in his schools, which are based on and teach one religion as true? Does he want the pupils to regard religious pluralism as something positive, or does he want them to believe that they have found the truth and want to share it with others?

The other topic that makes me uncertain about this is his tendency to talk about the religious basis as just a starting point. The tradition is used 'as a substantial basis from which pupils might be launched on their own search for autonomous agency' (McLaughlin 1991, 199).

In his discussion of Hirst's distinction between 'education' and 'catechesis' (ibid., 228-37), he suggests that Christianity as a starting point in education could be a means towards the more fundamental aim of auton-omy (ibid., 232-3). Understanding in the religious area is an aim in liberal education, and he argues that this can be gained from the 'inside', i.e. in a liberal religious school, as well as from the 'outside', i.e. in a common values school. But the understanding gained from the inside has to be located 'in due course ... in a broader framework which goes beyond the particular tradition' (ibid., 234-5).

What is this 'broader framework', how is it to be understood? Does it just mean that they get knowledge about other traditions and learn that their own framework is not the framework of everybody? Or does it mean that they change frameworks to a 'broader' one, whatever that is? If the latter, it may again be this notion of the 'from nowhere'-view that is lurking underneath. Taking Catholic education as an example, is it to be based throughout on a view of reality and human nature that is related to Christ and concerned with salvation and faith, or is this only a primary culture that has to give way to something more 'neutral' for the pupils to attain autonomy?

Is it in the end essentially a comprehensive liberal education where it is to be conveyed that the meaning of life is not given, that it is up to the individual to find or choose or make his or her own? Or is it at heart, right through, a Christian education, where it is conveyed that the meaning of life is total commitment to Jesus Christ, that we exist for God's glory?

McLaughlin claims that the British Council of Churches is in danger of making autonomy instrumental to faith (ibid., 250). I am not sure whether his account is any better, to me it sounds very much like making Christianity, or faith, instrumental to autonomy. If Christianity is regarded as true in the first place, with its teaching about salvation, this seems incoherent. It is a result of trying to make Christianity, or other religions, with their own presuppositions, fit into the liberal framework, with its liberal notion of autonomy and of what is important in human life.

Maybe one thing that contributes to this unclear relationship between truth, autonomy and neutrality is that he seems to think that either the school transmits one view as true, or it leaves the choice with the pupils. If the former, they are formed in a certain way, they have no choice, or at least this choice is made very difficult. This view is more strongly expressed in other writers than McLaughlin, but he might also be understood in this way, for instance in the following quotation:

> At least in common schools, no substantial 'holistic' view of life should be transmitted to pupils, nor should they be shaped 'as whole persons' in the light of any such theory. Rather, schools should open up views of this kind for critical assessment and exploration. Schools should therefore be suspicious of aiming at 'wholeness' for pupils (McLaughlin 1996a, 15).

The 'rather' here is misleading, as if opening up views is an alternative to transmitting a holistic view. They can certainly both be done simultaneously. The opening up does not have to be done from 'nowhere', maybe it can even be done better if they have a 'holistic' view of life to compare other views with. It is easier to understand other views if we know where we are looking from. Neutrality is not a precondition for autonomy.

The concern to make the liberal religious education no more influential than necessary is probably due to neutrality being regarded as a safeguard for autonomy. Making this education as similar as possible to the common, no-standpoint education is seen as making it more acceptable from a liberal and autonomy-promoting perspective.

McLaughlin's conception of 'liberal' is understood as a quality, and therefore the basic presuppositions in the liberal, religious education come from the religion. This is not altogether right. Apart from the uncertainty already mentioned about the framework in the later stages of education, the overall flavour of the argument is that the perspective is from liberalism and it is autonomy that is important. The very fundamental understanding of 'autonomy' he gets from common liberal education. He does not discuss its world view presuppositions at all, probably thinking it is neutral, although in other contexts he suggests that Catholicism has a particular understanding of both 'freedom' and 'personal autonomy' (McLaughlin 1996b, 144).

Autonomy in a Christian sense has to reckon with God. It is not a question of either making all your decisions yourself or just following somebody else, God included, without reasoning. There is a third possibility, namely to want to do God's will because we know it is the best, and to base all our thinking and decision-making on his word. Christian autonomy acknowledges dependence on and responsibility towards God. Man is dependent on God, Beck says in his Catholic, Neo-Thomist account of education. But, given this, man 'has a relative autonomy higher than that of any other creature' (Beck 1964, 115-16).

Both parents and children are under God's authority and responsible to him, the parents' responsibility is to help the children to get to know God as Creator and Saviour and to teach them, in theory and practice, what it is like to live as his child and servant. It is part of the Bible's message that every one is responsible for him- or herself. Parents are only God's helpers. Nobody, not even parents, has the right to determine a child's future, to make it impossible or even difficult for children to make their own decisions and create their own life, in all areas. This God-dimension seems to be absent in McLaughlin's liberal, religious autonomy.

A particular problem is the relationship between autonomy and faith. McLaughlin says that parents who would give 'a clear priority to faith' are obviously not interested in his version of liberal, religious education (McLaughlin 1990, 119). This is not necessarily true. When Lutherans want children to make autonomous decisions about their life with God or not, it is not primarily because they want to be liberal, because they so desperately want the children to be autonomous, but simply because this is the only option.

Faith is the most important thing in the world, the question of being liberal or not is irrelevant in this matter. If parents could have dragged the children into fellowship with God, they probably would have done so. But, as McLaughlin also says, '*built into* the parents' faith are conditions requiring the toleration of error freely embraced by their offspring' (McLaughlin 1991, 89). Faith in the Lutheran sense cannot but be autonomous, otherwise it is not faith. So for Lutheran parents, liberal education that aims at autonomy, at least concerning faith, would be the only option. Whether this would be the same version of liberal religious education as McLaughlin argues for is however not quite certain.

In nearly all his writings, McLaughlin writes as if it is only religious upbringing and education that have problems with liberal autonomy, only this kind of upbringing and education that transmits beliefs. He argues for all children's need of a primary culture, including a 'substantive set of practices, beliefs and values' (ibid., 16-17). But then, whether he writes about common values education or liberal religious education, it is the religious parents and schools who have problems: 'It is impossible for parents who practise a religious faith to insulate their children from that faith' (ibid., 24). About the content of education he says that 'the general curriculum of the religious school might have a particular flavour or series of emphases' (McLaughlin 1987, 77).

What about parents who practise a non-religious world view? They can no more insulate their children from the fact that they do not go to church, do not pray, do not give God any room in their life. And the curriculum in non-religious schools will also have a certain 'flavour or series of emphases', only different. In a reply to Gardner, McLaughlin claims that atheists and agnostics also have a certain framework and persistent beliefs. They may not be as substantial as religious ones, but still there are fundamental presuppositions that influence upbringing and education (McLaughlin 1990, 112). But this is a view that is not to be found in his main work on this topic, his thesis, neither in any of the other documents I have read. When nurture is discussed, it is as something that happens in religious homes and schools. Religion is part of the family's culture and impossible to separate from the moral domain, therefore it cannot be left out until the children can think for themselves (McLaughlin 1991, 24-5). But the same is also true about any world view.

When such arguments are repeated again and again in relation to religious parents and schools, it rather gives the impression that it is these who are in danger of indoctrinating instead of promoting autonomy, not the secular ones. This is even more puzzling since we are talking about pluralist societies, fairly secular societies, where religious people, including children, cannot but be aware that they are different.

A number of times McLaughlin uses the argument that it is good for children to experience religion from the inside, it will help them to evaluate religion for themselves, it will give them a concrete understanding of what it is (McLaughlin 1984, 82).[72] Again, here is the assumption that children in non-religious homes are not on the inside of anything, that they are in a sort of nowhere-position. Another way to understand religion, he says, is '[f]rom the "outside in" - an exploration into the religious domain from the position of non-belief' (McLaughlin 1991, 234). If discussing beliefs and autonomy is to have any meaning at all, it is time we stop talking as if only religious people have perspectives. Everybody is on the inside of some view about reality and the meaning of life. Everybody has beliefs and convictions, everybody needs to learn and be aware of their own view and also to learn about others.

Writing about both liberal religious education and liberal common education, McLaughlin says that he is writing from within a liberal framework and not addressing questions about this framework itself. I think this is what makes it all somewhat confusing, because he ignores one of the important factors in the discussion, namely that all education will convey some world view presuppositions, even the presumably 'thin', liberal one. Trying to combine two traditions without discussing the presuppositions involved in both of them, or at least looking at the conceptions in focus (e.g. autonomy) from both points of view, will necessarily lead to some shortcomings.

5.1.4 Are 'common' and 'separate' useful labels?

It is common to talk about 'common' and 'separate' schools. The common school is the one that the majority of pupils are supposed to attend, and it should not be based on any particular world view, only on values we can all agree on. Separate schools are for those who are not happy with the common school for some reason, for instance because they want a particular religious upbringing, or because they want an upbringing that is based on a particular educational theory. Such schools are by many regarded as divisive, likely to indoctrinate, and as something to be avoided as far as possible.

But there are other solutions, and in an article about liberalism and common education, McLaughlin argues for the possibility of a non-neutral common school, a common school that is based on and promotes a particular culture or religion (McLaughlin 1995b). He uses M. Walzer's distinction between Liberalism 1 and Liberalism 2. Liberalism 1 is committed to a 'rigorously neutral state', but in Liberalism 2, 'nation states are non-neutral with regard to the cultural survival of the majority nation, but liberal principles are satisfied by a "strong theory of rights" ' (ibid., 245-6).

This Liberalism 2-school is something in between the kinds of school he otherwise defends. It is not neutral between world views as the common school he usually describes. This is because the society or community is so homogeneous that it is not necessary.[73] There are 'shared beliefs and cultural practices' which can be transmitted, as long as this is done in a non-repressive way. These may include religion, in societies with little religious diversity the majority religion may be presented as normative within the common school (ibid., 246).

It is interesting to note that it is not religion as such that should not be transmitted in the common school, only religion that is controversial. Is this then the same as a 'separate' religious school, only it is for the majority? No, not quite, because the religion is not to be transmitted in the same way. It should 'stop short of the sort of substantial religious formation that might take place in a religious school' (ibid.). He says that the reason for this is that Liberalism 2 is committed to non-repression, obviously then as opposed to religious schools. But he cannot mean that substantial religious formation is repressive, not necessarily anyway. The way he further explains the non-neutral liberal school's relation to religion is very similar to his liberal religious school: religion is part of the primary culture, and critical reflection should be encouraged.

He also says that it may only be the cultural aspects of the religion that can be normative in this common school, not the religious beliefs. If this is the case, what is left are some cultural religious values only. The only difference between a Liberalism 1-school and a Liberalism 2-school will then be that the latter has a few more public, or common, values. In principle they are both the same: schools that try to educate without wanting to transmit one religion or secular world view as true.

When McLaughlin argues for common education that is neutral between world views or theories of the good, it is not primarily because he thinks this is a good and desirable kind of education, but because it is necessary in a democratic, pluralistic society. People disagree in these questions, and no one group can force its own world view or faith on others.

If my argument is valid, the liberal no-standpoint school will also transmit to the pupils certain world view presuppositions, particularly a God-less and purpose-less reality. Then any kind of school will 'force' a view on its pupils. This makes the distinction between common and separate schools problematic. All schools are 'separate' in having a particular world view ethos. The only difference is in numbers, the common school is the one where the majority goes.

Maybe it would be better to talk about majority and minority schools, emphasizing that when it comes to what they convey, none is more neutral or separate than the others. Using such notions might be a push towards being more aware of and explicit about the influence the majority school gives. This might in turn help us away from the fear of indoctrination, of transmitting something that binds the pupils. B. Mitchell quotes Gilbert Murray:

Every man who possesses real vitality can be seen as the resultant of two forces. He is first the child of a particular age, society, convention; of what we may call in one word a tradition. He is secondly, in one degree or another, a rebel against that tradition. And the best traditions make the best rebels. (Mitchell 1980a, 144)

And Mitchell goes on:

Gilbert Murray, I suggest, gets the balance right. We have, as educators, to make our pupils heirs to a tradition in such a manner that in due course, they are free to appropriate it, modify it, develop it or reject it. If we decline to do this, through fear of exerting undue influence upon them, they will not thereby be enabled to discover some genuinely original alternative of their own; they will simply absorb uncritically the current fashions of the day and make what they can of them. (Ibid.)

CHAPTER 6

Christianity in the Non-Neutral State School

Having argued that liberal education is no more neutral in terms of transmitting world view aspects than Christian or any other education, the question is: What then about the common, or majority, school? We may have separate schools for the minorities, but my main concern is with the school where the majority of the children will be. When it cannot be neutral, what ought the basis to be, what kind of world view presuppositions should the education be based on and transmit? If it is right that all children are brought up believers, secular or religious, and that school cannot but contribute, what should this contribution be? There are only two kinds of choice, says the Norwegian theologian P. Gravem. One is which tradition the school should adhere to, the other whether this should be done openly or not (Gravem 1992, 114).

My reply to this is in four parts. First, I claim that the question about the school's upbringing is the parents' responsibility. Then, given that Christian education is not an obvious choice for all parents, I argue that it has many advantages compared to liberal education, that it is better as education. In the third part of my reply, which occupies the main part of this chapter, I discuss in what areas and to what extent it is possible to give Christian education in a state school with teachers of any faith. I also ask whether some of the Christian influence might be kept if the school's basis were made secular. Finally, I reflect on the consequences a 'watered down' Christian education might have for people's understanding of Christianity and Christian education.

Although this chapter, in particular the third part, is primarily related to the situation in Norway with its Christian basis for the state school, much of the discussion is relevant for other countries as well, including England and other countries where the majority denomination is not Lutheran. Most western countries have a large majority of people who are what Asheim would call cultural Christians (see above, p. 30). Although they would not call themselves practising or committed Christians, their thinking is to a smaller or larger degree influenced by a Christian world view, and they would not necessarily want a secular upbringing for their children.

6.1 Deciding the basis of state education

6.1.1 Parents' rights and responsibility

The starting point for my deliberations is that it is the parents' right and responsibility to decide the upbringing for their children, also in schools and other institutions. It is common to argue that parents should be responsible for the religious upbringing of their children. My claim throughout this argument has been that the religious upbringing, and similarly upbringing within a secular world view, is something that cannot be separated from education in general. Therefore parents are responsible for the world view influence in all education.

The state can require that a certain content be taught, and it can also put some limits to which values may be transmitted, barring an education that conveys violence, racism or other attitudes that will harm individuals and the society. But apart from this, the underlying view of reality and purpose of life are outside its 'legitimate province', to borrow an expression from Hirst (Hirst 1965/1974, 181).

Strike admits that his pragmatic liberalism is not enough as a basis for education. But he cannot see any alternative, because separate schools will not be able to make the pupils good citizens, and they are likely to indoctrinate (Strike 1994,18). McLaughlin says that from within the liberal point of view, liberal education is regarded as significantly objective and is therefore to be made compulsory.

> Whilst full 'objectivity' is unattainable in practice - and maybe theoretically too - this form of education is seen as one which approaches most closely to the ideal. This claim licenses the conclusions that (a) it should be made available to, and compulsory for, all children - in the face, if necessary, of parental objections; and that (b) such a requirement gives rise to no substantial worries about indoctrination or illicit 'moulding'. (McLaughlin 1991, 142)

To find out where the limit is for what society cannot accept, is not straight forward. To require the education to be liberal may lead into what Skjervheim calls 'the liberal dilemma': forcing people to be liberal (see above, p. 65). But this again certainly depends on what is meant by liberal, whether it means more than not harming the child 'by actually preventing the development of her autonomy' (Taylor 1996, 142).

The state can require education, but not direct it, says J. S. Mill (Hull 1982, xi). It is illiberal to force everybody into any kind of education, saying 'this is the good education'. Thus, the question of the basis of education is a question that the state should not decide, particularly not a liberal state. The parents must be responsible and make the decision.

This is in line with international conventions, and it is also stated in the first clause in the Norwegian 1969 Education Act. Crittenden advocates parents' right to choose the fundamental values for their children's education, also in school. He says that preventing such choice

> would seriously violate the pluralist principle of respect for diversity in areas of belief where people may reasonably differ. It would also shift the authority to make educational decisions on the important values at issue from parents to other adults in the society. Apart from the undesirable conflict between informal family education and schooling, there is no good reason to assume that on the matters being considered other adults would generally choose more wisely for children than their own parents. (Crittenden 1988, 126)

So the parents' own decision about faith or conviction is the starting point, that is what the school should be based on and transmit. The obvious problem, however, is that in our societies, parents have different faiths and convictions, pupils have different backgrounds. How do we come to terms with this? As far back as 1965, P.H. Hirst said that the only consistent alternative is 'the thorough-going pluralist system mentioned earlier in which maintained schools offering education according to different religious principles are readily available to all children' (Hirst 1965/1974, 184).

In a liberal democracy, the only solution is the provision of different schools. This is also the best guarantee against institutional indoctrination (Thiessen 1993, 273-5).

On the other hand, there are advantages in having a school for all, particularly in a country like Norway, where in many places communities are small and far apart. So I would argue for the same school for all children as long as possible, without forcing anybody. On one side, we should try to make the majority school attractive for as many as possible, without making its basis inconsistent, and being very clear and explicit about this basis. On the other side, there should be freedom and economical support to start minority schools for those who find that the majority school gives an upbringing that they do not want.

6.1.2 Arguments for Christian education in the state school

Some countries have many large religious or world view groups (Germany, the Netherlands), and it may be natural to have parallel state school systems. Other countries, like Norway, have one majority and several minorities, here it is more natural to have one state school and allow for minority schools in addition.

If the majority of parents actually want secular liberal schools, then that is what they should get, although such schools might be argued against on educational grounds. If they want Christian state schools, neither can there be any objection to that. The point is that the parents are responsible, not the state. But not all parents are convinced what they want for their children.

Although most people in Norway are members of Christian churches, far from all of them are practising Christians, and there is a continuum within the state church from practising Christians at one end to people with hardly any contact with the church and only a vague belief in some kind of God at the other.[74] Similar situations may be found in many countries. A. Brown says about England that '[a] number of parents who choose not to attend church themselves still believe it important for their children to be inducted into the teachings and beliefs of Christianity'. He quotes the archbishop of Canterbury, Dr George Carey, from 1991: 'Most of our fellow citizens do believe in God, do pray and do believe that Christian morality is important, however tenuous their links may be with the local church' (Brown 1992, 12).

Thus, having left the decision with the parents, there is still room for argument about the basis for the state school. Not everybody knows what the different alternatives imply, and much information is needed. In many countries the idea of the liberal, world view neutral school is so prevailing that even if it is shown not to hold water, this education may still be thought to be the best.

I would argue that Christian education is not only as good as secular liberal education, it is actually better. In such an argument, I certainly have to use 'public' reasons, i.e. arguments that make sense also to non-Christians and which they may agree with. I would argue that Christian, Lutheran education has more potential in counteracting the negative forces of selfishness and materialism in today's society and will therefore give better lives both to individuals and societies.

Christian education is better according to educational criteria: better for personal development, better for citizenship, and with a more realistic view of human nature, including autonomy. It also makes it easier for the pupils to understand what Christianity - and therefore also other religions and world views - are about, and thus challenges them to take a stand.

These may sound like very pragmatic arguments - where is the claim about this being the Truth? T.S. Eliot said that the worst thing we can do is to advocate Christianity because it is benevolent, not because it is true. Is it not as bad to advocate Christian education because it is useful instead of because it is true? That is not quite my line of thought. I *am* advocating Christianity, or Christian education, because it is true. That is the main reason. But this would not be a reason for non-believers. Believing, however, that it is true, includes believing that it is the best education for anybody, for individuals and society. There are many reasons for this, some of which will be focused on in the following.

CHRISTIAN EDUCATION IS REALISTIC

When it comes to the view of human nature and the place of good and evil, Christianity corresponds better with the facts than most forms of humanism.[75] The way Christianity describes people as able to do good, but also as self-centred, as wilfully harming others, gives a more realistic picture of humankind than a belief that people are basically good and that it is the circumstances that are the source of all evil.

This means that in terms of happiness, success and well-being as aims in life, Christianity is fairly modest. It teaches that evil and suffering will always be there, and that the pupils must not believe that they will always be able to follow their plans and wishes. Christian education will teach that it is possible to lead a good life without success in worldly terms. The real happiness depends on our relationship with God, which is not dependent on good health, a good job, wealth, etc. Happiness is also a result of giving rather than receiving, which is something that is independent of the outer circumstances too. It is a question of loving God and our neighbour. Christian happiness can be found in poor families, in poor countries, in circumstances where there is little choice in any area.

This realistic view of life and human nature is also important for teachers in a number of ways. However good teachers they are, the pupils will never become angels. They know that both the pupils, their colleagues and they themselves are not only caring and loving, but also selfish and proud. They can help the pupils to learn to know themselves in this way, learn that there are impulses they have to strive to resist, learn that they have to work hard to become good people, it is not something they automatically are. This is a better starting point for personal growth and development than humanism's more optimistic view of human nature.

IT IS OTHER-CONCERNED

Liberal education could probably be more other-concerned than how it is often described, but Christian education will restrain selfishness more than liberal education ever could. Love, mercy and compassion are central. There is a focus on responsibility towards other people, responsibility to God for how we use our resources, a focus away from self and towards our neighbour's good life. It should not be necessary to argue that less self-centred people are better citizens.

Protestant Christianity, particularly in a conservative or evangelical version, has sometimes been said to be very individualistic. And in one sense it is right and should be so, because the emphasis is on the individual's relationship with God, not on formally belonging to the church. Ethically, however, the tendency to regard individual ethics as more important than social ethics has been more problematic, but is recognized and being re-thought.

There is a strong potential in Christianity for solidarity and anti-individualism. This needs to be brought out and put into practice to counter today's individualistic liberalism. Attitudes to alcohol is a good example. Norwegian Labour leaders in the thirties argued for people becoming tee-totallers in solidarity with all the workers who had drink problems. Making it normal to refrain from drinking would make it easier for the latter to avoid problems. Today, a very common attitude is that everybody is responsible for keeping their own drinking under control, with no interest for the influence each person has on what is normal and which problems this 'normality' might create for others. Liberalism's limit for pursuing one's own well-being is that it should not harm others or limit their opportunities to pursue their own well-being. This is often understood in a very individualistic way, as if the only way I may harm others is directly, person-to-person.

It is not only the individuals' morality that makes up the society's morality, it also works the other way round: society's morality, also as expressed in mass media, becomes the individuals' morality. Communitarianism seems to have a point here, against liberalism, and maybe Christianity has been too much influenced by liberalism, too much focused on the individual. We have not realized, or not been willing to see, how individual, separate decisions together create the ethical ethos of society, and how this ethos influences the next generation, changes attitudes, changes laws, etc. The Bible's strong emphasis on loving our neighbour includes influencing society so it becomes a better place to live for everybody, particularly those who are weak in one sense or another.

IT IS FOR EVERYBODY, NOT ONLY THE MOST CAPABLE

Liberal education requires critical, rational thinking. Even the good life, at least according to J. White, requires critical, rational thinking. We lead a good life to the extent that we have chosen it ourselves, critically. This seems to mean that our intellectual capacity strongly influences to what degree we may get a good life. W. Galston says that '[a]t the heart of much modern liberal democratic thought is a (sometimes tacit) commitment to the Socratic proposition that the unexamined life is an unworthy life, that individual freedom is incompatible with ways of life guided by unquestioned authority or unswerving faith' (Galston 1989, 99).

If liberal education is about helping pupils to make rational, autonomous choices, then it cannot be of much help to those who have little of such capacities. According to White's theory, for instance, it is very difficult to see how mentally retarded children can get a good life at all, dependent as they are on others. But these are not the only ones, few are capable of becoming autonomous in the strong sense, at least not in more than a few areas. And we know that for all the upbringers' struggles to make the children reflect and make rational autonomous choices, a lot of them will nevertheless more or less continue within the framework and the thought patterns they were brought up within, thus not leading a good life, at least not in a pluralistic society.

Christianity claims that it is possible to lead a good life even if you depend on other people's choices, because the focus is not on who made the decision, but on the content of it. This does not mean that we may let our intellectual capacities sleep - they ought to be fully exercised, to the glory of God - but that such capacities are not necessary for a good life. The emphasis in the purpose of life and education in Christianity is on love, not on knowledge (Davis 1994, 6). Everybody can be a channel for God's love and thus serve him. Christian education can help everybody to a good life in service of others. Christianity tells us that everybody has the same worth, also those who cannot be 'useful' in the common sense of the word. It teaches us to love them and serve them and thus contribute to their good life.

CHRISTIAN EDUCATION IS EXPLICIT

Christian education does not pretend to be neutral. It is explicit about its presuppositions, it is explicit about its truth claims and its challenge to find and follow the Truth. World view pluralism is not regarded as something positive, as 'cherished pluralism', but as a challenge to assessing and comparing views, finding the truth. All this makes autonomy easier than in liberal education, because the alternatives are clearer and the personal challenge goes deeper.

In a different - for instance a thoroughly Christian - society, liberal education might stand out as something special and challenging. But even in our society it should be possible for it to be clearer, more distinct, if it stopped pretending to be neutral between world views. But whatever the society, Christianity is more well-defined and more concerned with truth than liberal humanism. It will therefore be a greater challenge to making a decision that goes right down to the question of what the meaning and purpose of life is. And this is necessary, for, as W. Galston says, 'the greatest threat to children in modern liberal societies is not that they will believe in something too deeply, but that they will believe in nothing very deeply at all' (Galston 1989, 101).

The Norwegian researcher on youth culture, P.O. Brunstad, says that today's children and young people are not concerned with truth and meaning.

> We might as well face it without delay: a great number of the next generation are neither seeking meaning, nor are they eager for knowledge or concerned about our culture in the traditional meaning. They have a very relaxed and easy attitude to the questions of absolute truths or fundamental meaning in life. As long as they have fun, feel fairly safe, can have exciting

experiences and have money enough to buy what they want, most of them
will think that life is good.
   ... They live to a large extent in the world of biology and senses and
show very little interest in binding political, cultural or religious systems
or institutions. To this is added an ironical attitude that makes it possible
for them to distance themselves and be free from most authorities and
connections. (Brunstad 1997, 6, my translation)

Young people have a multi-identity, says Brunstad. The idea that each
individual has an identity based on a coherent system of values, seems to be
disappearing (ibid.). It is possible to ask how far this is a result of so-called
neutral upbringing and education, of the influence from liberal humanism.
The view of the good life that he describes is not too unlike White's satisfaction of desires.
   I am not claiming that this is the result liberal education would want,
both White and others want certain basic, common values inculcated. It
might nevertheless be the result they are likely to get, given a realistic view
of human nature and its tendencies towards selfishness and materialism.
Autonomy's claim not to follow authorities blindly has turned into not being
bound to systems and authorities at all.
   A view of life like the one described by Brunstad is both individualistic
and irresponsible. A society cannot survive if everybody wants to be free
from all commitments. Explicit Christian education, with focus on truth,
love, and service, would have a different influence. It would also be explicit
about the purpose and meaning of life being to serve, trying to get the pupils
into the habit of looking for opportunities to serve others. To know that life
has a meaning is also educationally good, it gives direction and meaning
also to education. As R.T. Allen says, if life has no meaning, maybe as
educators we ought to pretend that it has, to give meaning to education
(Allen 1991, 50-55).

6.2 Christian education in the state school

One thing is what is desirable, another what is actually desired, and a third
question is what is possible. If the majority of parents should want Christian
education in the state school, could the school provide it?
   K. Williams argues that a religious ethos is justifiable in state schools.
Neutrality is impossible, liberal education transmits not only certain values,
but a world view (Williams 1992, 565). On the other hand, many of the
central values in Christianity are also acceptable to non-believers (ibid.,
569). In any case it is important to take into account that the ethos of a
school 'is not something which can be imposed ... A school ethos must
emerge from the genuinely held convictions and aspirations of parents and
teachers' (ibid., 562-3). Therefore what the law says about the ethos or

basis for the school is only of limited importance. Whatever the parents want, if a school's Christian basis is to be more than empty words on a piece of paper, it has to be in line with the teachers' own beliefs and values, at least to a certain extent.

In Norway, Christianity has always been an important part of the education in the state school. For most of the time, most teachers have not found this difficult, even if they were not believers. Christianity was part of the culture and something that everybody was part of. Non-Christian teachers would think and teach that Christian ethics was right, and they would more or less live according to it. They would say set prayers (e.g. Our Father) with the children, and they would teach Christianity without questioning its truth. They were so-called cultural Christians. According to Asheim's distinction, their 'tro' was belief, not faith (see above, pp. 30-31).

It was common to say that as long as the teachers were loyal and showed respect for the Christian basis, this was enough. Even from a Christian point of view, it was said that as long as teachers taught Christianity properly, having good knowledge and understanding, it was not crucial whether they believed or not. And maybe it did not matter all that much, say fifty years ago, when society was fairly homogeneous and a Christian world view was shared by a vast majority. A Christian understanding of the world, with God as the centre, would often be assumed by the pupils, even if it was not made explicit. Christianity was in a way the default position, the position that was assumed if nothing else was clearly conveyed, the framework all knowledge was understood within. There could be a kind of Christian ethos in the school even without teachers who were practising Christians.

This is no longer the case, although Christianity still seems to have a stronger position in Norway than in England. Adults, including teachers, who are not practising Christians, will more often than not convey a non-Christian view of life and reality, a view where God is, at the best, marginal. It probably seems unlikely that in such a situation, the majority of parents would want Christian education, but that is the case.

More than 80% have their children baptized (Årbok for Den norske kirke 1997, 8), declaring that they want them to be brought up in the Christian faith. Whether they really mean this has been discussed, some people argue that they only want the traditional 'christening' and family gathering. However, the clergy are aware of this and normally discuss it with parents and godparents beforehand. Research shows that parents want more of a Christian upbringing for their children than they feel they can provide themselves (Evenshaug & Hallen 1981, 125). What parents think Christian education actually consists in, is difficult to tell, but a vast majority clearly want some sort of Christian education for their children.

So if ever it were true, it is true today that Christian education requires Christian teachers, Christian role models, otherwise it can hardly be conveyed that God is a living reality. But since the state school cannot require a specific faith in its teachers, it seems to be impossible to expect Christian education in such schools in general.

What then? Is the conclusion that the school has to give secular education after all, whatever the parents want? Some may argue like that, but that is again an example of 'religion as icing on the cake'-thinking. If the school were to be agnostic, that would create similar problems for non-agnostic teachers. They would have to convey something that they did not believe was true.

Are the options only two - either a fully Christian education such as I described in chapter two, or a fully secular education? I believe it is possible to have something in between, a kind of 'watered down', culturally Christian education. In some ways that is what we have in Norway today, but I believe it is possible to have a stronger Christian influence than we find in many schools. It is not only possible, but also good that education should be as Christian as possible. According to Luther's model of the two governments, good citizens is a worthwhile aim, even if they do not believe in God. And good citizens are basically people who are concerned with the good of others more than with their own. Whether this should actually be called Christian education is a different matter, to which I shall return later.

It is obvious that the world view influence of a school does not depend on the teachers only. Although other staff will normally not spend so much time with the pupils, they too influence the ethos of the school. Choice of subjects and content are important, so are textbooks and other material, and rules and regulations. When I, nevertheless, in the following focus on the teachers, it is because there lies the greatest challenge. 'Skulen er læraren' - 'the school is the teacher', is an old saying (Kvam 1993, 8).

An ethos cannot be imposed, K. Williams said. Subjects may be chosen and books written from a Christian perspective, but the choosers and writers will not be in the classroom. The teachers are there, they cannot avoid being role models,[76] they have to a large degree to *live* what is to be conveyed. And they must be honest more than anything, says M. Donley. 'All one can do is be aware in one's own mind of what it is that one is committed to ... and, secondly, to make no secret of one's commitment to one's pupils ... Total honesty and openness is what children deserve, and all they will respect' (Donley 1992, 188-9).

Christian education in state schools raises a lot of questions: How do we avoid inconsistencies for the pupils between what the teachers say and what their lives say? How is it possible to ask teachers to give Christian education without infringing on their integrity? What is it possible - and right - to ask non-Christian teachers to do? Part of the answer is to look for aspects of a Christian world view that might be consistent with other world views that teachers might have, aspects that are not exclusively Christian. It is also, however, important to keep in mind that the teachers, like the rest of the population, are not either committed Christians or committed atheists. Most of them will be somewhere in between, with some kind of belief in God. This will be the background against which I shall discuss some of the most important aspects of Christian education.

6.2.1 Ethical values

In many ways, ethics may be the easiest area to come to terms with. There are a lot of Christian values and norms that are found both in other religions and in secular world views. The Norwegian National Curriculum has since the early seventies used the phrase 'Christian and humanistic' about the values the school is to transmit. The new National Curriculum mentions 'human equality and the dignity of man, ... charity, brotherhood and hope' (Core Curriculum 1993/1997, 7). The old one had the well-known list of truth, justice, loyalty, love of one's neighbour, solidarity, responsibility and tolerance (Curriculum Guidelines 1987/1990, 18).

Christian ethics is based on the Bible. It is also rational and possible to defend from within many other frameworks. So there should not be any impossible obstacles to having biblical values and norms as a guide for life in school, both for the teachers themselves, and as norms for the habits they try to get the pupils into. It is important, though, thinking of the teachers as role models, that the difference there often is between how we live and how we think we ought to live, is emphasized with the pupils. Teachers are also struggling to do what they think right, and not always succeeding. If something wrong is done against pupils, asking for forgiveness is both necessary and a good opportunity to talk about the difference between ideals and practice.

Although in many ways Christian ethics is not a problem in state schools, I would like to draw attention to three areas that may create problems.

The first is that there are central Christian values that are not central in other world views, notably in secular humanism. These may be either ignored or given a very low priority. Values like humility, moderation, self-control and obedience might be mentioned, and also the notions of going the second mile and turning the other cheek. H. Bringeland has coined the concept 'bremseverdier' - 'brake-values' - for values such as these, which set limits and ask us to refrain from doing or saying things (Bringeland 1993, 37).

These 'brake-values' are aspects of Christian ethics that may be particularly important to transmit in our society. Although they may not be central in the teacher's world view, they are fairly likely to be consistent with it and therefore something it might be possible for him or her to convey with integrity. Another side of this is that values like the ones mentioned are quite contrary to materialism and therefore to a lot of teachers' practised world view, whatever their confessed one is. An emphasis on them may even help teachers of many convictions, including Christians, to live accordingly.

The second problem is the subjectivism and relativism found in many people's thoughts on ethics, not always backed by much reasoning or reflection. There is a fear of saying that anything is absolute, particularly in areas where people disagree. In school, this is most obviously a problem in what is taught and talked about explicitly, when the focus is on what we *say* about true and right. In Christian education pupils should be taught to base their ethical reflection on the Bible. Some teachers might find this unproblematic, others might teach how to think from the Bible as a basis but would say that this is only one way among others.

Other religions certainly also believe in objective, given norms. And forms of humanism too argue for objectively given values and norms, although they are not given by any god (Aadnanes 1992, 64-5). Teachers who believe that certain norms and values that are to be taught are objectively given, should say so, whatever their reason for believing it. From a Christian point of view, and from an educational point of view in general, it is better that they state what they believe is right and give both their own and other reasons for it, than that they convey a vague 'it is all up to you' or 'it is not really important what you believe' attitude.

If teachers find that they disagree with Christian ethics, the only solution seems to be that they try to go along with it as long as they can, and then are honest and open about their own conviction, both to pupils and to parents. The way this is done should certainly take into account the age and maturity of the pupils, and also the diversity of the backgrounds in the classroom. Such openness can - and must - be combined with respect for parents and children and their convictions, and also with close co-operation with the parents so that they can follow up at home what is said at school.

The last problem or challenge concerns motivation. It is important to emphasize that there are common values, that whatever our background we agree on values and norms that should be basic in society. Christian ethics explains this by what is called 'natural law', i.e. that morality is part of how we are created and therefore this law, 'in principle, can be discovered by all persons who use their reasons' (Langford 1985, 26). To regard the common values as common is part of being human.

But it is also important to underline that these values are part of different frameworks of belief and therefore may have different priorities and motivations. The basic motivation in Christian ethics is that it is for the good of our neighbour, which should be possible to use in any framework. The pupils must be taught how the Bible explains and motivates, but all pupils should also be helped to see the values and norms taught from within their own framework, related to their own motivation. Christian education should certainly help Muslim pupils to understand love, honesty, tolerance, etc. as part of their own faith, and similarly for others.

Nothing of what has been discussed in this section requires faith, although an emphasis on the Bible may require fairly strong beliefs about Christianity being the true or right religion. It requires, however, teachers who see other-concern as an important purpose of education. It also requires that teachers are willing to work on their own ethics and morality, to make clear to themselves where they stand in relationship to what they are asked to teach and convey. They might also reflect on the possibility to make the gap between the two smaller by changing their own theory or practice.

6.2.2 Service as the meaning of life

In Christian education, service is to be taught as the meaning and purpose of life. Is this something non-Christian teachers could be asked to do? If they have no personal relationship with God, they would hardly believe that service for God is the meaning of life. But most people might regard serving others, or doing good to them, as meaningful, which is how service for God is understood in the secular government. Both cultural Christians, people of other religions and people with a secular humanistic world view might find that serving their neighbours is meaningful and consistent with their conviction about the purpose of life. I can see no reason why well-being as desire satisfaction is a more natural aim than service for others, even in secular education.

If we think of habits and actions, serving others would normally mean the same as doing good to them. But for some people there may be a difference in attitude, because 'service' to them includes a notion of subservience or submissiveness: the others tell me what they want, and I do it. Also, if I 'turn the other cheek' to somebody, he or she may abuse me. 'Doing good', however, is more active. It is my own initiative, I am in control. I may also, with such an attitude, claim my own rights.

I think the reason why 'service' gets this meaning is that God is out of the picture. It is the same setting as with autonomy: if there is no God to relate to, I am either my own master or I am ruled by other people. If, on the other hand, God is my master, neither of these is true (see above, 2.2.3). When it comes to service, the important difference is that Christians primarily serve God and are responsible to him. That is the perspective that makes it impossible to be a doormat for others.

If it is the case that the concept of 'service' has these - non-biblical - connotations of subservience or submissiveness for many teachers, it may be impossible to have it as an aim for education. But at least aspects of it could be conveyed: solidarity, concern for others, the habit of looking for ways of helping people, etc. There is, however, a danger in the 'doing good to others'-attitude too, in that it may include a feeling not only of being in control, but also of knowing best, which may lead to paternalism and forcing things on others.

One thing is to talk about serving, doing good to or helping others as something good and worthwhile. It is stronger to say that it is the meaning of life. But here, too, teachers may have and convey a view that has more or less Christian thinking in it. Even if they do not regard it as the ultimate meaning, or the over-arching purpose, it might be one among others. And even if they see it as primarily a duty, something they ought to do, it is a common experience that helping others is rewarding. This experience they can help the pupils to get by leading them into other-concerned habits and attitudes, and it may in turn give at least a feeling of meaning or purpose, even if they do not believe that this is what they are created for.

It should not be necessary to argue that a society of other-concerned, serving people will be a better one than one of self-centred people concerned primarily with their own rights. But Brunstad's description of today's youth culture gives cause for concern and is a challenge to upbringers and educators. Service is mainly taught by example and habit formation, through the school ethos. But it is probably also necessary to talk about, to make the pupils aware of the consequences of various kinds of behaviour. Teachers should be servants themselves, or at least other-concerned people.

It is a question of focusing not only on others rather than myself, but on the weakest others, those who have nobody else to help them, those who are lonely, poor, strangers. This attitude may also be learned through the teachers' way of helping the pupils and talking about helping, and talking about others in general. Creativity is important, both on the teacher's part, and helping the pupils to develop their own creative thinking related to giving help and joy to others.

S. Fowler claims that in secular education, mastery is the most valued aim. '[T]he chief end of learning is increased power for human mastery. Behind this dominant educational value is the life value that values human life by the power to exercise mastery' (Fowler 1990b, 70-71). Changing this for the service of love, he says, will transform the whole of our educational practice, for instance what we think about assessment.

> It will transform our approach to the assessment of student learning. No longer will we be satisfied to assess students on their mastery of concepts and skills alone. We will want to assess how effectively these concepts and skills have been integrated in a wisdom that shows understanding and appreciation leading to responsible action.
>
> No longer will we single out the student with a superior power of knowledge for special honour and acclaim. We will help that student to recognise the responsibility for the service of others in this superior power of knowledge. (Ibid., 72)

Without going into the discussion about which aspects should be formally assessed, I would argue that an emphasis on responsibility for using one's talents for the good of others, individually and as a society, would contribute to better persons and better citizens being the result of education.

It is also something any teacher could do, regardless of their world view. As well as J. White wanting to inculcate certain basic values and dispositions that are not to be questioned, trying to balance self-interested desire satisfaction and other-concern, the school might want to inculcate a disposition to focus on other people's needs.

6.2.3 The curriculum

Although the curriculum has not been a topic in my discussion so far, it would make sense to include a few comments about it now, since education being Christian also will influence the content. McLaughlin says that 'the general curriculum of the religious school might have a particular flavour or series of emphases' (see above, p. 129). Teachers spend most of their time teaching certain subjects, and the question is whether non-Christian teachers might be expected to give this flavour or these emphases to their teaching.

I. Asheim talks about values being conveyed and taught through the school subjects (Asheim 1978, 126). And Allen shows how choice of both subjects and subject content carry with them metaphysical standpoints (Allen 1989, 162-8). The subjects, the content, shape the pupils' view of what the world is like and who they are, both by what is taught and what is not taught, if not explicitly, so by implication.

There is no one Christian curriculum, it is a question both of what the pupils need in the particular society they live in and of their individual abilities and interests.[77] But the purpose of service, the other-concernedness, will also permeate the way the curriculum is presented. It will not be as something they primarily need to get good exam results, or a good job, but as something they need to be able to understand other people and the society, to be able to help and to influence. In order to do that, it might be necessary to get good exam results, but these are means, not ends. This attitude to learning might be difficult for many people to actually convey, but that would, I suggest, be more due to the influence of materialism in our society than to any world view principle.

But how would Christianity actually influence the choice of subjects and their content? One example is that in Mathematics, instead of using examples about people buying and spending money on themselves, the examples could for instance be about giving to charities (Charis Mathematics 1996, 31-45). Such changes could hardly be any problem for non-Christian teachers.

The other example I would like to use is about the teaching of foreign languages, commenting on J. White's view in his discussion of what the curriculum in education for the good life should be. White does not see any need for a foreign language to be compulsory (White 1990, 153). In most other countries, this is a necessity if you want to be able to communicate with foreigners, this is not so for English people. But there is another argument for learning a foreign language, even more important for those who do not have to, and that is that it is a marvellous help in understanding other people better.

English people who always talk to others in their own language, cannot understand what it is like for others to try to express themselves in a foreign language. It is not only the words, the language is also the key into understanding culture, ways of thinking, beliefs, etc. Trying to master another language will make them aware of how easily misunderstandings can occur, and how likely they themselves are to misunderstand. This is extremely important in a small, but fragmented world where conflicts and wars are the order of the day.

Even learning French or Spanish for going on holiday would help, but better still would be Croatian, or another language spoken by refugees or minorities who have problems finding their feet in England. The weak, the poor, the strangers. Maybe teaching an Asian or African language instead of French would help combat racism? The pupils would learn not only the language, but also other aspects of the culture, to help understand and build relationships. It is not only a question of which language is taught, but also why, and therefore how, it is taught. Even French does not have to be motivated by and focused on going on holiday and buying things, it may be focused on French people we meet at home and how we may show them kindness and hospitality.

Focusing on content, this is an example of what it means that the education is Christian. Obviously faith is not required to teach like this. The education belongs in the secular government, the government of reason, where we are trying to help the pupils to become good citizens. Starting from the biblical thought of love and service helps us to see different reasons for and approaches to teaching ordinary subjects.

6.2.4 View of human nature

Is it necessary to be a Christian to convey a Christian view of human nature to the pupils? The answer depends both on which aspect we focus on and on the individual teacher's conviction. For secular teachers, being created by God would hardly make sense, neither would eternal life. This means that it cannot be expected that such teachers convey these aspects as part of the ethos of the school. They may certainly talk about them as something Christians believe, but they will not be naturally integrated in the life as a whole.

When it comes to conveying the equal and infinite worth of every person, the situation is a little more complex. From a Jewish perspective, A.J. Heschel claims that belief in God is necessary for giving the individual unique value:

In terms of the cosmic process, all of human history counts as much as a match struck in the darkness, and the claim that there is unique and eternal value to the life of the individual must be dismissed as an absurdity ... Only if there is a God who cares, a God to whom the life of every individual is an event - and not only a part of an infinite process - then our sense for the sanctity and preciousness of the individual man may be maintained. (Heschel 1959/1972, 161)

Because of the long Christian tradition in Norway, this view of the individual's value and preciousness, even sanctity, is more or less taken as read, whatever people's relation to God is. Many of the teachers have some kind of belief in God, but even without, the belief that every person has infinite value is still there. Some of them may express this belief using biblical terms, others not. For the pupils, it is more important that they feel treated as unique and of equal worth than how the teachers express their belief.

Many pupils feel, for different reasons, that they are failures in school. They are worthless, or at least worth less than others. There is a constant danger of identifying people's worth with their reasoning, their abilities, their actions, their morality, thus making some people more worth than others. In Christianity there is a constant reminder that this is wrong, both in the fact that we are created in the image of God, and also in Jesus' lifting up and loving the children, the poor, the outcast. All differences between us are irrelevant compared to what is similar: God created each one and loves each one.

Secular humanism is not always clear about what makes a person a person, why people are different from and worth more than animals. Often it is said that it is rationality that makes us human. Other religions and world views have other answers. But even if there is uncertainty and disagreement about the 'why', most people would agree that everybody has the same value. It should therefore be no problem for teachers to convey this with integrity, at least in action and attitudes. It should be demonstrated in the way they relate to the pupils by loving them all, respecting them, trying to give every one tasks that can help them to grow.

The structures of school and society sometimes prevent us from conveying what we want and ought to convey. In today's school the danger of valuing pupils according to their academic abilities and achievement is great. They are put in different groups and thereby labelled, explicitly or implicitly. '[T]here is little purpose in telling pupils that they are all valued equally when all the signals the children receive from the organisation of the school tells them this isn't true' (Price, no date, 17). Christianity, with its focus on the value and dignity of the weak, can help to counteract the thinking that bright people are more valuable than others.

A Christian view of autonomy is one aspect that might be difficult to transmit for teachers who do not believe in God, because they are left with only the two options of being governed by oneself or by other people. Nothing can replace God, but from a Christian point of view, in ethical matters it is important for individuals to have something objective outside themselves, something to hold on to when selfishness or group pressure gets strong. Some objective, inculcated values might serve as such a 'governing body'. To be rational is not enough, our rationality must be based on something that helps us to view ourselves and society from the outside. According to what I argued in 6.2.1 and 6.2.2, it should be possible for teachers of any faith and conviction to inculcate some Christian values for this purpose.

I have argued that Christian education would emphasize responsibility more than autonomy. At least in Norway, this is not a problem, whatever the teacher's world view. Responsibility and learning to be responsible have been focused on over the last ten - fifteen years. Books have been written and projects run.[78] All teachers may not be able to talk about being responsible to God, but habits and attitudes of responsibility may be formed.

6.2.5 Teaching of Christianity

It is necessary in Christian education that Christianity is taught explicitly. The ethos of the school is important, the understanding that our whole life is related to God. But for the pupils to get to know God and understand what it means to believe in him, the Bible must be taught. They also need to be given the chance to take part in worship, although their integrity should be respected, allowing them to be onlookers rather than participants.

Other religions and secular world views should certainly also be taught, either in the same or in a different subject. They should be taught from the inside, so the members of each group can recognize and approve of what is said. The overall framework will, however, be Christianity. Pupils from non-Christian backgrounds should be offered an alternative subject to Christian RE. It should primarily teach their own faith or conviction, but Christianity and other religions and secular views should also be taught.

Non-Christian teachers should not be asked to lead worship, that would show lack of respect both for them and for Christians. But they can certainly teach Christianity, as long as they have enough knowledge, and respect. They can teach Bible stories and the Bible story, read the Bible with the pupils, let the stories stand on their own, and try to create a setting for a Bollnowian meeting (see above, p. 34). They can teach church history and ethics, and they can teach what the Christian faith is about, explain and discuss dogmas, help them to grasp the essence.

Nobody should be forced to teach Christianity if they feel it is difficult for them. But again, many teachers who would not call themselves practising or committed Christians, feel very strongly that Christianity is their own tradition, their own culture, even their own religion, and they see no great problems in teaching it. They would go to the Bible with respect.

It is possible for non-believers to a very high degree to present Christianity from the inside. This should also include teachers who have strong, non-Christian convictions, because they know something about the importance of faith and the necessity to present it correctly. Teachers who have made an autonomous decision about what to believe will have tried to understand other views from the inside before making up their mind and should thus be able to be good teachers in any view. Although teachers without faith cannot explain what the personal relationship with God is like from their own experience, they can use other people's experience to help the pupils understand.

But what do they do when the pupils start asking whether it is true? They are not good role models if they say it is the truth without believing it themselves. Also, the explicit answer will be compared with what they say and do outside the Christianity lessons. So they should be honest about their own beliefs and faith.

When the pupils ask, they deserve honest answers. According to their age and maturity, they should be told both the arguments about its truth and that in the end it is a question of faith, not of scientific proof. There are different ways of knowing something, knowing God is not the same as scientific knowledge. The presentation should not be full of 'but this is only belief', 'this is what the Christians mean', 'we do not know', etc. When they are presenting it from the inside, they are presenting it from the inside. With the older pupils, however, it is appropriate also to look at it from the outside, reflecting on what Christianity is and what the alternatives are.

Christian education cannot teach that all faiths and beliefs are equally good or right or true, but it can teach - and show - that all pupils are equal and of infinite value. It cannot say that 'your god is as good as my god', but saying this is not to show respect for other people's faith, it is rather to reduce it to something less important. Christianity's exclusive truth claim implies that in Christian education both teachers and pupils of non-Christian background are to be respected for what they believe is the truth.

Whether the teachers are Christians or not, a humble attitude towards the question of truth is crucial. Respect, love and creativity will help them to find good, individual solutions to dilemmas where the school's truth is not their own, and also where the school's truth is not the pupil's. If we want a state school for the cultural Christian majority, creative attempts to find individual solutions is the only way forward.

6.2.6 God-centred education

We have seen that in Christian education in a secularized society like ours, it is particularly important to make God's presence and relevance explicit.

That reality is God-centred and not human-centred is the central difference between Christianity and humanism, and this is the crucial question in the discussion about how far education can be Christian without Christian teachers.

If teachers do not believe in God, they cannot convey a view of life that is God-centred, because their life will not be God-centred. They cannot give an education where God is experienced as a living reality, a loving God to talk to and listen to, if they have no personal relationship with him. They cannot transmit in their life with the pupils that God has given us life with a purpose and a perspective beyond death. There is no way society can ask atheistic and agnostic teachers to provide this kind of Christian education, because they cannot do it.

What they could do towards this is to teach about God-centred lives in literature and history. If there are textbooks that do not exclude God from different topics, they can follow this up and in that way show how some people believe that God is relevant to various sides of life. It is possible to do something to make God visible, if not as the focus of reality, at least as the focus of reality for others, and as a possibility.

If this is the case about secular teachers, what then about teachers from other religions? The document 'Faith as the basis of education in a multi-faith multi-cultural country' (1990)[79] argues that a faith-based education ought to be an alternative to the secularist common education in Britain. It lists some beliefs and values that are common for various religious groups.
–   belief in a Transcendental Reality, in most religions called 'God'
–   belief in the existence of spirit in each human being
–   belief in primary, eternal, unchanging, fundamental values, such as Truth, Justice, Righteousness, Mercy, Love, Compassion and care towards all creation, etc.
–   belief in the need for Divine Guidance (Faith as ... 1990, 6)

Some aspects in Christian education could be easier to promote for believers in other religions than for secular people. Since both Judaism and Islam 'believe in one transcendent Deity' (ibid., 10), they may be able to convey a God-centred view of life with integrity. The problem is that the picture they will give of their God is different from the one the Bible gives. They have a more distant God, not one who became incarnate in Jesus of Nazareth, so even such a God-centred education would not be Christian. Even these monotheistic religions are so different in their most central beliefs that it is hardly possible to have education that is based on a general faith.

Non-Christian teachers might be able to do a lot towards making the education Christian. But would they want to do it? How would they think and feel about it? An important presupposition for them to keep in mind is that the reason why they are asked to do it is that they are the parents' helpers, and the parents want it. In this context it is not a question of Christianity being true or better than their own or any other view, but of being professional.

We might wonder whether some would feel inferior if they are asked to do their best to transmit a view of reality that is different from their own. I do not think this is a common feeling, but it is difficult to tell, it being an empirical matter where hardly any research is done. A couple of thoughts might be mentioned that are, at least, relevant in Norway. First, most teachers actually think that what they are giving is a kind of Christian education. That is what the law says, and that is their cultural tradition. Second, if they were asked to make education much more Christian than it is, they would probably object, claiming that they are teachers, not preachers. To change this attitude is, I believe, a long process.

I would like to add that my argument certainly does not imply that education being Christian is a guarantee for its being good education. For that, the teachers must also be good teachers. How good or bad the teachers are will normally rub off on the beliefs they confess, whatever these are. A bad atheistic teacher, for instance, does not make atheism attractive. This is probably even more crucial in Christian than in secular education, because Christians confess to believe in a God of love and mercy. If the Christian teachers do not show love and mercy, the education is neither Christian nor good, and the pupils may discard Christianity before even learning very much about it.

The Norwegian sociologist S. Skirbekk has argued that a society where religion gives meaning to reality and culture, functions better in many respects than our present naturalistic, hedonistic and individualistic culture. But to be useful, in the long run religion must be more than useful. It must be regarded as true, otherwise it will dissolve itself. P. Gravem says in his discussion of Skirbekk's claim that for a perspective to be plausible it is not enough that it functions. It must also be regarded as true (Gravem 1992, 122). Thus, Christianity cannot in the long run be transmitted in school just because it is useful, there must be at least some people who believe in its truth.

Faith in God is crucial to Christian education. It is God that is the centre of Christianity and makes it all coherent. It is this perspective that holds the secular and the spiritual governments together. How coherent the world view would be which an education based on cultural Christianity only would give, is not a topic to go into at this stage. But without the faith dimension, Christianity may well be perceived as a set of beliefs and practices only (see above, 4.1.1 and 4.1.2).

6.3 Christian education in a secular state school?

If the vast majority of Norwegian parents decided that they want secular humanistic education for their children, not Christian, and the law was changed according to this, what then about Christianity in school? Would that mean that all of the above would have to go? A parallel question to this is whether the English state school in some ways could give Christian education? There is no explicitly stated world view basis for the school, but secular humanism seems to be the *de facto* one.

It is implicit in my argument that a school based on a secular world view could give a kind of Christian education in certain areas. Because there are overlaps between Christianity and other world views, a number of aspects of Christian education could still have room there, only with a different label. Some of the ethical values, focus on other-concern, the uniqueness and worth of persons, and teaching about Christianity could all be there. From a Christian educational point of view, this is valuable, because Christian education is regarded as the best education.

There are overlaps, but the aspects would be part of different wholes. The ethos of a secular humanistic school would be different from a Christian one, based on a different view of reality. Content would be chosen and textbooks written from a human-centred perspective on life. But secular humanism is less well defined than Christianity. It may be atheistic, or it may be agnostic. It may have a materialistic orientation, but it may be influenced in a more spiritual direction. It may be very individualistic, but it may also be focused on the community. In societies which for centuries have had a Christian and humanistic tradition, it is possible to argue for a fairly 'Christianized' humanistic education, although secular.

Also in a secular humanistic state school there will be teachers who do not share the school's basis. The same argument that was made for Christian education is valid here, namely that the teachers should try to be loyal as far as possible, but also honest and open. This school's basis will give a framework for understanding Christianity that does not convey it as the truth. But Christian pupils, and all others who are not secular humanists, should be offered a separate subject where their own faith is taught from its own perspective.

Is it important what the 'label' of the state school's education is? Because of the teachers, and also because of the parents being somewhere 'in between', the school may more or less convey the same ethical values, the same view of human nature, etc., whatever it is called in formal documents. Is it necessary to call it anything at all?

R.T. Allen writes about metaphysical beliefs and assumptions acting as pumps or as filters in relation to education. If they act as pumps, they require certain policies, all the decisions about education are deduced from the philosophical premises. If, however, the beliefs act as filters, they only permit or debar educational policies, they stop or do not stop a certain content or certain methods from being part of the education (Allen 1989, 164). In the same way, a formal link to Christianity or secular humanism would make different filters, letting different things through.

In many areas humanism would be a coarser filter, letting through both Christian and non-Christian values and attitudes. It would for instance allow for more materialism, more individualism, more atheism, more openness towards various New Age types of spirituality (astrology, occultism, etc.). Many of these openings would not help the school in its work towards good citizens. So its being defined as Christian or secular humanist does make a difference, if not so much to how the school is at the moment, then at least to its development.

I have so far, because of the situation in Norway, regarded the alternative to Christian education as being education based on traditional, secular humanism, where the humanistic basis is made explicit and regarded as a particular world view. Another possibility is to choose Mitchell's liberal humanism, with its few basic values and its professed neutrality between versions of the good life. This may be more similar to England's liberal, pluralistic education that tries not to take a stand between world views. Then the picture will be different. A few Christian values may still be conveyed as common values, necessary for our life together in a society. But many values, along with the view of human nature and the meaning of life, will have to be presented as options, as something the pupils may choose if they are meaningful for them. The question of truth becomes irrelevant.

Liberal humanistic education might seem more positive to religion than straight forward and explicit secular humanistic education, but that is only on the surface. Not only will the ethos of such a school be atheistic, but it will prevent thorough understanding of both Christianity and other world views. They will not even be presented as what they are - total and fundamental perspectives on life and death. Different world views may certainly be taught from the inside, giving a fair presentation of each. But the fact that they are all presented as equally valid will add to the general ethos of the school and make the claims from them seem less serious. As L. Newbigin says,

> A 'religion' which is simply one of a class, is no longer an ultimate commitment, a stance for living ... The Hindu acknowledges many ways to salvation ... but he understands them from the standpoint of the *Sanatanadharma*, the eternal order to which the ultimate key is found in the Upanishads. To suggest that the *Sanatanadharma* is itself just one of the possible ways of looking at things would be to cease to be a Hindu. (Newbigin 1977/1982, 98)

With its lack of emphasis on truth, liberal humanistic education still teaches something about truth, namely that in most areas there is none. People who believe that they are right, are wrong. They cannot have found the truth about reality and the meaning of life, because there is none. The fact that this kind of education tries to be silent about its own world view presuppositions, makes it difficult for the pupils to see this influence and be autonomous in relation to it. It is also hard to discover where it is contrary to their own faith or conviction. Also the parents may have difficulties in actually understanding what is going on and exercising their responsibility.

Also in this school the teachers will be role models, and they ought to be honest and open about their own view. But because of the setting, it may be harder for the pupils to understand how fundamentally different the world views are. The liberal humanist version of education has more difficulties than many others in including Christian aspects as something given, not just options.

6.4 Negative consequences of labelling common education 'Christian'

Will education given by mainly non-Christian teachers be Christian enough to carry this label? This would depend on many things, including how close to or distant from Christianity the teachers' own world views are. In Norway today, we find all degrees from very clearly Christian schools to definite secular ones.

That the school is by law required to give Christian upbringing is a filter that has, at least from a Christian point of view, positive educational consequences. This basis should guide choice of subjects, content, textbooks, etc., and also give some guidelines for what the teachers ought to say and do - or refrain from saying and doing. From the perspective of the secular government, the more Christian the education is, the better.

But there may also be negative consequences of having 'Christian' state schools. Not because of the Christian substance in the education, but because it is labelled 'Christian'. These consequences are mainly to do with the understanding people get of Christianity and Christian education, and they are worth taking into account when deciding whether to argue for the majority state school being called Christian or to work for it to be as Christian as possible without calling it so.

If education is called Christian and does in fact only have a few Christian aspects, one of the problems is that pupils may get a wrong picture of what Christianity is all about. This could particularly be a problem for non-Christian pupils who may not learn more about God and what it is to be a Christian than what they learn at school. If they do not have a teacher who is a practising Christian and who does not try to be neutral, the picture they get could be fragmented and wrong.

The most likely impression may be that Christianity consists of ethical values and rules and of a faith that is kept in a separate area and has nothing to do with everyday life. Or, in a time when many are looking for something else than materialism, Christianity may be regarded as something spiritual, something to fill people's need for harmony and wholeness. It could then become a means towards the aim of personal, spiritual satisfaction.

The teaching about Christianity may be good, but if the life of the school conveys a human-centred reality and not a God-centred one, the pupils may not see any connection between what is taught and their own lives. The school's ethos is an important influence as to the relevance of the Bible for people's lives. If not lived, what is taught easily becomes theoretical, abstract and irrelevant. If talking about God is limited to RE lessons, the pupils' understanding of God may be limited too. A faith that only adds something and does not change the whole of life is very little of a challenge to think about one's own life. Such education gives a very thin background for making a decision about following Christ or not.

If the school's basis is said to be Christian, this may also give a biased understanding of what Christian upbringing or education is. Parents, for instance, may believe that what the school gives is actually Christian upbringing. Many of them, though not practising Christians themselves, have at baptism promised to give their child a Christian upbringing. If formally this is what the school does, they may never learn that Christian upbringing is much more.

Teachers may also think like this, that Christian upbringing or education is what they give. Christian values and the explicit teaching of Christianity are often mentioned as what make today's Norwegian school Christian. From one point of view it is true, these aspects do make the education more Christian than if they had not been there. But this does not mean that these are all there is to Christian education. Non-Christian teachers may see that there is a personal aspect that they cannot convey, but they may think that it is a question of adding it to the ethical values etc., not of the faith being the centre of and transforming everything else.

Also pupils from Christian homes will be influenced by the way the school practices its Christian basis. They need a strong Christian influence at home to counteract the school's conveying that there are lots of areas of life where God and their faith are irrelevant. Christianity may become something that primarily belongs in home and church, not in schools and other places where they mix with non-Christians.

A different problem is that even Christian teachers and educationalists may be very influenced in their thinking about Christian education by what it is or can be in the state school. Most of the scholarly writing on Christian education in Norway is related to the state school, there is hardly anything done to explore what a Lutheran school might be like if we could start from scratch, with Christian teachers and with only the school laws setting limits.

The very few Lutheran Christian schools there are in Norway seem to be very similar to the state schools, only with more lessons in Christianity and more periods of worship. New Christian school movements in countries with secular state schools seem much more creative in defining and running their schools (e.g. Lambert 1994). This may partly have theological reasons, these movements often being influenced by Baptist or Reformed theology, but it is not unlikely that it also is due to their not being limited in their thinking by Christian state school traditions.

If we think radically, it may not only be the ethos of the school that should be different in Christian education. The whole structure may have to be changed, it may for instance not be possible to work towards service and love in a school structured for competition and mastery. Writing about Catholic education, A. Price claims that '[t]eachers should devote more time to talking to pupils - than to writing about them. Pastoral structures should be designed to create relationships and not to complete administration or to deal with problems'. And further: 'A distinctive school has a carefully worked out grouping policy - a distinctive school is one which knows that there is no such thing as a homogeneous group of human beings'[80] (Price, no date, 16-17).

A dilemma in Norway is that on the one hand, some Christians want to start separate Lutheran schools because they do not think the state schools, at least not in their area, are Christian enough. On the other hand, starting separate Christian schools will be a good argument against the Christian basis for the state school for those who want to get rid of it. It also sends out signals saying that the Christian education state schools can give, or at least are giving, is not good enough, and thus deprives state school teachers, Christians and non-Christians alike, of much-needed support as they try to do their best in a difficult situation.

The state school having a Christian basis may limit our thinking about Christian education, and so may the desire to keep this basis. It may stop us from working fundamentally on what Lutheran education could and should be in today's society. If the state school had a secular basis and people wanted to start separate Christian schools, we might even be forced into working more fundamentally than we do today on what Christian education is.

6.5 Conclusion

I started this work being puzzled by people's belief in world view neutral education. I still find it puzzling that such belief is possible, but I can see some reasons for it. One is purely pragmatic: in a democratic, pluralist society, which is also heavily influenced by individualism, it is important to have a common school, and this school must not give any specific world view influence. So the desire to have such a school makes people believe that although it is difficult, it is possible.

The second reason is that this desire for neutrality finds support in liberalism, in the theory that there are basic, common values that are binding for all, and then there are various theories of the good which are not so fundamental, between which we may choose. Although this may only be thought of as a political theory, it seems to influence basic educational thinking. This supports the idea that religion can be taught separately and just added on.

These two reasons are probably more prominent in England than in Norway, but with the third reason it is the other way round. This reason lies in how the tradition of the state school's Christian basis makes teachers - and others - think that Christian education is only different from secular education in having Christian RE and worship. Maybe church schools in England have had the same effect on what people think special about Christian education. I believe that an important reason for belief in world view neutrality in education is that Christian education has, in practice, failed to show people that Christianity is 'yeast' that ought to permeate all parts of education, rather than merely added 'icing'.

In a country like Norway, the 'common' school has to cater for pupils from many different world view backgrounds. Even if a majority want some kind of Christian education, it obviously cannot be as thoroughly Christian as in a homogeneous society or in a minority school. It has to be 'watered down', made more 'common'. The teachers' different faiths and convictions will contribute to this. This 'watering down' may become an ongoing process. Claims about equality, tolerance and respect are often used against an education that actually takes a stand and claims that Christianity is true. The Bible may be reduced to cultural heritage, faith to something private, and we may be left with a secular school, transmitting practical atheism, in spite of the Christian label. What then?

Attempts to have a kind of world view neutral education will not solve any problems. No other solution will be satisfying for everybody either. As K. Williams says from an Irish perspective: 'We inhabit the corner of the universe in which we find ourselves rather than a perfect world where all conflicts between rights can be harmoniously reconciled to the complete satisfaction of everyone' (Williams 1997, 150).

Whichever solution a society chooses, the first requirement is to be explicit and open about it. There should be discussion, aimed at finding the basis that most people think is best. It is the parents' responsibility to choose for their children, and to do this, they ought to know the alternatives. The world view presuppositions in 'neutral' education should be pointed out. Parents should be helped to see how the basis differs from their own faith and conviction, and provision should be made for minority schools for those who think the majority school is too different from their own view to give them any help with the upbringing.

Making clear what the school is likely to transmit, will not necessarily lead to more minority schools. Reasons for keeping all children in one school are many and should not be ignored. If the basis for the majority school is explicit, the parents may find that they can counteract it in their upbringing at home. If they know which world view presuppositions that are likely to be transmitted, they can talk about them and help the children to see the differences.

If the majority want something 'slightly' Christian, something in between Christianity and secular humanism, one possibility may be to state this in more detail than just 'Christian and humanistic values'. There could be a basis that specified values and aspects of views of human nature that should be transmitted. It could be stated how and in which areas Christianity and humanism should function as pumps and as filters. It would be difficult, and maybe a default position ought to be decided for all the areas that were not included.

Such a more detailed basis should also say something about what parents could possibly expect and what the school cannot help with, most notably that even with a Christian basis it is next to impossible for a state school with teachers of all backgrounds to convey a Christian, God-centred view of reality.

Whatever the state school's basis, if we are to succeed in preventing people from thinking in terms of neutrality, teacher education is an important factor. Teachers first of all have to learn, and admit, that they are role models, whether they want to or not. They must know what their own beliefs and convictions are, so that they know what they will convey. Teacher education ought to help the student teachers to work on the relationship between their own world view and what they are asked to transmit as professional teachers. It may be challenging for many of them, but they are after all going to be responsible for bringing up other people's children.

I would argue that in a society that is so influenced by liberalism as ours, teachers need to be able to talk to pupils about what they believe themselves, they cannot 'hide' behind neutrality or the school's basis. The pupils need adults who have standpoints, convictions, who have thought through who they are and what the purpose of life and education is. They need adults who show them how serving others gives meaning to life, who help them to understand and listen to the Bible, and who walk with them in search for truth.

NOTES

Chapter 1

[1] In Norway, it is primarily the Humanist Association, (Human-Etisk Forbund) which has advocated a world view neutral school and a neutral presentation of religions and world views in Religious Education (RE) (e.g. Lingås 1997, Gule 1999). In the recent discussion about RE, however, people from various backgrounds, including theologians, have argued - more or less explicitly - for a subject where the school is silent about truth (Gravem & Mogstad 1997, see also Eidsvåg 1997, Furre 1997, Møse in Ot prp nr 38, 1996-97).

[2] There has also been a lot of debate in England about RE over the last decades. But this has not been linked to a discussion about the basis of the school in general and is therefore not discussed here.

[3] In his book 'Teaching for Commitment' (1993), E.J. Thiessen defends Christian nurture, and confessional religious education in general, against the charge of indoctrination.

[4] For an account from a different religious perspective, see for instance Ashraf (1985) or Al-Attas (1979) about a Muslim view.

[5] N. Smart questions the division we normally make between religious and secular world views, claiming that this is a western perspective. If we look to China, he says, 'we find that Maoism comes as a direct alternative to the old tradition of Confucius, which likewise contained a philosophy on how to run society' (Smart 1983, 21-2).

[6] A. Jeffner was from the sixties leading a project on world view research ('livs-åskådningsforskning'). He suggested various definitions of the concept, moving from a more subjectivist and emotional understanding at the early stages to a more ideological and cognitive one later on (Aadnanes 1997, 65-8). According to Aadnanes, who himself has a hermeneutic approach in his world view research, Jeffner's approach could be characterized as positivist (ibid., 74, 69).

[7] B. Crittenden uses the notion 'way of life', referring to three overlapping categories of belief and practice:

> (a) shared moral, religious, philosophical and other basic beliefs that interpret human life and provide ideals and rules for how people should act as individuals and as members of society; (b) important customs and other practices related to occupation, social class, region, ethnic background and so on (e.g. language, child-rearing practices, manners, male and female roles, ...); (c) matters of personal taste and style, usually in such areas as clothing, food, sport, the arts. (Crittenden 1988, 108)

> It seems to me that a) and b) are related to Aadnanes' 'traditions' and 'framework', but that c) is different from his 'inside', which Crittenden does not include in his concept.

[8] Consistency is one aspect of coherence, says McLaughlin, but coherence also involves ' "making sense" in a way that goes beyond consistency. A notion of *justification* therefore lurks within coherence' (McLaughlin 1994, 458).

[9] Norway has had compulsory education for everybody in rural areas since 1739, in
towns since 1848. Since 1920 we have had one common school for all children aged
seven to fourteen. There are no independent schools, 1% are in what in Britain would
be called voluntary aided schools (in Norway called free or private schools), with
85% financial support from the state. These are basically schools run by various non-
Lutheran churches and Steiner schools. The law says that free schools can be started
if parents want a religious, moral or educational basis for their children's education
that is different from the state school's. A group of Muslims in 1994 applied to start
their own school, but the Department refused to give permission. In the wake of this,
there has been a debate about free schools in general, with voices wanting to make it
harder to start such schools.

The Declaration of Human Rights is often quoted in debates, claiming that it is the
parents' right to bring up their children according to their own belief and philosophical conviction or view of life. School is not compulsory in Norway, only education, so
parents may in principle teach their own children.

Primary school has since the mid-sixties been from seven to thirteen, secondary from
thirteen to sixteen years old. From 1997 a pre-school year is compulsory as well, and it
is legislated that there shall be an upper secondary place (sixteen to nineteen) for everybody who wants one. There is a long tradition for a National Curriculum, with a new
one (1997) being implemented at the moment. It has plans for all subjects, but also
general chapters (about eighty pages, a fourth of the total) about aims, co-operation,
integration, general thoughts underlying the particular plans, etc. The subject plans
are more detailed than they have been for some decades.

[10] The constitution from 1814 claims that Evangelical-Lutheran Christianity is the
state's religion. In 1997 about 88% of the population (which is 4.4 mill.) were members of the state church. About 4% were members of other Christian denominations,
only 1.5-2 % were members of other religions. The Humanist Association organized
about 1.5% of the remaining 6% (Årbok for Den Norske Kirke 1997, 19 and Statistisk
Årbok 1996, 190).

[11] The 'church geography' in Norway is very peculiar, and a number of practising
Christians meet at other times and in other places, so the 10% figure is probably too
low as an estimate for 'practising Christians'. About 75% (1996) of the fifteen year
olds are confirmed in church, another 11% choosing the secular alternative, organized by the Humanist Association (Årbok for Den norske kirke 1997, 13-14).

[12] The English version of the new Core Curriculum translates the clause slightly
differently:

> Primary and lower secondary education shall, with the understanding of
> and in cooperation with the home, assist in providing pupils with a Christian
> and ethical upbringing, develop their mental and physical abilities, and give
> them a broad general education so that they can become useful and
> independent persons in their private lives and in society.

Schools shall promote intellectual freedom and tolerance, and emphasize the establishment of cooperative climate between teachers and pupils and between school and home. (Core Curriculum 1993/1997, I)

[13] Until 1969 RE, called 'Christianity', was also, formally, the church's responsibility, it was regarded as the church's way of teaching the baptized children about their faith. Now it is solely seen as a help for the parents in their religious upbringing. The 1987 national syllabus said that the subject 'does not only pass on a religious and cultural heritage. What the pupils learn can also guide them and help them to clarify their own faith and beliefs' (Curriculum Guidelines 1987/1990, 113).

Until 1997, Christianity was compulsory unless at least one of the parents was not a member of the state church. For those who were exempted, there was the option of a subject called World Views, or 'General religious and moral education' as it is called in the English version of the curriculum. This, at least in theory, was more like English RE, only with less emphasis on Christianity. Parents with non-religious world views seemed to be those most content with it, but a lot of Muslims, for instance, did not want it for their children. The Curriculum Guidelines also offered the teaching of particular religions or ideologies as an option, in co-operation with the respective communities, but this was not much used. The alternatives were not compulsory, so a number of pupils were not taught religion or world views at all at school.

[14] The common school in Norway was at the beginning run by the church, and close links have always remained. The 1969 Education Act's purpose of helping to give Christian upbringing is a continuation of what has always been - there was a similar clause already in 1889 (Skottene 1994, 46). There was some discussion in Parliament over this clause in 1969, some claiming that it might produce intolerance. Therefore the promotion of tolerance was added, by some seen as a counterbalance, by others as part of the Christian upbringing. The National Curriculum has also been emphasizing that the school is based on Christian values. In 1985 this was changed to 'Christian and humanistic values', but the committee behind it made it clear that this was not a change in values, rather an acknowledgement that a lot of the Christian values are also humanistic.

Lately, there has been relatively little discussion at all about this paragraph from the Act, and the nineties have seen a renewed awareness and valuing of the Christian heritage. It has been said repeatedly by both the Minister of Education and others that Christianity is an important part of Norwegian culture, and everybody should learn about it, whether they believe or not.

[15] In spring 1995 the Department had a committee set up to look into what RE ought to be like in the new National Curriculum. The main guideline for the committee was that they had to solve the problem of so many classes being split when taught about religion and ethics, this being negative for the dialogue between people of different faiths and convictions.

The resulting subject is described in vague and partly contradictory formulations. Sometimes it is emphasized that the subject should strengthen the identity every child has from home, at other times the claim is that there must be no indoctrination, the pupils must choose for themselves. Some groups argue that the Christian basis for the school as a whole means that Christianity is regarded as the truth, others claim that all views should be presented from within, without the school taking any stance. Both Christians, other religious groups and secular humanists have threatened to take the question of it being compulsory to the European Court of Human Rights.

[16] The Norwegian Parliament has decided that the subject should be evaluated after three years. Three educational institutions have been given the task, and reports are to be submitted by 1 November 2000.

Chapter 2

[17] In Norway it would be more common to call it 'conservative', but this seems to have more political overtones in English. 'Orthodox' is used, not to refer to seventeenth century orthodoxy, but to distinguish it from what is loosely labelled liberal theology.

[18] For an account of the model in English, see for instance Althaus 1972, chapter 4. Among theologians, the model has been heavily criticized, but most of the criticism has been against misunderstandings and misuse, particularly because it has not been taken into account that Luther lived in a society very different from ours. He also changed the model, so there are different versions of it.

Although I have read some of Luther's works, particularly where he writes about education, it would be arrogant of me as a non-theologian to try to engage directly with his writings, which so many competent people have discussed and disagreed about.

[19] It is difficult to find recent writings about Lutheran education outside Norway. The Germans seem not to be too concerned about being Lutheran, their schools are 'evangelical' and interdenominational (Arbeitsgemeinschaft ..., 1985). The American Lutherans seem to be most concerned with some of Luther's practical suggestions (Bruce 1928/1979, Harran 1990).

[20] It is not possible to judge one's own faith in the same way as other religions, from the outside so to speak. In contrast to how a person views other religions, N.P. Blake says,

> he cannot see his own religion as any more than marginally corrigible, otherwise he would not be a believer. I am not denying that he may occasionally doubt his own faith. But it is one thing to experience moments of religious doubt; quite another to hold one's claimed religious beliefs constantly open to radical revision. In Christianity, for instance, to believe is to fear the loss of faith. That is the difference between a committed Christian or Muslim and someone who simply suspects that Christianity or Islam is true. A true believer chooses the very direction of his life in the light of his faith. Religious beliefs are of their very nature more deep-rooted than other kinds of belief. They are not available for disinterested reexamination and revision in the sense in which economic or historical or scientific beliefs are. (Blake 1983/1993, 104)

[21] See for instance Nipkow 1993.

[22] In Norwegian, we have the word 'menneske' as a gender-neutral word for 'man', like the German 'Mensch'. This makes it sound very clumsy to me to use 'human being' or other expressions. I try, but some places - like here - it sounds impossible.

[23] Luther seemed to think that schools are primarily for teaching various subjects, upbringing is the parents' task. This is easy to understand when we think of the relative amount of time spent in school then compared to our days. Also, society was fairly homogeneous, and aspects like growing up within a tradition, being formed as a person, and taking on various roles were things that just happened, without being thought of as tasks for upbringers.

[24] Before the reformation the pupils met Christianity through their readers, in music and in compulsory church going as part of their education, but there was no subject where they were actually taught the content of the Christian faith. The Bible should now be the centre of the school, taught as a separate subject, Luther said, and the other subjects would naturally be judged critically from this centre, so that they did not oppose it. Christianity and secular subjects ran parallel, both having their own value. But it was still obvious to Luther that together they created a unified education, with faith in God, the Creator and Saviour, keeping it all together (Asheim 1961, 71-86).

[25] The curriculum in Luther's schools might well have been called humanistic, says Asheim, with its emphasis on languages and classical literature. But he wanted a biblical humanism, a humanism that gave room for God's word, the Bible, without creating doubt in the children (Asheim 1961, 79). So Christianity was to be a subject alongside others, the Bible to be read alongside classic Greek works.

[26] About a Christian way of teaching subjects like mathematics, history, science, literature, etc., see for instance Niblett (1960).

[27] An example of this thinking is the Lutheran teacher education college 'Norsk Lærerakademi' that was started in Norway in 1968 for the explicit purpose of educating teachers for the state schools. It offers degree courses in Christianity and Educational Theory, and there is no requirement of Christian faith in its students.

[28] 'Positive Partnership' is a document that expresses the Church of England's policy on education. It contains a few paragraphs on a theological basis for partnership between church and state in education (Positive Partnership 1985, 23-4 and 39-40). The purpose for the church, whether through its own schools or through 'the way in which "the secular authorities" operate the education system nationally', is said to be to witness to the Kingdom of God (ibid., 23). The church should be a sign of the presence and promise of his kingdom (ibid., 39).

Chapter 3

[29] Kymlicka argues that a lot of communitarian criticism has misinterpreted liberalism (Kymlicka 1991).

[30] According to Bailey, liberally educated persons are intellectually and morally autonomous, they are free choosers of beliefs and actions, 'a free moral agent, the kind of entity a fully-fledged human being is supposed to be and which all too few are!' (Bailey 1984, 21). This may sound like a belief in a completely free chooser, with no restrictions, but the contrast that Bailey presents makes the claim sound more moderate: they do not *have* to be determined in actions and beliefs by origins and

conditioning, but by knowledge and reason they can come to understand the forces
acting upon them from the inside and the outside and thereby become independent of
them (ibid., 22).

[31] In the preface of his book 'The Aims of Education Restated', White says that to his
knowledge no book at all has been written (in Britain, I suppose he means) on the
topic of what aims of education should be. He has missed out at least one, namely
M.V.C. Jeffreys' (1950) 'Glaucon. An inquiry into the Aims of Education'. Jeffreys'
approach is very influenced by Christian thoughts, but he nevertheless presents his
view as something common to all, writing at a time when Britain was more Christian
than it is today.

[32] R. Marples wants to replace desires with real-interests, arguing that the latter is more
objective (Marples 1993, 12-13). J. Griffin says that we have to 'get behind desires
and expectations to the deeper considerations that show which desires and expectations have moral force' (Griffin 1988, 40), and wants to focus on basic needs. J. Raz
bases his account of well-being on personal goals. A person's well-being depends on
both the value of his or her goals and the degree to which they are reached (Raz
1988).

[33] The only place it is found is in (1990, 156), about evil consequences of two conflicting desires.

[34] Dispositions seem to be the same as firmly built-in higher-order desires.

[35] Doing good then, being attentive to others' needs, seems in itself to contribute to well-
being, at least most of the time. White suggests that both (narrow) self-interest and
other-concern can be put under the same heading of self-interest (White 1990, 69).
There will still be conflicts, but he reconceptualizes them to be between two self-
interested desires instead of between self-interested and other-regarding ones. It is
difficult to see what this means, apart from showing the children that their own and
other people's well-being are interconnected at point after point. They should be
'encouraged to see others' flourishing as inextricably entwined with their own' (ibid.,
162).

If this just means that they should be given dispositions that do not make the conflicts between self-interest and other-concern more numerous and bigger than necessary, most people would agree. If it means that he wants to bring up children in such
a way that they notice no difference between satisfaction from getting a very much
wanted job themselves and satisfaction from seeing a friend - or even an enemy -
happy from getting that same job, I think he is too optimistic as to what upbringing
can do about people's selfishness. His whole account of this seems all too smooth,
harmonious and strugglefree. Maybe it is an example of what Hollinger calls 'more
"altruistic" models of utilitarianism', where they start from rational self-interest but
'convince people that it is in each person's enlightened self-interest to care about
others and to take the general welfare into account when acting' (Hollinger 1994, 23).

Raz has a slightly different approach, saying that '[i]ndividuals define the contours of their own lives by drawing on the communal pool of values. These will, in
well-ordered societies, contribute indiscriminately both to their self-interest and to
other aspects of their well-being. They also define the field of moral values. There is

but one source for morality and for personal well-being' (Raz 1986/1988, 318-19). So society defines the values, what is worth pursuing. To the extent that the social forms are morally sound, people will have goals that promote both morality (i.e. other people's well-being) and their own well-being. There will be conflicts between well-being and morality, but they do not have to be there (ibid.).

In a way Raz's account reminds me of Luther's orders or stations (Ordnungen) where, by living in them (social forms), we promote other people's and our own good, even the good of the society. The difference is that for Luther, the final authority for what is right and good is found in the Bible, and all orders and moral rules are given by God to restrain our egoism. Neither Raz nor White seem to have room in their theory for the battle between good and evil both in the society and in every individual.

[36] I am not going into the debate about the difference between strong and weak autonomy or between autonomy and autarchy, because this is not directly relevant to the focus for my work.

[37] This does not mean, as White seems to believe, that 'the good for man consists in one thing only, faith in our Lord' (White 1990, 110). Faith is fundamental for living the really good life, but there are innumerable good things and ways of living this life, and also people without faith can experience many of these, although their life basically is lived contrary to what they are created for.

[38] After this was written, another article by K.A. Strike was published (autumn 1998), where he seems to be more aware of the importance in education of what he calls comprehensive doctrines and cultures. He says that 'schools in which comprehensive doctrines are themselves chosen (as opposed to criticized, modified, or abandoned) make little sense. They assume a view from nowhere - a transcendent rationality that can be wielded by children' (Strike 1998, 225). But still he holds that this does not mean the end of the public school (ibid., 228).

[39] It is an interesting observation that sex education is not regarded as part of moral education.

[40] I suppose that the same is true if we compare no-standpoint education with education within other religions, but they will have other presuppositions and will therefore have to be discussed separately.

Chapter 4

[41] Hirst understood some of this:

> Surely we must distinguish between on the one hand those natural experiences of the ultimate mystery of the existence of things and their contingency and on the other the experience of worship as an intentional act in church or school assembly. The former experiences may well be basic to any understanding of what religion is about. The latter, however, are experiences of a kind that are meaningful only on the basis of commitment to some specific religious beliefs. In this sense one can no more simply worship than one can simply think. One must necessarily worship something or somebody just as one must necessarily

think about something. If this is so there is no experience of mere worship, but only the experience of worshipping some particular object or being. (Hirst 1965/1974, 183)

[42] The Bible tells us, says Hirst, that it is possible for 'natural man' to find out what is right and wrong - and do it - without revelation, therefore morality is autonomous (Hirst 1974, 52). But the Bible also says that although this is possible, it does not always happen, people are able to argue rationally - or so we think - also for immoral actions. So our rationality has to be corrected or adjusted by revelation, by the Bible, not to find answers that are a-rational or irrational, but to find the true rational answers that correspond to the rationality God gave us. The problem with Hirst's supreme reason is not that it never can find out what is right and wrong, but that Hirst has no room for sin, for egoism, for the self-centredness that often blinds our reasoning.

[43] Hirst outlines four different kinds of religious education, from the traditional to the rational and critical. None of them is similar to Christian education as I outlined it in chapter two. This is basically because of his view of rationality as something 'neutral', he thinks we can have education that is neither Christian (or any other kind of religious) nor secular, it is only 'open, critical and rational'. E.J. Thiessen has given a thorough criticism of Hirst's model (Thiessen 1987/1993 and 1993).

[44] Traditions may be religious or moral, political, economic, aesthetic or geographical. (See Mulhall & Swift 1992, 90)

[45] See Crittenden 1993, 136-7.

[46] The other four marks are awareness of evil, acceptance of authority, concern for the person, and sacramental cast (Blamires 1963).

[47] Although our views are different, they are not so much so that it is impossible to understand each other. We are, after all, created by the same God and with the same kind of mind. It is possible to change perspective. From a Christian point of view, the only rational way of relating to the world is one that is based on faith in God the creator and reckons with him.

[48] If secular means non-religious, a society that is for instance Marxist or Fascist could be called secular. More common today, though, is to take 'secular' to mean a society which has not committed itself as a society to one religion or ideology. It is pluralist 'in the sense that it embraces people who differ in regard to their adherence to ultimate beliefs and values. A secular, pluralist society is not secular in the sense of embodying an ideology hostile to religion' (Davis 1994, 2). G. Haydon would use the term about a society where religious concepts are in very limited use - secularization is always a matter of degree (Haydon 1994, 65-6).

[49] 'This understanding of justice is intuitive rather than rational. Yet neither is it *irrational*. The religious conviction can be elaborated in laws marked by consistency, predictability and generality. Perhaps it is best described as a *trans-rational* understanding of justice, as reason fired by passion, as faith worked out in rational forms.' (Wren 1986, 46)

50 Whether Hirst's rejection of his former belief in the 'rationalist' myth (Hirst 1993, 193) gives him a different view of the fundamentality of world views in education is not clear. 'There can be no detached clean slate position from which all possibilities can be assessed', he says, but he may regard wants and 'the practical knowledge of available satisfactions that goes with these' (ibid.) in a similar way to J. White, where world view beliefs are not fundamental.

51 The claim, says Crittenden, that impartiality between different religions and between religious and non-religious ways of life is not neutral, and, in fact, endorses secularism, is not given enough attention by Hirst (Crittenden 1993, 144).

52 The same is true about S. Macedo, who does not seem to see any difference between 'exposing the children to a variety of religious points of view' and doing so 'in an even-handed manner' (Macedo 1995, 224 and 227). A. Gutman, writing about the same case as Macedo (Mozert v Hawkins), calls the parents fundamentalists because they require that when exposed to beliefs and values that contradict their own, it should be explained to the children 'that the other views are incorrect and that their views are the correct ones' (Gutman 1992/1996, 297).

53 I owe the example of vegetarianism, including the suggestion of this link to the treatment of animals, to G. Haydon.

54 Newbigin says that this personal knowledge in many languages 'is designated by a different word. It is the kind of knowing that we seek in our relations with other people. In this kind of knowing we are not in full control. We may ask questions, but we must also answer the questions put by the other' (Newbigin 1995, 10). Newbigin discusses the possibility of having certain knowledge of God, claiming that the dualism between objective and subjective knowledge is false. In this he refers to M. Polanyi who, he says, 'used the term "personal knowledge" with the precise intention of affirming that the objective-subjective dualism is false and that all knowing of reality involves the personal commitment of the knower as a whole person' (ibid., 39).

55 Thiessen mentions as criteria for assessing belief systems 'simplicity, explanatory comprehensiveness, aesthetic elegance, internal consistency, and empirical accuracy' (Thiessen 1993, 111-12).

56 'Trua er korkje blind tru eller prova tru.' Norwegian theologian A. Brunvoll in public defence of his doctoral thesis, Bergen 14 Nov. 1997.

57 See R.J. Royce (1983) for an argument along these lines concerning moral education.

58 Although postmodernists would hardly argue for a world view neutral, or 'narrative neutral', education, they would have education within each narrative.

59 He shows how Kuhn and Feyerabend often in their rejection of objective truth in science use concepts that assume the same objectivism. 'We have already seen some of the consequences of this kind of view when examining Wittgenstein's remarks about religion. There can be no understanding of one system by those committed to another. As a result, it is not only impossible in principle to resolve fundamental disagreement, it is impossible even to formulate it ... it becomes impossible for an atheist to disagree with a Christian.' (Trigg 1973, 119)

60 One of the important arguments against liberal education, and against liberalism in general, from the communitarian tradition, is how impossible the liberal notions of free choice and autonomy are. The communitarians claim that we are so determined by the community, the culture, where we are brought up, that free choice is an illusion.

61 See for instance Nome (1970, 93-4 and Strike's recent article (Strike 1998, 225) about how a world view or a comprehensive doctrine is not something we choose as a result of thinking, but something that is necessary for our thinking to get started.

62 See also Thiessen's criticism of Gardner's position (Thiessen 1993, 170-71).

63 G. D'Costa argues in a similar way about a pluralist view of religions. Orthodox religions that claim that they alone are right and all others wrong, will by pluralists be regarded as exclusive and therefore wrong. Religious pluralism, the view that all religions are more or less equally true, is also a form of exclusiveness, D'Costa says, because it claims that this is the only way to understand religions (D'Costa 1996).

64 Thiessen mentions different ways of manipulating the subject matter or the pupils: non-evidential teaching, misuse of evidence, misuse of authority, failure to cultivate 'a critical spirit', etc. (Thiessen 1993, 89-91). These are non-rational and regarded as ways of indoctrinating and therefore by many as common in religious nurture (ibid., 87-8). To use such methods is not Christian, because it is not honest. Another question is whether these methods are also found in liberal education: is for instance evidence given for the belief in a God-less world, or the subjective meaning of life? Is science used as evidence against God?

Chapter 5

65 McLaughlin uses 'significant disagreement' and discusses what this means (McLaughlin 1995a, 24-6).

66 The second assumption, b), is 'that the most justifiable form of society is an open, pluralist, democratic one where there is maximum toleration of diversity and a commitment to free critical debate as the most rational means of advancing the pursuit of truth in all its forms' (McLaughlin 1991, 11).

67 A school cannot be culture-neutral, he says, it must have a 'cultural content' (McLaughlin 1995b, 245). This must mean, given that he is consistent, that some common parts of the culture will be included, but not religion or world view.

68 See for example p. 83 above about justice.

69 And therefore are not autonomous anyway, at least according to J. White's view of autonomy.

70 The latter quotation is taken from the Second Vatican Council's Declaration on Christian Education 'Gravissimum educationis'.

71 He quotes from Sacred Congregation for the Clergy, 1971.

72 Laura & Leahy use the same argument for a religious upbringing (1989, 253).

[73] He refers to Walzer who uses Norway as an example of such a homogeneous country. The same does Tamir (1995, 163). This is only partly true, which has been made abundantly clear in the recent discussion about RE in the state schools. Although there is a large majority, there are some strong minorities too, particularly the Humanist Association, which has been actively working against any Christian influence in school.

Chapter 6

[74] Figures from 1984 tell that 30% of the population believe in God, heaven and hell, resurrection, and eternal life for those who believe in Jesus Christ. Another 30% believe in God, heaven, and some form of eternal life. In addition there are 15% who believe in God only. 20% do not believe in any of the traditional beliefs, and 5% do not know. (Tveiten 1994, 178-9)

[75] D. Cook analyses humanism, postmodernism, scientific materialism and a few other world views in relation to Christianity, using three tests: 'Is it self-consistent? Does it correspond with the facts? Is it the best alternative available?' (Cook 1996, 6)

[76] T. Bergem has done some interesting research on student teachers' thinking about being a role model. See for instance Bergem (1990).

[77] There are numerous books and articles dealing with a Christian view of curriculum, of which I might mention *Livssyn i Skolen* (1970), Niblett (1960), and Van Brummelen (1994). There is also the Charis project (1996), which is a curriculum development project, promoting spiritual and moral development across the curriculum.

[78] See for instance Foros (1989), which has been very influential.

[79] This is a discussion document based on a seminar for Christian and Muslim scholars and educationalists.

[80] 'Distinctive' is what he wants the Catholic schools to be, meaning not necessarily different, but explicit on what is important.

Bibliography

Ackerman, B. (1980). Social Justice in the Liberal State. New Haven: Yale University Press.

A Future in Partnership. A green paper. (1984). London: The National Society (Church of England) for Promoting Religious Education.

Al-Attas, S.N. (1979). Aims and Objectives of Islamic Education. Jeddah: King Abdulaziz University / Hodder and Stoughton.

Allen, R.T. (1989). Metaphysics in Education. Journal of Philosophy of Education, 23, 159-69.

Allen, R.T. (1991). The meaning of life and education. Journal of Philosophy of Education, 25, 47-58.

Althaus, P. (1972). The Ethics of Martin Luther. (R.C. Schultz, trans.) Philadelphia: Fortress Press. (Original work published 1965)

Andersen, W.E. (1990). A biblical view of education. In L. Francis & A. Thatcher (eds.), Christian Perspectives for Education (pp. 37-49). Leominster: Gracewing. (Reprinted from Journal of Christian Education, 1983, 26)

Arbeitsgemeinschaft Evangelischer Bekenntnisschulen (AEBS). (1985). Schule auf biblischer Basis. Neuhausen-Stuttgart: Haenssler-Verlag.

Asheim, I. (1961). Glaube und Erziehung bei Luther. Heidelberg: Quelle & Meyer.

Asheim, I. (1967). Hva er kristen oppdragelse? Prismet, 18, 134-41.

Asheim, I. (1970). Orientering i religionspedagogikken. Oslo: IKO.

Asheim, I. (1978). Tro - Dannelse - Oppdragelse. Unpublished work. Oslo: Menighetsfakultetet.

Asheim, I. (1991). Øyet og horisonten. Oslo: Universitetsforlaget.

Ashraf, S.A. (1985). New Horizons in Muslim Education. Hodder & Stoughton / Cambridge: The Islamic Academy.

Astley, J. (1994). The Philosophy of Christian Religious Education. Birmingham, Alabama: Religious Education Press.

Austad, T. (1972). Luthers lære om de to regimenter og dens aktualitet. Ung Teologi, 5, 1-13.

Baier, A. (1985). Postures of the Mind. Essays on mind and morals. London: Methuen.

Bailey, C. (1984). Beyond the Present and the Particular. London: Routledge & Kegan Paul.

Ball, W.B. (1967). Religion and the public education: the post-Schempp years. In T.R. Sizer (ed.), Religion and Public Education. Boston: Houghton Mifflin Company.

Beck, G.A. (1964). Aims in education: Neo-Thomism. In T.H.B. Hollins (ed.), Aims in Education. The Philosophic Approach (pp. 109-32). Manchester: Manchester University Press.

Bergem, T. (1990). The teacher as moral agent. Journal of Moral Education, 19, 88-100.

Berger, P.L. & Luckmann, T. (1967). *The Social Construction of Reality*. New York: Doubleday, Anchor Books.

Bible, the Holy (1984). New International Version. Grand Rapids, Michigan: Zondervan.

Blake, N.P. (1993). Church schools, religious education and the multi-ethnic community: a reply to David Aspin. In L. Francis & D.W. Lankshear (eds.), *Christian Perspectives on Church Schools* (pp. 102-15). Leominster: Gracewing. (First published in *Journal of Philosophy of Education*, 1983, *17*)

Blamires, H. (1963). *The Christian Mind*. London: SPCK.

Bollnow, O.F. (1969). *Eksistensfilosofi og pedagogikk.* (R. Myhre, trans.) Oslo: Fabritius og Sønner. (Original work published 1959)

Bringeland, H. (1993). *Verdiar og verdikrise.*Unpublished work. Bergen: NLA.

Brown, A. (1992). *The Multi-Faith Church School*. The National Society (Church of England) for Promoting Religious Education.

Bruce, G.M. (1979) *Luther as an Educator*. Minneapolis: Augsburg. (Original work published 1928)

Brunner, E. (1948). *Christianity and civilization*. First part. London: Nisbet.

Brunstad, P.O. (1997, 18th November). Kameleon i en oppløst verden. *Vårt Land*, p. 6.

Butler, J. (1964). *Fifteen sermons*. London: G. Bell & Sons. (Original work published 1726.)

Callan, E. (1985). McLaughlin on parental rights. *Journal of Philosophy of Education, 19*, 111-18.

Callan, E. (1996). Common schools for common education. In W. Hare & J.P. Portelli (eds.), *Philosophy of Education. Introductory Readings* (pp. 267-288). Calgary: Detselig Enterprises. (Reprinted from *Canadian Journal of Education*, 1995, *20*, 251-71)

Carson, D.A. (1996). *The Gagging of God. Christianity Confronts Pluralism*. Grand Rapids, Michigan: Zondervan.

Charis. *Mathematics.* (1996).The Charis Project. St Albans: The Association of Christian Teachers.

Cook, D. (1996). *Blind Alley Beliefs*. Leicester: Inter-Varsity.

Core Curriculum for Primary, Secondary and Adult Education in Norway. (1997). Oslo: The Royal Ministry of Education, Research and Church Affairs. (Original work published 1993)

Crittenden, B. (1988). *Parents, the State and the Right to Educate*. Carlton, Victoria: Melbourne University Press.

Crittenden, B. (1993). Moral and Religious Education: Hirst's perception of their scope and relationship. In R. Barrow & P. White (eds.), *Beyond liberal education* (pp. 129-149). London: Routledge.

Curriculum Guidelines for compulsory education in Norway. (1990). Oslo: Aschehoug. (Original work published 1987)

D'Costa, G. (1996). The impossibility of a pluralist view of religions. *Religious Studies, 32*, 223-32.

Davis, C. (1994). *Religion and the Making of Society*. Cambridge: Cambridge University Press.

Donley, M. (1992). Teaching discernment: an overview of the book as a whole from the perspective of the secondary school classrom. In B. Watson (ed.), *Priorities in Religious Education* (pp. 183-94). London: Falmer.

Dunn, J.D.G. (1993). *Christian liberty. A New Testament perspective*. Carlisle: Paternoster.

Education for All. (1985). The Report of the Committee of Inquiry into the Education of Children from Ethnic Minority Groups. Chairman: Lord Swann FRS, FRSE. London: Her Majesty's Stationery Office.

Eidsvåg, I. (1997, 18th February). Nøytralt og objektivt. *Vårt Land*, p. 6.

Evenshaug, O. & Hallen, D. (1981). *Barnedåp og oppdragelse*. Oslo: Pedagogisk forskningsinstitutt, University of Oslo.

Faith as the Basis of Education in a Multi-faith Multi-cultural Country. A discussion document. (1990). Cambridge: The Islamic Academy.

Feinberg, W. (1995). Liberalism and the aims of multicultural education. *Journal of Philosophy of Education, 29*, 203-16.

Fjelde, J. (1970). Lærerens frihet og lojalitet i lys av skolens formålsbestemmelse. In *Livssyn i skolen* (pp. 166-85). Oslo: IKO.

Foros, P.B. (1989). *Læring av ansvar. Fra handling til holdning*. Oslo: Universitetsforlaget.

Fowler, S. (1990a). Christian schooling as prophetic witness. In S. Fowler, H.W. Van Brummelen & J. Van Dyk, *Christian Schooling: Education for Freedom* (pp. 47-61). Potchefstroom: Potshefstroom University.

Fowler, S. (1990b). Schooling for the service of love. In S. Fowler, H. W. Van Brummelen & J. Van Dyk, *Christian Schooling: Education for Freedom* (pp. 70-80). Potchefstroom: Potshefstroom University.

Furre, B. (1997, 8th February). Det nye religionsfaget i stampesjø. *Aftenposten*.

Galston, W. (1989). Civic education in the liberal state. In N.L. Rosenblum (ed.), *Liberalism and the Moral Life* (pp. 89-101). Cambridge, MA: Harvard University Press.

Gardner, P. (1988). Religious upbringing and the liberal ideal of religious autonomy. *Journal of Philosophy of Education, 22*, 89-105.

Gardner, P. (1991). Personal autonomy and religious upbringing: the problem. *Journal of Philosophy of Education, 25*, 69-81.

Gravem, P. (1992). Fast forankring og vid horisont. In S.D. Mogstad & L. Østnor (eds.), *Forankring og forandring* (pp. 113-26). Oslo: Universitetsforlaget.

Gravem, P. & Mogstad, S. (1997, 10th February). Det nye kristendomsfaget - 'nøytralt og objektivt'? *Vårt Land*, pp. 19-20.

Griffin, J. (1988). *Well-being*. Oxford: Clarendon. (Original work published 1986)

Groome, T.H. (1996). What makes a school Catholic? In T.H. McLaughlin, J. O'Keefe SJ & B. O'Keeffe (eds.), *The Contemporary Catholic School* (pp. 107-25). London: Falmer.

Gule, L. (1999). Er livssynsnøytralitet i skolen umulig? *Humanist, 25*, 111-18.

Gutman, A. (1987). *Democratic education*. Princeton: Princeton University Press.

Gutman, A. (1992). Democratic education in difficult times. In W. Hare & J.P. Portelli (eds.), *Philosophy of Education. Introductory Readings* (pp. 289-302). Calgary: Detselig Enterprises. (Reprinted from *Teachers College Record*, 1990, *92*(1))

Gutman, A. (1995). Civic education and social diversity. *Ethics, 105*, 557-79.

Habgood, J. (1990). Are moral values enough? *British Journal of Educational Studies, 38*, 106-15.

Haldane, J. (1996). Catholic education and Catholic identity. In T.H. McLaughlin, J. O'Keefe SJ & B. O'Keeffe (eds.), *The Contemporary Catholic School* (pp. 126-35). London: Falmer.

Halstead, M. (1996, May). Editorial. *SPES, 4*.

Harbo, S. (1989). *Barndomserfaringer og voksentro*. Oslo: Universitetsforlaget.

Hareide, B. (1955). *Pedagogikk og evangelium*. Oslo: Land og Kirke.

Harran, M.J. (1990). The contemporary applicability of Luther's pedagogy: education and vocation. *Concordia Journal, 16*, 319-32.

Haworth, L. (1986). *Autonomy*. New Haven / London: Yale University Press.

Haydon, G. (1994). Conceptions of the secular in society, polity and schools. *Journal of Philosophy of Education, 28*, 65-75.

Hebblethwaite, B. (1988). *The Ocean of Truth. A defence of objective theism*. Cambridge: Cambridge University Press.

Heschel, A.J. (1972). *The Insecurity of Freedom: Essays on Human Existence*. New York: Schockers Books. (Original work published 1959)

Hill, B.V. (1990). A more visible presence: agenda for Christian teachers. In L. Francis & A. Thatcher (eds.), *Christian Perspectives for Education* (pp. 100-109). Leominster: Gracewing. (Reprinted from *Journal of Christian Education*, 1982, 25)

Hirst, P.H. (1965). Liberal education and the nature of knowledge. In R.D. Archambault (ed.), *Philosophical Analysis and Education* (pp. 113-38). London: Routledge & Kegan Paul.

Hirst, P.H. (1974). Morals, religion and the maintained school. In P.H. Hirst, *Knowledge and the curriculum* (pp. 173-89). London: Routledge & Kegan Paul. (Reprinted from *British Journal of Educational Studies*, 1965, *14*(1))

Hirst, P.H. (1974). *Moral Education in a Secular Society*. London: Hodder & Stoughton.

Hirst, P.H. (1993). Education, catechesis and the church school. In L. Francis & D.W. Lankshear (eds.), *Christian Perspectives on Church Schools* (pp. 2-16). Leominster: Gracewing. (Reprinted from *British Journal of Religious Education*, 1981)

Hirst, P.H. (1985). Education and diversity of belief. In M. Felderhof (ed.), *Religious Education in a Pluralist Society* (pp. 5-17). London: Hodder & Stoughton.

Hirst, P. (1993). Education, knowledge and practices. In R. Barrow & P. White (eds.), *Beyond Liberal Education* (pp. 184-99). London: Routledge.

Hollinger, R. (1994). *Postmodernism and the Social Sciences*. Thousand Oaks, CA: Sage.

Holmes, A.F. (1983). *Contours of a world view*. Grand Rapids: Eerdmans.

Hull, J.M. (1982). Introduction: new directions in religious education. In J. Hull (ed.), *New Directions in Religious Education* (pp. xi-xvi). Lewes: Falmer.

Jeffreys, M.V.C. (1950). *Glaucon. An inquiry into the aims of education*. London: Sir Isaac Pitman & Sons.

Jeffreys, M.V.C. (1969). *Truth is not Neutral*. Oxford: The Religious Education Press.

Kvam, B. (1993). Ordet og danningsarbeidet. In *Ordet og mennesket* (pp. 7-20). Bergen: NLA-forlaget.

Kymlicka, W. (1991). *Liberalism, community, and culture*. Oxford: Clarendon. (Original work published 1989)

Lambert, I.P.M. (1994). *The new Christian schools' movement in Britain - a case study*. PhD-thesis, Department of Education University of Cambridge.

Langford, M.J. (1985). *The Good and the True*. London: SCM.

Laura, R.S. & Leahy, M. (1989). Religious upbringing and rational autonomy. *Journal of Philosophy of Education, 23*, 253-65.

Lewis, C.S. (1968). *The Magician's Nephew*. Harmondsworth, Middlesex: Penguin Books. (Original work published 1955)

Lewis, C.S. (1977). *Mere Christianity*. Collins: Fount Paperbacks. (Original work published 1952)

Lingås, L.G. (1997, 28th January). Stortinget og menneskerettigheter. *Dagbladet*, p. 37.

Livssyn i Skolen (1970). Oslo: IKO.

Læreplanverket for den tiårige grunnskolen. (1996). Oslo: Det kongelige kirke-, utdannings- og forskningsdepartement.

MacIntyre, A. (1988). *Whose Justice? Which Rationality?* London: Duckworth.

McLaughlin, T.H. (1984). Parental rights and the religious upbringing of children. *Journal of Philosophy of Education, 18*, 75-83.

McLaughlin, T.H. (1987). 'Education for All' and religious schools. In G. Haydon (ed.), *Education for a pluralist society* (pp. 67-83). London: Institute of Education University of London, Bedford Way Papers.

McLaughlin, T.H. (1990). Peter Gardner on religious upbringing and the liberal ideal of religious autonomy. *Journal of Philosophy of Education, 24*, 107-125.

McLaughlin, T.H. (1991). *Parental Rights in Religious Upbringing and Religious Education within a Liberal Perspective*. PhD-thesis, Institute of Education University of London.

McLaughlin, T.H. (1992). Fairness, controversiality and the common school. *Spectrum, 24*, 105-18.

McLaughlin, T.H. (1994). Values, coherence and the school. *Cambridge Journal of Education, 24*, 453-70.

McLaughlin, T.H. (1995a). Public values, private values and educational responsibility. In *Values, Education & Responsibility*. Centre for Philosophy and Public Affairs, University of St Andrews.

McLaughlin, T.H. (1995b). Liberalism, education and the common school. *Journal of Philosophy of Education, 29*, 239-55.

McLaughlin, T.H. (1996a). Education of the whole child? In R. Best (ed.), *Education, Spirituality and the Whole Child* (pp. 9-19). London: Cassell.

McLaughlin, T.H. (1996b). The distinctiveness of Catholic education. In T.H. McLaughlin, J. O'Keefe SJ & B. O'Keeffe (eds.), *The Contemporary Catholic School* (pp. 136-54). London: Falmer.

Macedo, S. (1995). Multiculturalism for the religious right? Defending liberal civic education. *Journal of Philosophy of Education, 29*, 223-38.

Marples, R. (1993, 18th sept.). *Education and Well-being*. Paper presented at the meeting of the Philosophy of Education Society Great Britain, Cambridge branch.

Middleton, J.R. & Walsh, B.J. (1995). *Truth is stranger than it used to be*. London: SPCK.

Mitchell, B. (1979). Religion and truth. *New Universities Quarterly, 33*, 459-471.

Mitchell, B. (1980a). Faith and reason: a false antithesis? *Religious Studies, 16*, 131-44.

Mitchell, B. (1980b). *Morality: Religious and Secular*. Oxford: Clarendon.

Mitchell, B. (1996). Postscript: conservation and criticism. In J. Astley & L.J. Francis (eds.), *Christian Theology & Religious Education* (pp. 271-7). London: SPCK.

Mollenhauer, K. (1996). *Glemte sammenhenger. Om kultur og oppdragelse.* (S. Wivestad, trans.) Oslo: Ad Notam. (Original work published 1985, *Vergessene Zuzammenhänge. Über Kultur und Erziehung.*)

Mulhall, S. & Swift, A. (1992). *Liberals and Communitarians.* Oxford: Blackwell.

Myhre, R. (1970). Oppdragelse til selvstendighet - og kristen oppdragelse. In *Livssyn i Skolen* (pp. 9-44). Oslo: IKO.

Newbigin, L. (1982). Teaching religion in a secular plural society. In J. Hull (ed.), *New Directions in Religious Education* (pp. 97-107). Lewes: Falmer. (Reprinted from *Learning for Living*, 1977, *17*(2))

Newbigin, L. (1995). *Proper Confidence.* London: SPCK.

Niblett, W.R. (1960). *Christian Education in a Secular Society.* London: Oxford University Press.

Niebuhr, R. (1964). *The Nature and Destiny of Man.* Vol 1. New York: Charles Scribner's sons. (Original work published 1941)

Nipkow, K.-E. (1993). Oikumene - the global horizon for Christian and religious education. *British Journal of Religious Education, 15*(2), 5-11.

Nome, J. (1953). Humanistisk eller kristent livssyn? *Kirke og Kultur 58*, 75-89.

Nome, J. (1970). Tro og fornuft i livssynet. In J. Nome, *Kunst og etikk* (pp. 88-107). Oslo: Universitetsforlaget.

NOU 1995:9. *Identitet og dialog.* Oslo: Statens forvaltningstjeneste.

Ot prp nr 38, 1996-97 (1997). Om lov om endringar i lov 13. juni 1969 nr. 24 om grunnskolen m.m. Oslo: Kyrkje-, utdannings- og forskingsdepartementet.

Pedersen, C.H. (1996). *Kulturoppgaven og missionsoppgaven som udfordring for kristne skoler.* Bergen: Norsk Lærerakademi. Hovedoppgave (Master's thesis).

Peters, R.S. (1966). *Ethics and Education.* London: G. Allen & Unwin.

Positive Partnership. A sequel to A Future in Partnership. (1985). London: The National Society (Church of England) for Promoting Religious Education.

Price, A. (No date). *Turbulent Times - A Challenge to Catholic Education in Britain Today.* Occasional Papers in Education No. 1. Glasgow: St. Andrew's College.

Raz, J. (1988). *The Morality of Freedom.* Oxford: Clarendon Press. (Original work published 1986)

Reese, W.J. (1993). Soldiers for Christ in the army of God: The Christian school movement in America. In L. Francis & D.W. Lankshear (eds.), *Christian Perspectives on Church Schools* (pp. 274-300). Leominster: Gracewing. (Reprinted from *Eduactional Theory*, 1985, 35)

Royce, R.J. (1983). Process and product in moral education. *Journal of Philosophy of Education, 17*, 73-83.

Sandel, M.J. (ed.)(1984). *Liberalism and Its Critics.* New York: New York University Press.

Sandsmark, S. (1992). Hva er et kristent menneskesyn? In *Mennesket på godt og ondt* (pp. 113-25). Bergen: NLA-forlaget.

Shortt, J. (1986). A critical problem for rational autonomy? *Spectrum, 18*, 107-121.

Skjervheim, H. (1996). The liberal dilemma. In H. Skjervheim, *Selected Essays* (pp. 85-97). Bergen: The Department of Philosophy, University of Bergen. (Original work published 1967)

Skoglund, R. (1991). *Barns livssynsdanning, grunnskolens verdigrunnlag og verdiformidling. Hvorfor, hva og hvordan?* Hovedoppgave (Master's thesis). Bergen: Norsk Lærerakademi.

Skottene, R. (1994). *Den konfesjonelle skole*. Stavanger.

Smart, N. (1983). *Worldviews*. New York: Charles Scribner's Sons.

Smith, A. (1985). Hva er et livssyn? *Kirke og Kultur, 90*, 412-21.

Statistisk årbok 1996. (Official statistics of Norway). Oslo / Kongsvinger: Statistisk sentralbyrå / Statistics Norway.

Stowe, H.B. (1955). *Uncle Tom's Cabin*. London: J.M. Dent & Sons. (Original work published 1851)

Strawson, P.F. (1974). Social morality and individual ideal. In P.F. Strawson, *Freedom and Resentment*. London: Methuen & Co. (Reprinted from *Philosophy, 1961, 36*)

Strike, K.A. (1992). Liberal discourse and ethical pluralism: an educational agenda. *Philosophy of Education, 48*, 226-36.

Strike, K.A. (1993a). Teaching ethical reasoning using cases. In K.A. Strike & P.L. Ternasky (eds.), *Ethics for Professionals in Education* (pp. 102-16). New York: Teachers College Press.

Strike, K.A. (1993b). Ethical discours and pluralism. In K.A. Strike & P.L. Ternasky (eds.), *Ethics for Professionals in Education* (pp. 176-88). New York: Teachers College Press.

Strike, K.A. (1994). On the construction of public speech: pluralism and public reason. *Educational Theory, 44*, 1-26.

Strike, K.A. (1998). Liberalism, citizenship, and the private interest in schooling. *Studies in Philosophy and Education, 17*, 221-9.

Tamir, Y. (1995). Two concepts of multiculturalism. *Journal of Philosophy of Education, 29*, 161-72.

Taylor, J. (1996). A plea for parental choice: a classical liberal critique of the detached school. *Papers of the Philosophy of Education Society of Great Britain, annual conference*. Oxford.

Thiessen, E. (1993). Two concepts or two phases of liberal education? In L. Francis & D.W. Lankshear (eds.), *Christian Perspectives on Church Schools* (pp. 17-32). Leominster: Gracewing. (Reprinted from *Journal of Philosophy of Eduction, 1987, 21*)

Thiessen, E.J. (1993). *Teaching for Commitment*. Montreal: McGill-Queen's University Press.

Trigg, R. (1973). *Reason and commitment*. Cambridge: Cambridge University Press.

Tveiten, T. (1994). Kristen oppseding og undervisning i et framtidsperspektiv. In *Oppseding mellom åpenbaring og medier* (pp. 174-82). Bergen: NLA-forlaget.

Van Brummelen, H. (1994). *Steppingstones to Curriculum*. Seattle: Alta Vista College Press.

Walsh, P. (1983). The church secondary school and its curriculum. In D. O'Leary (ed.), *Religious Education and Young Adults* (pp. 4-19). Slough: St Paul Publications.

Walsh, B.J. & Middleton, J.R. (1984). *The Transforming Vision. Shaping a Christian World View*. Downers Grove, Ill.: InterVarsity.

Ward, K. (1986). *The Turn of the Tide*. London: BBC.

Watson, B. (1988). Children at school: a worshipping community? In B. O'Keeffe (ed.), *Schools for Tomorrow. Building Walls or Building Bridges* (pp. 101-24). Lewes: Falmer.

Weeks, N. (1988). *The Christian School*. Edinburgh: The Banner of Truth Trust.

White, J. (1982). *The Aims of Education Restated*. London: Routledge & Kegan Paul.

White, J. & White, P. (1986). Education, liberalism and human good. In D.E. Cooper (ed.), *Education, Values and Mind* (pp. 149-71). London: Routledge & Kegan Paul.

White, J. (1989). The aims of personal and social education. In P. White (ed.), *Personal and Social Education: Philosophical Perspectives* (pp. 7-18). London: Institute of Education University of London, Bedford Way Series.

White, J. (1990). *Education and the Good Life.* London: Kogan Page.

White, J. (1995). *Education and personal well-being in a secular universe.* London: Institute of Education University of London, Bedford Way Series.

White, J. (1997). Education, work and well-being. *Journal of Philosophy of Education, 31*, 233-47.

Williams, K. (1992). Religious ethos and state schools. *Doctrine and Life, 42*, 561-70.

Williams, K. (1997). Parents' rights and the integrated curriculum. *Doctrine and Life, 47*, 142-50.

Williams, K. (1998). Religion, culture and schooling. In J.M. Feheny (ed.), *From Ideal to Action: The Inner Nature of a Catholic School Today* Dublin: Veritas.

Wren, B. (1986). *Education for Justice.* (2nd ed.). London: SCM.

Øystese, O. (1983). *Religionspedagogikk.* Lectures, volume 1. Unpublished work. Bergen: NLA.

Øystese, O. (1985). Hva er en kristen skole? In J. Kvalbein (ed.), *Foreldrerett og friskolekamp* (pp. 54-65). Oslo: Lunde.

Øystese, O. (1989). Religionspedagogiske konsekvenser av den lutherske regimentslære. *Fast Grunn, 42*, 298-305.

Aadnanes, P.M. (1992). *Livssyn.* Oslo: Tano.

Aadnanes, P.M. (1997). *Det nye tusenårsriket. New Age som livssyn.* Oslo: Scandinavian University Press.

Årbok for Den norske kirke 1997. Oslo: Kirkens Informasjonstjeneste.

Index

Paternoster Biblical Monographs

(All titles uniform with this volume)
Dates in bold are of projected publication

Joseph Abraham
Eve: Accused or Acquitted?
A Reconsideration of Feminist Readings of the Creation Narrative Texts in Genesis 1–3
Two contrary views dominate contemporary feminist biblical scholarship. One finds in the Bible an unequivocal equality between the sexes from the very creation of humanity, whilst the other sees the biblical text as irredeemably patriarchal and androcentric. Dr Abraham enters into dialogue with both camps as well as introducing his own method of approach. An invaluable tool for any one who is interested in this contemporary debate.
2002 / 0-85364-971-5 / xxiv + 272pp

Octavian D. Baban
Mimesis and Luke's on the Road Encounters in Luke-Acts
Luke's Theology of the Way and its Literary Representation
The book argues on theological and literary (mimetic) grounds that Luke's on-the-road encounters, especially those belonging to the post-Easter period, are part of his complex theology of the Way. Jesus' teaching and that of the apostles is presented by Luke as a challenging answer to the Hellenistic reader's thirst for adventure, good literature, and existential paradigms.
2005 / 1-84227-253-5 / *approx. 374pp*

Paul Barker
The Triumph of Grace in Deuteronomy
This book is a textual and theological analysis of the interaction between the sin and faithlessness of Israel and the grace of Yahweh in response, looking especially at Deuteronomy chapters 1–3, 8–10 and 29–30. The author argues that the grace of Yahweh is determinative for the ongoing relationship between Yahweh and Israel and that Deuteronomy anticipates and fully expects Israel to be faithless.
2004 / 1-84227-226-8 / xxii + 270pp

Jonathan F. Bayes
The Weakness of the Law
God's Law and the Christian in New Testament Perspective
A study of the four New Testament books which refer to the law as weak (Acts, Romans, Galatians, Hebrews) leads to a defence of the third use in the Reformed debate about the law in the life of the believer.
2000 / 0-85364-957-X / xii + 244pp

Mark Bonnington
The Antioch Episode of Galatians 2:11-14 in Historical and Cultural Context
The Galatians 2 'incident' in Antioch over table-fellowship suggests significant disagreement between the leading apostles. This book analyses the background to the disagreement by locating the incident within the dynamics of social interaction between Jews and Gentiles. It proposes a new way of understanding the relationship between the individuals and issues involved.
2005 / 1-84227-050-8 / approx. 350pp

David Bostock
A Portrayal of Trust
The Theme of Faith in the Hezekiah Narratives
This study provides detailed and sensitive readings of the Hezekiah narratives (2 Kings 18–20 and Isaiah 36–39) from a theological perspective. It concentrates on the theme of faith, using narrative criticism as its methodology. Attention is paid especially to setting, plot, point of view and characterization within the narratives. A largely positive portrayal of Hezekiah emerges that underlines the importance and relevance of scripture.
2005 / 1-84227-314-0 / approx. 300pp

Mark Bredin
Jesus, Revolutionary of Peace
A Non-violent Christology in the Book of Revelation
This book aims to demonstrate that the figure of Jesus in the Book of Revelation can best be understood as an active non-violent revolutionary.
2003 / 1-84227-153-9 / xviii + 262pp

Robinson Butarbutar
Paul and Conflict Resolution
An Exegetical Study of Paul's Apostolic Paradigm in 1 Corinthians 9
The author sees the apostolic paradigm in 1 Corinthians 9 as part of Paul's unified arguments in 1 Corinthians 8–10 in which he seeks to mediate in the dispute over the issue of food offered to idols. The book also sees its relevance for dispute-resolution today, taking the conflict within the author's church as an example.
2006 / 1-84227-315-9 / approx. 280pp

Daniel J-S Chae
Paul as Apostle to the Gentiles
*His Apostolic Self-awareness and its Influence on the Soteriological Argument
in Romans*
Opposing 'the post-Holocaust interpretation of Romans', Daniel Chae competently demonstrates that Paul argues for the equality of Jew and Gentile in Romans. Chae's fresh exegetical interpretation is academically outstanding and spiritually encouraging.

1997 / 0-85364-829-8 / xiv + 378pp

Luke L. Cheung
The Genre, Composition and Hermeneutics of the Epistle of James
The present work examines the employment of the wisdom genre with a certain compositional structure and the interpretation of the law through the Jesus tradition of the double love command by the author of the Epistle of James to serve his purpose in promoting perfection and warning against doubleness among the eschatologically renewed people of God in the Diaspora.

2003 / 1-84227-062-1 / xvi + 372pp

Youngmo Cho
Spirit and Kingdom in the Writings of Luke and Paul
The relationship between Spirit and Kingdom is a relatively unexplored area in Lukan and Pauline studies. This book offers a fresh perspective of two biblical writers on the subject. It explores the difference between Luke's and Paul's understanding of the Spirit by examining the specific question of the relationship of the concept of the Spirit to the concept of the Kingdom of God in each writer.

***2005** / 1-84227-316-7 / approx. 270pp*

Andrew C. Clark
Parallel Lives
The Relation of Paul to the Apostles in the Lucan Perspective
This study of the Peter-Paul parallels in Acts argues that their purpose was to emphasize the themes of continuity in salvation history and the unity of the Jewish and Gentile missions. New light is shed on Luke's literary techniques, partly through a comparison with Plutarch.

2001 / 1-84227-035-4 / xviii + 386pp

Andrew D. Clarke
Secular and Christian Leadership in Corinth
A Socio-Historical and Exegetical Study of 1 Corinthians 1–6
This volume is an investigation into the leadership structures and dynamics of first-century Roman Corinth. These are compared with the practice of leadership in the Corinthian Christian community which are reflected in 1 Corinthians 1–6, and contrasted with Paul's own principles of Christian leadership.

2005 / 1-84227-229-2 / 200pp

Stephen Finamore
God, Order and Chaos
René Girard and the Apocalypse
Readers are often disturbed by the images of destruction in the book of Revelation and unsure why they are unleashed after the exaltation of Jesus. This book examines past approaches to these texts and uses René Girard's theories to revive some old ideas and propose some new ones.

2005 / 1-84227-197-0 / approx. 344pp

David G. Firth
Surrendering Retribution in the Psalms
Responses to Violence in the Individual Complaints
In *Surrendering Retribution in the Psalms*, David Firth examines the ways in which the book of Psalms inculcates a model response to violence through the repetition of standard patterns of prayer. Rather than seeking justification for retributive violence, Psalms encourages not only a surrender of the right of retribution to Yahweh, but also sets limits on the retribution that can be sought in imprecations. Arising initially from the author's experience in South Africa, the possibilities of this model to a particular context of violence is then briefly explored.

2005 / 1-84227-337-X / xviii + 154pp

Scott J. Hafemann
Suffering and Ministry in the Spirit
Paul's Defence of His Ministry in II Corinthians 2:14–3:3
Shedding new light on the way Paul defended his apostleship, the author offers a careful, detailed study of 2 Corinthians 2:14–3:3 linked with other key passages throughout 1 and 2 Corinthians. Demonstrating the unity and coherence of Paul's argument in this passage, the author shows that Paul's suffering served as the vehicle for revealing God's power and glory through the Spirit.

2000 / 0-85364-967-7 / xiv + 262pp

Scott J. Hafemann
Paul, Moses and the History of Israel
The Letter/Spirit Contrast and the Argument from Scripture in 2 Corinthians 3
An exegetical study of the call of Moses, the second giving of the Law (Exodus 32–34), the new covenant, and the prophetic understanding of the history of Israel in 2 Corinthians 3. Hafemann's work demonstrates Paul's contextual use of the Old Testament and the essential unity between the Law and the Gospel within the context of the distinctive ministries of Moses and Paul.
2005 / 1-84227-317-5 / xii + 498pp

Douglas S. McComiskey
Lukan Theology in the Light of the Gospel's Literary Structure
Luke's Gospel was purposefully written with theology embedded in its patterned literary structure. A critical analysis of this cyclical structure provides new windows into Luke's interpretation of the individual pericopes comprising the Gospel and illuminates several of his theological interests.
2004 / 1-84227-148-2 / xviii + 388pp

Stephen Motyer
Your Father the Devil?
A New Approach to John and 'The Jews'
Who are 'the Jews' in John's Gospel? Defending John against the charge of antisemitism, Motyer argues that, far from demonising the Jews, the Gospel seeks to present Jesus as 'Good News for Jews' in a late first century setting.
1997 / 0-85364-832-8 / xiv + 260pp

Esther Ng
Reconstructing Christian Origins?
The Feminist Theology of Elizabeth Schüssler Fiorenza: An Evaluation
In a detailed evaluation, the author challenges Elizabeth Schüssler Fiorenza's reconstruction of early Christian origins and her underlying presuppositions. The author also presents her own views on women's roles both then and now.
2002 / 1-84227-055-9 / xxiv + 468pp

Robin Parry
Old Testament Story and Christian Ethics
The Rape of Dinah as a Case Study

What is the role of story in ethics and, more particularly, what is the role of Old Testament story in Christian ethics? This book, drawing on the work of contemporary philosophers, argues that narrative is crucial in the ethical shaping of people and, drawing on the work of contemporary Old Testament scholars, that story plays a key role in Old Testament ethics. Parry then argues that when situated in canonical context Old Testament stories can be reappropriated by Christian readers in their own ethical formation. The shocking story of the rape of Dinah and the massacre of the Shechemites provides a fascinating case study for exploring the parameters within which Christian ethical appropriations of Old Testament stories can live.

2004 / 1-84227-210-1 / xx + 350pp

Ian Paul
Power to See the World Anew
The Value of Paul Ricoeur's Hermeneutic of Metaphor in Interpreting the Symbolism of Revelation 12 and 13

This book is a study of the hermeneutics of metaphor of Paul Ricoeur, one of the most important writers on hermeneutics and metaphor of the last century. It sets out the key points of his theory, important criticisms of his work, and how his approach, modified in the light of these criticisms, offers a methodological framework for reading apocalyptic texts.

2006 / 1-84227-056-7 / approx. 350pp

Robert L. Plummer
Paul's Understanding of the Church's Mission
Did the Apostle Paul Expect the Early Christian Communities to Evangelize?

This book engages in a careful study of Paul's letters to determine if the apostle expected the communities to which he wrote to engage in missionary activity. It helpfully summarizes the discussion on this debated issue, judiciously handling contested texts, and provides a way forward in addressing this critical question. While admitting that Paul rarely explicitly commands the communities he founded to evangelize, Plummer amasses significant incidental data to provide a convincing case that Paul did indeed expect his churches to engage in mission activity. Throughout the study, Plummer progressively builds a theological basis for the church's mission that is both distinctively Pauline and compelling.

2006 / 1-84227-333-7 / approx. 324pp

David Powys
'Hell': A Hard Look at a Hard Question
The Fate of the Unrighteous in New Testament Thought
This comprehensive treatment seeks to unlock the original meaning of terms and phrases long thought to support the traditional doctrine of hell. It concludes that there is an alternative—one which is more biblical, and which can positively revive the rationale for Christian mission.

1997 / 0-85364-831-X / xxii + 478pp

Sorin Sabou
Between Horror and Hope
Paul's Metaphorical Language of Death in Romans 6.1-11
This book argues that Paul's metaphorical language of death in Romans 6.1-11 conveys two aspects: horror and hope. The 'horror' aspect is conveyed by the 'crucifixion' language, and the 'hope' aspect by 'burial' language. The life of the Christian believer is understood, as relationship with sin is concerned ('death to sin'), between these two realities: horror and hope.

2005 / 1-84227-322-1 / approx. 224pp

Rosalind Selby
The Comical Doctrine
The Epistemology of New Testament Hermeneutics
This book argues that the gospel breaks through postmodernity's critique of truth and the referential possibilities of textuality with its gift of grace. With a rigorous, philosophical challenge to modernist and postmodernist assumptions, Selby offers an alternative epistemology to all who would still read with faith *and* with academic credibility.

2005 / 1-84227-212-8 / approx. 350pp

Kiwoong Son
Zion Symbolism in Hebrews
Hebrews 12.18-24 as a Hermeneutical Key to the Epistle
This book challenges the general tendency of understanding the Epistle to the Hebrews against a Hellenistic background and suggests that the Epistle should be understood in the light of the Jewish apocalyptic tradition. The author especially argues for the importance of the theological symbolism of Sinai and Zion (Heb. 12:18-24) as it provides the Epistle's theological background as well as the rhetorical basis of the superiority motif of Jesus throughout the Epistle.

2005 / 1-84227-368-X / approx. 280pp

Kevin Walton
Thou Traveller Unknown
The Presence and Absence of God in the Jacob Narrative
The author offers a fresh reading of the story of Jacob in the book of Genesis through the paradox of divine presence and absence. The work also seeks to make a contribution to Pentateuchal studies by bringing together a close reading of the final text with historical critical insights, doing justice to the text's historical depth, final form and canonical status.
2003 / 1-84227-059-1 / xvi + 238pp

George M. Wieland
The Significance of Salvation
A Study of Salvation Language in the Pastoral Epistles
The language and ideas of salvation pervade the three Pastoral Epistles. This study offers a close examination of their soteriological statements. In all three letters the idea of salvation is found to play a vital paraenetic role, but each also exhibits distinctive soteriological emphases. The results challenge common assumptions about the Pastoral Epistles as a corpus.
2005 / 1-84227-257-8 / approx. 324pp

Alistair Wilson
When Will These Things Happen?
A Study of Jesus as Judge in Matthew 21–25
This study seeks to allow Matthew's carefully constructed presentation of Jesus to be given full weight in the modern evaluation of Jesus' eschatology. Careful analysis of the text of Matthew 21–25 reveals Jesus to be standing firmly in the Jewish prophetic and wisdom traditions as he proclaims and enacts imminent judgement on the Jewish authorities then boldly claims the central role in the final and universal judgement.
2004 / 1-84227-146-6 / xxii + 272pp

Lindsay Wilson
Joseph Wise and Otherwise
The Intersection of Covenant and Wisdom in Genesis 37–50
This book offers a careful literary reading of Genesis 37–50 that argues that the Joseph story contains both strong covenant themes and many wisdom-like elements. The connections between the two helps to explore how covenant and wisdom might intersect in an integrated biblical theology.
2004 / 1-84227-140-7 / xvi + 340pp

Stephen I. Wright
The Voice of Jesus
Studies in the Interpretation of Six Gospel Parables
This literary study considers how the 'voice' of Jesus has been heard in different periods of parable interpretation, and how the categories of figure and trope may help us towards a sensitive reading of the parables today.
2000 / 0-85364-975-8 / xiv + 280pp

Paternoster
9 Holdom Avenue,
Bletchley,
Milton Keynes MK1 1QR,
United Kingdom
Web: www.authenticmedia.co.uk/paternoster

Paternoster Theological Monographs

(All titles uniform with this volume)
Dates in bold are of projected publication

Emil Bartos
Deification in Eastern Orthodox Theology
An Evaluation and Critique of the Theology of Dumitru Staniloae
Bartos studies a fundamental yet neglected aspect of Orthodox theology: deification. By examining the doctrines of anthropology, christology, soteriology and ecclesiology as they relate to deification, he provides an important contribution to contemporary dialogue between Eastern and Western theologians.

1999 / 0-85364-956-1 / xii + 370pp

Graham Buxton
The Trinity, Creation and Pastoral Ministry
Imaging the Perichoretic God
In this book the author proposes a three-way conversation between theology, science and pastoral ministry. His approach draws on a Trinitarian understanding of God as a relational being of love, whose life 'spills over' into all created reality, human and non-human. By locating human meaning and purpose within God's 'creation-community' this book offers the possibility of a transforming engagement between those in pastoral ministry and the scientific community.

2005 / 1-84227-369-8 / approx. 380 pp

Iain D. Campbell
Fixing the Indemnity
The Life and Work of George Adam Smith
When Old Testament scholar George Adam Smith (1856–1942) delivered the Lyman Beecher lectures at Yale University in 1899, he confidently declared that 'modern criticism has won its war against traditional theories. It only remains to fix the amount of the indemnity.' In this biography, Iain D. Campbell assesses Smith's critical approach to the Old Testament and evaluates its consequences, showing that Smith's life and work still raises questions about the relationship between biblical scholarship and evangelical faith.

2004 / 1-84227-228-4 / xx + 256pp

Tim Chester
Mission and the Coming of God
Eschatology, the Trinity and Mission in the Theology of Jürgen Moltmann
This book explores the theology and missiology of the influential contemporary theologian, Jürgen Moltmann. It highlights the important contribution Moltmann has made while offering a critique of his thought from an evangelical perspective. In so doing, it touches on pertinent issues for evangelical missiology. The conclusion takes Calvin as a starting point, proposing 'an eschatology of the cross' which offers a critique of the over-realised eschatologies in liberation theology and certain forms of evangelicalism.
2006 / 1-84227-320-5 / approx. 224pp

Sylvia Wilkey Collinson
Making Disciples
The Significance of Jesus' Educational Strategy for Today's Church
This study examines the biblical practice of discipling, formulates a definition, and makes comparisons with modern models of education. A recommendation is made for greater attention to its practice today.
2004 / 1-84227-116-4 / xiv + 278pp

Darrell Cosden
A Theology of Work
Work and the New Creation
Through dialogue with Moltmann, Pope John Paul II and others, this book develops a genitive 'theology of work', presenting a theological definition of work and a model for a theological ethics of work that shows work's nature, value and meaning now and eschatologically. Work is shown to be a transformative activity consisting of three dynamically inter-related dimensions: the instrumental, relational and ontological.
2005 / 1-84227-332-9 / xvi + 208pp

Stephen M. Dunning
The Crisis and the Quest
A Kierkegaardian Reading of Charles Williams
Employing Kierkegaardian categories and analysis, this study investigates both the central crisis in Charles Williams's authorship between hermetism and Christianity (Kierkegaard's Religions A and B), and the quest to resolve this crisis, a quest that ultimately presses the bounds of orthodoxy.
2000 / 0-85364-985-5 / xxiv + 254pp

Keith Ferdinando
The Triumph of Christ in African Perspective
A Study of Demonology and Redemption in the African Context
The book explores the implications of the gospel for traditional African fears of occult aggression. It analyses such traditional approaches to suffering and biblical responses to fears of demonic evil, concluding with an evaluation of African beliefs from the perspective of the gospel.
1999 / 0-85364-830-1 / xviii + 450pp

Andrew Goddard
Living the Word, Resisting the World
The Life and Thought of Jacques Ellul
This work offers a definitive study of both the life and thought of the French Reformed thinker Jacques Ellul (1912-1994). It will prove an indispensable resource for those interested in this influential theologian and sociologist and for Christian ethics and political thought generally.
2002 / 1-84227-053-2 / xxiv + 378pp

David Hilborn
The Words of our Lips
Language-Use in Free Church Worship
Studies of liturgical language have tended to focus on the written canons of Roman Catholic and Anglican communities. By contrast, David Hilborn analyses the more extemporary approach of English Nonconformity. Drawing on recent developments in linguistic pragmatics, he explores similarities and differences between 'fixed' and 'free' worship, and argues for the interdependence of each.
2006 */ 0-85364-977-4 / approx. 350pp*

Roger Hitching
The Church and Deaf People
A Study of Identity, Communication and Relationships with Special Reference to the Ecclesiology of Jürgen Moltmann
In *The Church and Deaf People* Roger Hitching sensitively examines the history and present experience of deaf people and finds similarities between aspects of sign language and Moltmann's theological method that 'open up' new ways of understanding theological concepts.
2003 / 1-84227-222-5 / xxii + 236pp

John G. Kelly
One God, One People
*The Differentiated Unity of the People of God in the Theology of
Jürgen Moltmann*
The author expounds and critiques Moltmann's doctrine of God and highlights
the systematic connections between it and Moltmann's influential discussion of
Israel. He then proposes a fresh approach to Jewish–Christian relations building
on Moltmann's work using insights from Habermas and Rawls.
2005 / 0-85346-969-3 / approx. 350pp

Mark F.W. Lovatt
Confronting the Will-to-Power
A Reconsideration of the Theology of Reinhold Niebuhr
Confronting the Will-to-Power is an analysis of the theology of Reinhold
Niebuhr, arguing that his work is an attempt to identify, and provide a practical
theological answer to, the existence and nature of human evil.
2001 / 1-84227-054-0 / xviii + 216pp

Neil B. MacDonald
Karl Barth and the Strange New World within the Bible
Barth, Wittgenstein, and the Metadilemmas of the Enlightenment
Barth's discovery of the strange new world within the Bible is examined in the
context of Kant, Hume, Overbeck, and, most importantly, Wittgenstein.
MacDonald covers some fundamental issues in theology today: epistemology,
the final form of the text and biblical truth-claims.
2000 / 0-85364-970-7 / xxvi + 374pp

Keith A. Mascord
Alvin Plantinga and Christian Apologetics
This book draws together the contributions of the philosopher Alvin Plantinga to
the major contemporary challenges to Christian belief, highlighting in particular
his ground-breaking work in epistemology and the problem of evil. Plantinga's
theory that both theistic and Christian belief is warrantedly basic is explored and
critiqued, and an assessment offered as to the significance of his work for
apologetic theory and practice.
2005 / 1-84227-256-X / approx. 304pp

Gillian McCulloch
The Deconstruction of Dualism in Theology
With Reference to Ecofeminist Theology and New Age Spirituality
This book challenges eco-theological anti-dualism in Christian theology, arguing that dualism has a twofold function in Christian religious discourse. Firstly, it enables us to express the discontinuities and divisions that are part of the process of reality. Secondly, dualistic language allows us to express the mysteries of divine transcendence/immanence and the survival of the soul without collapsing into monism and materialism, both of which are problematic for Christian epistemology.
2002 / 1-84227-044-3 / xii + 282pp

Leslie McCurdy
Attributes and Atonement
The Holy Love of God in the Theology of P.T. Forsyth
Attributes and Atonement is an intriguing full-length study of P.T. Forsyth's doctrine of the cross as it relates particularly to God's holy love. It includes an unparalleled bibliography of both primary and secondary material relating to Forsyth.
1999 / 0-85364-833-6 / xiv + 328pp

Nozomu Miyahira
Towards a Theology of the Concord of God
A Japanese Perspective on the Trinity
This book introduces a new Japanese theology and a unique Trinitarian formula based on the Japanese intellectual climate: three betweennesses and one concord. It also presents a new interpretation of the Trinity, a co-subordinationism, which is in line with orthodox Trinitarianism; each single person of the Trinity is eternally and equally subordinate (or serviceable) to the other persons, so that they retain the mutual dynamic equality.
2000 / 0-85364-863-8 / xiv + 256pp

Eddy José Muskus
The Origins and Early Development of Liberation Theology in Latin America
With Particular Reference to Gustavo Gutiérrez
This work challenges the fundamental premise of Liberation Theology, 'opting for the poor', and its claim that Christ is found in them. It also argues that Liberation Theology emerged as a direct result of the failure of the Roman Catholic Church in Latin America.
2002 / 0-85364-974-X / xiv + 296pp

Jim Purves
The Triune God and the Charismatic Movement
A Critical Appraisal from a Scottish Perspective
All emotion and no theology? Or a fundamental challenge to reappraise and realign our trinitarian theology in the light of Christian experience? This study of charismatic renewal as it found expression within Scotland at the end of the twentieth century evaluates the use of Patristic, Reformed and contemporary models of the Trinity in explaining the workings of the Holy Spirit.
2004 / 1-84227-321-3 / xxiv + 246pp

Anna Robbins
Methods in the Madness
Diversity in Twentieth-Century Christian Social Ethics
The author compares the ethical methods of Walter Rauschenbusch, Reinhold Niebuhr and others. She argues that unless Christians are clear about the ways that theology and philosophy are expressed practically they may lose the ability to discuss social ethics across contexts, let alone reach effective agreements.
2004 / 1-84227-211-X / xx + 294pp

Ed Rybarczyk
Beyond Salvation
Eastern Orthodoxy and Classical Pentecostalism on Becoming Like Christ
At first glance eastern Orthodoxy and classical Pentecostalism seem quite distinct. This ground-breaking study shows they share much in common, especially as it concerns the experiential elements of following Christ. Both traditions assert that authentic Christianity transcends the wooden categories of modernism.
2004 / 1-84227-144-X / xii + 356pp

Signe Sandsmark
Is World View Neutral Education Possible and Desirable?
A Christian Response to Liberal Arguments
(Published jointly with The Stapleford Centre)
This book discusses reasons for belief in world view neutrality, and argues that 'neutral' education will have a hidden, but strong world view influence. It discusses the place for Christian education in the common school.
2000 / 0-85364-973-1 / xiv + 182pp

Hazel Sherman
Reading Zechariah
The Allegorical Tradition of Biblical Interpretation through the Commentary of Didymus the Blind and Theodore of Mopsuestia
A close reading of the commentary on Zechariah by Didymus the Blind alongside that of Theodore of Mopsuestia suggests that popular categorising of Antiochene and Alexandrian biblical exegesis as 'historical' or 'allegorical' is inadequate and misleading.
2005 / 1-84227-213-6 / approx. 280pp

Andrew Sloane
On Being a Christian in the Academy
Nicholas Wolterstorff and the Practice of Christian Scholarship
An exposition and critical appraisal of Nicholas Wolterstorff's epistemology in the light of the philosophy of science, and an application of his thought to the practice of Christian scholarship.
2003 / 1-84227-058-3 / xvi + 274pp

Damon W.K. So
Jesus' Revelation of His Father
A Narrative-Conceptual Study of the Trinity with Special Reference to Karl Barth
This book explores the trinitarian dynamics in the context of Jesus' revelation of his Father in his earthly ministry with references to key passages in Matthew's Gospel. It develops from the exegeses of these passages a non-linear concept of revelation which links Jesus' communion with his Father to his revelatory words and actions through a nuanced understanding of the Holy Spirit, with references to K. Barth, G.W.H. Lampe, J.D.G. Dunn and E. Irving.
2005 / 1-84227-323-X / approx. 380pp

Daniel Strange
The Possibility of Salvation Among the Unevangelised
An Analysis of Inclusivism in Recent Evangelical Theology
For evangelical theologians the 'fate of the unevangelised' impinges upon fundamental tenets of evangelical identity. The position known as 'inclusivism', defined by the belief that the unevangelised can be ontologically saved by Christ whilst being epistemologically unaware of him, has been defended most vigorously by the Canadian evangelical Clark H. Pinnock. Through a detailed analysis and critique of Pinnock's work, this book examines a cluster of issues surrounding the unevangelised and its implications for christology, soteriology and the doctrine of revelation.
2002 / 1-84227-047-8 / xviii + 362pp

Scott Swain
God According to the Gospel
Biblical Narrative and the Identity of God in the Theology of Robert W. Jenson
Robert W. Jenson is one of the leading voices in contemporary Trinitarian theology. His boldest contribution in this area concerns his use of biblical narrative both to ground and explicate the Christian doctrine of God. *God According to the Gospel* critically examines Jenson's proposal and suggests an alternative way of reading the biblical portrayal of the triune God.
2006 / 1-84227-258-6 / approx. 180pp

Justyn Terry
The Justifying Judgement of God
A Reassessment of the Place of Judgement in the Saving Work of Christ
The argument of this book is that judgement, understood as the whole process of bringing justice, is the primary metaphor of atonement, with others, such as victory, redemption and sacrifice, subordinate to it. Judgement also provides the proper context for understanding penal substitution and the call to repentance, baptism, eucharist and holiness.
2005 / 1-84227-370-1 / approx. 274 pp

Graham Tomlin
The Power of the Cross
Theology and the Death of Christ in Paul, Luther and Pascal
This book explores the theology of the cross in St Paul, Luther and Pascal. It offers new perspectives on the theology of each, and some implications for the nature of power, apologetics, theology and church life in a postmodern context.
1999 / 0-85364-984-7 / xiv + 344pp

Adonis Vidu
Postliberal Theological Method
A Critical Study
The postliberal theology of Hans Frei, George Lindbeck, Ronald Thiemann, John Milbank and others is one of the more influential contemporary options. This book focuses on several aspects pertaining to its theological method, specifically its understanding of background, hermeneutics, epistemic justification, ontology, the nature of doctrine and, finally, Christological method.
2005 / 1-84227-395-7 / approx. 324pp

A Comparative Study of the Relationship between the Doctrine of Revelation and Pneumatology in the Theology of Eberhard Jüngel and of Wolfhart Pannenberg

The relationship between revelation and pneumatology is relatively unexplored. This approach offers a fresh angle on two important twentieth century theologians and raises pneumatological questions which are theologically crucial and relevant to mission in a postmodern culture.

2005 / 1-84227-104-0 / xxii + 232pp

Nigel G. Wright

Disavowing Constantine

Mission, Church and the Social Order in the Theologies of John Howard Yoder and Jürgen Moltmann

This book is a timely restatement of a radical theology of church and state in the Anabaptist and Baptist tradition. Dr Wright constructs his argument in dialogue and debate with Yoder and Moltmann, major contributors to a free church perspective.

2000 / 0-85364-978-2 / xvi + 252pp

Paternoster:
thinking faith

Paternoster
9 Holdom Avenue,
Bletchley,
Milton Keynes MK1 1QR,
United Kingdom
Web: www.authenticmedia.co.uk/paternoster